W9-AOE-324

Same Song—Separate Voices

We four Lennon Sisters today. Left to right, Janet, Dianne, Peggy, and Kathy. *(Courtesy of Harry Langdon)*

Same Song— Separate Voices

The Collective Memoirs of
THE LENNON SISTERS

Dianne, Peggy, Kathy, and Janet Lennon

ROUNDTABLE PUBLISHING, INC.
Santa Monica   California

ROUNDTABLE PUBLISHING, INC.
933 Pico Boulevard
Santa Monica, CA 90405

Second Printing, 1985

Library of Congress Catalog Card Number—84-60761

PRINTED IN THE UNITED STATES OF AMERICA

To Mom

*She looketh well to the ways of her household, and eateth
not the bread of idleness. Her children rise up, and call
her blessed . . . .*

—Proverbs 31: 27-28

Acknowledgements

While we have made efforts to be consistent, by choice we are not always chronological. We have written about most of the people and events of our lives to this time. We apologize to those who may feel slighted by not being included in these pages. Surely, it is understood that lack of mention is sometimes unintentional (except when it is intentional). To some persons we can say we did write about you, but you've obviously been edited out of our memoirs. To those men and women who are within these pages, we can only hope that we got things right from their points-of-view.

We are indebted to so many for their aid and encouragement during the years of preparing our memoirs. We express our gratitude with a singular "thank you" to:

Harold Cohen, for his determined guidance.

Jeremy Tarcher, for encouraging us to tell our story.

Larry Welk, Jr., our founder, friend, and Mini-Mogul.

Warren Bayless, for his "fixings," and for making us go on.

Florence Levy, for coordinating with care.

Bob Eubanks, Steve Wolf, and Jim Rismiller, for opening new doors.

Ruth Bullington, for the countless public and private moments she has captured on film for us.

Eve Baxter and Shari Steere Feducia, for their technical aid.

Our children, for trying to understand our long hours, our unpredictable moods, and tired evenings.

Our husbands (all six of them), for loving us, in spite of our family; and to

Dad and Mom, for helping us to see the simplicity of God's love.

Contents

Christopher Lennon
b. 3/12/1960

Anne Lennon
b. 1/24/1959
m. Michael Suzuki

Mary Macias
b. 4/17/1978

Joseph Lennon
b. 5/9/1957
m. Ellyn Neumeier

Elizabeth Macias
b. 11/7/1982

William Lennon
b. 7/29/1954

Miriam Lennon
b. 10/16/1955
m. Daniel Macias

Carrie Cathcart
b. 12/27/1952
m. Toby Sadasky

William Bernhardi
b. 6/6/1967

Patrick Lennon
b. 11/9/1952
m. Nancy Conterno

John Cathcart
b. 5/28/1955—
d. 5/19/1983
m. Denice Hilbert

Mary Lennon
b. 3/5/1953—
d. 7/20/1954

John Bernhardi
b. 10/31/1968

Danforth Lennon
b. 2/8/1950
m. Virginia Mathews

Janet Lennon
b. 6/15/1946
m. 1, Lee Bernardi
m. John Bahler

Kristin Bernhardi
b. 1/17/1970

George Cathcart
b. 8/27/1960

Margaret Lennon
b. 4/8/1941
m. Richard Cathcart

Gregory Bahler
b. 12/23/1963

Michele Bahler
b. 12/26/1966

Julianne Cathcart
b. 3/17/1965

Kathleen Lennon
b. 8/2/1943
m. James Daris

Christopher Cathcart
b. 2/27/1966

Mary Gass
b. 1/7/1964

Joseph Cathcart
b. 6/29/1967

Jennifer Cathcart
b. 1/22/1973

Dianne Lennon
b. 12/1/1939
m. Richard Gass

Diane Gass
b. 10/10/1964

Michael Cathcart
b. 7/7/1968

Elizabeth Cathcart
b. 6/21/1974

Thomas Gass
b. 3/31/1966

John Lennon
b. 2/4/1910

James Lennon
b. 4/12/1913

Isabelle Denning
b. 7/25/1919

Thomas Lennon
b. 6/14/1917

Robert Lennon
b. 11/12/1918

Theodore Lennon
b. 10/23/1920

Patrick Lennon
b. 4/27/1926

Danforth Denning, Jr.
b. 2/8/1921—
d. 7/1977

Mary Lennon
(Blaser)
b. 10/13/1928

William Lennon · m. 2/19/1939
b. 4/20/1915—
d. 8/12/1969

Herbert Lennon
b. 5/24/1886—
d. 1/11/1931

m.

Barbara Heinrich
b. 3/2/1887—
d. 6/21/1957

Danforth Denning
b. 6/2/1892—
d. 9/1954

m. Reina Ysabel Alvarez
b. 7/8/1894

John Lennon
Minna Lehman
Valentine Heinrich
Margaret
William Charles Denning
Emily Chaplin
Peter Paul Alvarez
Marguerite Camacho

The Lennon Family Tree

Foreword

We were fortunate to be born in the twentieth century. During this remarkable era enormous advances were made in the development of mass communications. Because of these advances, we—The Lennon Sisters—instantly reached an audience of millions with our very first television appearance.

In our profession we have followed a path established by The Boswell Sisters, The Andrew Sisters, The King Sisters, and The Maguire Sisters. After us came the Osmonds, the Carpenters, the Pointer Sisters, and the Jacksons. Each has a different sound, exuding its own energy and personality. But all of us are part of a twentieth-century musical phenomenon, "the recorded group sound." We four sisters have been performing our unique style of harmony for over thirty years.

In 1973, we undertook a new challenge when we decided to write our memoirs. Motivated by managers, producers, editors, fans, friends, and our family, we realized we did have much to share; most importantly, how we, as sisters, relate to one another.

We—Dianne, Peggy, Kathy, and Janet Lennon—started out discussing those things that would be included in our book. Though we have spent most of our lives singing together, we are also individuals with different personalities and separate achievements.

If nothing else, this book serves as a testament to our parents and our families. It is intended for our audiences, those who have watched us growing up before their eyes on their television screens. Our memories have served us well, too. We tell as much as we are able. We are great talkers, and admittedly we've written as we speak.

We considered many titles for this, and that discussion alone took nearly a year. Our work habits for writing did not reach our levels of discipline for rehearsal and performance. This tome took so long to write it nearly ruined our lives. We considered calling it "How To Write A Book And Wreck A Family." Summers ran into autumns, then another Christmas was upon us, and before we could blink it was another Easter season, and in a few short weeks, summer again and onward, year after year . . . .

It was war and peace. (Tolstoy got to the printer first, so we had to give up that title.) We listed as possibilities "The Lennon Sistory," "The Lennon Tree," "A Twist of Lennon," and "Four Girls and Twenty Years Ago." That one lost out because it became 24 years ago, 25 years ago, 26 years . . . .

How can four people write a book, one autobiography? Each of us remembers something different, each has a viewpoint that might conflict with another's. Who writes what part? This book may well be the only "collective" autobiography in print—by four authors, all related. Separate voices singing one song.

We did one thing right for our book. We began with an outline:

1) An Introduction by all of us.
2) Family Ancestry and Family Life.
3) Childhood Days, our dating, our school years.
4) The Lawrence Welk Show years.
5) The Tours, the Fairs, the Nightclubs, the Benefits.
6) Our parents, our brothers and sisters, our fear of flying, our other fears.
7) Our Dad's life, our Dad's death.
8) Our marriages and our family life, then and now.

Well, it was a beginning . . . .

Our early childhood was easy to put down on paper, as it brought back only fond memories. We found it impossible to write all we remembered and felt about Lawrence Welk and our years with his organization. Some memories were happy, yet many were not. Recalling our personal tragedies left us emotionally drained, but we felt that people would want to read our account of those sad days and perhaps it might be helpful to others coping with deep personal loss. We realized that we had blocked much from our minds, and it was with painstaking effort that we managed to slowly drag out all the memories.

The difficulty completing the Book continued over the years because there were always other things to do. We would not allow the Book to get in our way. We had rehearsals, performances and benefits, costume fittings, photo sessions, recordings, husbands and children to nurture, and CARPOOLS.

We arranged—at least for a time—to work on the Book weekdays between 9:00 a.m. and 2:00 p.m. Six hours may seem like a long period, but it took more than an hour just to make the coffee, drink it, and get past the chit-chat. We would reach a good level of discussion and writing when one of our husbands would telephone. "How's it going?" So one of us would answer "fine," and then we would try to get back on track. After that it was, "Jan, would you trim my hair? I brought my scissors—it'll take only a few minutes."

"Sure Peg. Wait, though. I just put another coat of polish on my nails."

"Say, did I tell you about running into . . . ."

"Did you watch 'Little House' last night?"

"No, I watched the Rams."

"What are you cooking tonight? I need a new idea."

"Did you know Jennie cut her first tooth yesterday?"

With effort and luck, we might settle down to work by 11 o'clock. Toward the end of the fourth or fifth year we had pretty much written a first draft of what we wanted included. Our collaboration took various turns and twists. We practiced a score of diets during this time of the Book. We tried everything to keep on track and in shape.

"Harold Cohen called last night. He said we'll be working for three weeks in July with Andy Williams in Las Vegas."

"Oh, no, we'll have to buy the kids new bathing suits. I'd be embarrassed to let them swim in what they now wear."

"I'll go shopping with you. There's this cute little kids' shop . . . ."

For a time we tried writing individually in four separate rooms. Then, at an appointed hour, we would meet to read one another's efforts.

"I got a lot done, did you?"

"No, everything I wrote came out boring."

"Speaking of boring, did you see the 'Movie of the Week' last night?"

Part of our problem was finding a place to work. Peg and Janet live in the San Fernando Valley. Dee Dee and Kathy live forty minutes away, near the beach. Our four meetings a week were split; two days in the Valley, two days at the beach. This sounded good. And it was fair.

However, it proved to be a disaster. Meetings at Jan's had us devouring her fresh fruit, homemade biscuits, and sweet rolls. So a good hour was lost eating and admiring her baking techniques; then subsequent discussion covered all foods and recipes, foreign and domestic, cooked or otherwise. At Dee Dee's house, people stopped by to visit for "just a minute," so we took long breaks that ended with lunch. The drop-ins finally sauntered off, leaving the dishes for us. Another day shot.

At Kathy's home the phone seldom stopped ringing because she handled all Lennon Sister business. After each interruption, Kathy would return to our free-for-all talk. At Peg's house, with preschoolers at home and older kids coming in from school, there was no peace.

We endured endless ribbing from the family about the Book. Would it ever end? Dee Dee's husband proclaimed continually, "It won't be through 'til '92!"

We didn't appreciate their humor because the Book was like a weight on our shoulders, always there waiting to be written. At one point we thought the title should be "Blood, Sweat, and Tears," but while we were writing they became a rock group.

In all fairness, there were legitimate gaps in our work on the Book. There were appearances in Las Vegas, Lake Tahoe, Atlantic City, television variety shows, Christmas holidays, state fairs, Easter holidays, summer and the living is easy because the kids are at home. There were dinners and lunches and meetings and family gatherings for birthdays, weddings, and baby showers . . . .

In a desperate effort to finish—having re-read three more years of our literary monster—we decided to go away somewhere and write, write, write.

Wrong!

We locked ourselves in a hotel room for six days—from 8:30 a.m. to 9:00 p.m. We infused ourselves with all our original enthusiasm and—as dedicated achievers—motivated to finish the Book with a flourish, we . . . .

RRRRRING: "Hello, Mommy? I got hit in the stomach with the kickball at school, so Grandma came to get me. I'm at her house now, in case you wanted to talk to me about anything."

RRRRRING: "Mom, I can't start my homework because as I was walking home a gust of wind accidentally blew my assignment papers away. I really tried hard to find them, but . . . ."

RRRRRING: "Hello, Jan? I'm sorry to bother you when you're so busy, but your Goober (John) hasn't come home from school yet, and his friend said he saw him down by the creek playing with some frogs. What should I do?"

RRRRRING: "Hi, Honey? So, how's it going?"

And the room service menu kept bothering us.

"Maybe we should order a big breakfast now, skip lunch . . . .

"No, I think we should order a light breakfast now and then take a break and go out for a big lunch."

"Now, listen. If we order light breakfasts, we can have coffee about 11:30, go out for a light lunch at 1:30, then come back and work five hours steady, and then have a big dinner."

"What time will we have dinner?"

It's sad, we admit, that the question most on our minds every fifteen minutes after 3:00 p.m. each day was: "What time is it now?"

"One hour until baked potato." Then, "half hour until baked potato." And naturally, "fifteen minutes to baked potato."

We were close to the end of the Book, but could no longer bear the claustrophobia of the hotel room. So this method didn't work either.

A light bulb went on in someone's head! Why not meet at Mom's. Then our brother Bill made us an offer we could not refuse. "Rather than pay hotel bills, why don't you pay me to clean my room, and you can isolate yourselves in Mom's backyard."

And so, for ten dollars a week payable to Billy Lennon, we reentered the old den in the backyard of the family homestead in Venice, California. Originally it had been our rehearsal room after we had moved from Garfield Avenue to Harding Avenue. Now it was our younger brother's uncontested possession. This deal afforded us isolation and indeed forced Billy to give his room a long, much overdue cleaning. Once again Mom proved there is an art *and* a science to mothering, when she offered to cook and serve us our meals. That clinched the deal.

We had spent many years in that room, rehearsing our songs, and we hoped we could recapture that creative aura to complete our memoirs. However, Billy's room was not quite as isolated as he had suggested, for Mom's house is never tranquil. Amidst the four dogs barking at the trashman in the alley (or at anyone or anything in the alley), brothers and sisters running into the room "just to see how you're doing," Mom's welcomed interruptions of freshly baked cookies and hot coffee, we finally managed to finish.

We're proud of our Book. We're proud of ourselves for completing it. It has been good therapy, and after so many hours, days, weeks, and years, we are proud to say we're still friends.

Finally, this is It! It is finished! It has been ours for years. Now it is yours.

Same Song—Separate Voices

We four Lennon Sisters, 1949. Left to right, Kathy, 6; Peggy, 8; Janet 3; Dee Dee, 9. *The Lennon Sisters Collection)*

Our first public appearance, Spring, 1954. The Lennon Sisters in *Roamin' Holiday*, St. Mark Church, Venice, California. *(The Lennon Sisters Collection)*

1

Getting To Know You

Dianne:

I can remember being looked up to by my younger sisters and brothers. And I always knew that Dad and Mom were proud of me. I was truly happy being the oldest child and enjoyed the responsibilities and advantages of that position. I loved being needed and was happiest when rocking one of the little ones or making peanut butter and grape jelly sandwiches. "Take off the crust and cut them into triangles." I recall Christmas Eve when I was about eleven years old. My sandwich-making capability was tested. Our family was undergoing its annual siege of stomach flu, and Mom and Dad were the last to fall—and on Christmas Eve. So I took over the kitchen and, with Peg as my assistant chef, made tuna sandwiches for all the little kids. After all, peanut butter and jelly sandwiches weren't for holidays.

As the oldest sister in a family of eleven, I guess I could have felt very overworked and overwhelmed by the multitude of diapers and bottles and babysitting. But I never felt burdened at all. My favorite recollections are of bathing chubby-bottomed toddlers, cuddling a soaking wet baby in bed with me in the early morning, or just rocking a new brother or sister. My stability and security was in and with my status as "oldest sister."

I learned much from our mother, who was a real mom. Her family was her life—and still is. Without any great to-do she gave lesson after lesson on the innumerable facets of motherhood. But while she carried out her everyday chores and concerns of rearing a large family, I was able to reap the harvest of laughter and tears that came from living among and spoiling all my sisters and brothers.

It was my gradual preparation for things that would come quickly to me in later years—three children in 27 months!

I was Dad's pal, and I learned to be a confidante and friend. We spent a lot of time together, just the two of us. Through our companionship, I feel I learned many of the qualities for being a good wife.

I have always been a shy person. Maybe that comes from the fact that I didn't have to leave my home to seek the company of others. My home and family was where I loved to be, and I always wanted to "grow up and be a wife and mother."

Basically, I, Dianne Gass, am just that. I often have to put her aside to become Dianne Lennon, singer and performer. Then I feel that I become someone I truly am not. Or am I? I did not seek to become a member of a famous singing group. It just fell into my lap. I am not forced to perform, and yet, after all these years, I'm still doing it. Why? It is a constant wonder to me that it never gets easier. Whereas my sisters can learn their individual harmony notes after only a few rehearsals, I spend hours and hours at home by myself trying to memorize simple phrases. My ear is definitely not tuned to harmonies. Peg, Kath, and Jan can actually *enjoy* learning new choreography, though they also work very hard. For me it is frustrating! My feet and hands and head all move in different directions and never come together until opening night—sometimes even later. I have learned to be a good faker—not out of laziness or not caring, but simply because "I don't have it!" I'm not really uncoordinated because I am a very good athlete. I feel that for the other three girls our rehearsals must be like that old golf saying, "Hit the ball and drag" Dee Dee. I am thankful for and respect their collective patience.

But not all aspects of our performing are trying for me. It is with a great deal of pride in the four of us—as a unit and as sisters—that I stand onstage and do my best in order to measure up to the others. (I keep waiting for the day when I can be performing onstage and planning my grocery list at the same time, as my sisters can!)

So why do I continue? There is always the financial aspect. The few weeks in the year that we work allow me the privilege of staying home with my family and doing what I like best the rest of the time. And I also am very pleased that my husband and children are proud of me. They really know how hard I work. They put up with my tears of frustration on rehearsal days and manage to bring me back to the comfortable reality of home and family. I don't know what I would do if I did not have their support.

I am truly fulfilled as both a wife and mother. I treasure each day with my family. I now find my security and stability in *them*. Few individuals have been afforded the wonderful events and people such as I have in my life. I accept each one and try to enjoy them.

Our children are almost grown now, and though they are all living at home and are still "underfoot," I often miss the days of their little clinging hands, warm cuddly hugs, and their constant need for "Mom."

I'm looking forward to having grandchildren—when again I'll know the joys of making peanut butter and jelly sandwiches. It is a most rewarding experience.

Peggy:

Whatever it is that causes members of a family to seem similar to each other in appearance, attitude, or temperament just didn't happen to me. I *was* different from my sisters. Perhaps I tended to emphasize all the differences. One has only to look at me and see the first difference. I carry several of the good, sturdy Mexican-Spanish genes of my grandmother, Nana.

During all the years we have been writing this book we have examined our performances, onstage and off. We found it easy to discuss the past with each other, but when it came to expressing ourselves as we are now, I had difficulty. I chalk that up to being different. This writing process has forced me to listen more closely to each of my sisters and to our brothers, who have such wonderful insights of their own. I found I focused on their observations of me. Some have surprised me, and I concede that many are true. But one of the truths I've always known is that I have so much more to do.

There is more searching to do, more growth to achieve in order to define the spirit that I am. Not necessarily seeking a greater religious life, but moving to a great spiritual experience.

When I was young, being alone was easy for me; I just made it happen. I was the last to clean my room and do the household chores. That was easier for others, not for me. I was surrounded by people at home, more than enough. I seemed to need no bond of friendship outside the family. But I did not think quite like any of my sisters. I was not listening for the sound of different drums, I *was* the different drummer. It took no persuasion from them, however, for me to join in with their abrupt plans or chaotic antics, but still they allowed me my aloneness and solitude.

Some parents and educational techniques have squelched the very uniqueness that every child possesses: be this, be that, do this, do that, don't feel this, watch out for . . . . I'm grateful no one in my family suppressed me. In the midst of a home filled with people, I read books. I had early on read *The Confessions of St. Augustine* and immersed myself in *The Imitation of Christ* and the works of Thomas Aquinas. This was not weird to my way of thinking. I just felt ahead of everyone else—no one stopped me from feeling this way.

I've never felt myself in competition with anything or anyone, especially not with my sisters. Our parents placed no demands on us to fulfill their expectations for us, but I believe one thing that pleased them was accomplishment. My kind of accomplishment had more to do with the mind and spirit than with physical achievements, except, of course, being one of The Lennon Sisters. I did develop my voice when Dee Dee and I sang during the household tasks we did together. Singing a second harmony, adding Kathy's third part when she grew into it, came quite easily and naturally. At least that's how it seemed.

My curiosity was for unseen things. Why did something happen the way it did? Or why did a series of events seem to work as if they had been planned by an architect? I spent many hours studying the planes on which spiritual growth can be attained. Reading filled my hunger for knowledge and for what I projected to be the truth of things. I found solace in books; I did not need much else—at least until I married and had a family of my own. And it was just a few years ago that I came to true friendship with other women. I like being a friend, and I love the reward of having friends.

In my youth I buried myself in learning. Whenever my sisters teased me about being lazy and hiding out in the bathroom to escape work, I could easily rationalize that I was feeding my mind with important things. I knew I would share my ideas with others in time. There weren't many places at home where one could get lost. If there were, I found them. Then I could be alone again, yet still seem to feel a part of the family. That was part of my spiritual development.

I expected to be teased and to receive nicknames, although it could not be said I was called St. Therese in derision. The name came to me because one Halloween I dressed as St. Therese rather than as a stupid gypsy. (After all, if you can't dress as a saint on All Saint's Eve, when can you?)

Too often it seemed I never had enough time to contemplate. So when I was invited to attend a weekend retreat—at age twelve, much younger than any of the other girls attending—to spend time in prayer and meditation, away from the frantic, everyday matters and noise, I leaped at the chance.

Our retreat master, Father Joel Gromowski, C.P., was just the kind of priestly guide I needed then. He spoke to me straight and to the point, with no sentiment. Plainly, what I achieved in that weekend experience, not only in the conferences and seminars, but in private talks with Father Gromowski, was the beginning of self-understanding. It was not the fulfillment of my continual spiritual thirst, but a course was set, with sound advice; although some of it was not what I may have desired or expected to hear.

Father Joel pointed out that I could not necessarily spend all my time in perpetual retreat. I told him I was seriously contemplating becoming a nun. He pointed out that perhaps God had other plans. One did not need to stop reading or searching, but by balancing study with experience in the outside world one might find many ways to contribute to the spiritual world of others. I was advised to examine the needs of my family and to cultivate friends. "Grow in all directions; then you will be able to make a sensible decision about your life course," he said.

After that I ceased saying, "When-I-grow-up-I'm-going-to-be-a-nun!" But I had not stopped thinking about it. It was not easy for

Dianne Lennon Gass, wife and mother, with husband Dick, baby Mary, and four months pregnant with Diane. *(Globe Photo/Lennon Family Collection)*

Peggy Lennon, age 8, expressing her desire to become a nun, as Saint Therese, Halloween, 1950. *(The Lennon Family Collection)*

Kathy Lennon in performance. "I might have been a solo performer, but I could not imagine being onstage without my sisters." *(The Lennon Sisters Collection)*

Little Janet, with Lawrence Welk, at ABC Studios, Hollywood, dancing their incomparable polka.

me to accept life's changing patterns. It meant I had to share my private world and open myself up.

Within a few weeks, we girls were to make our first public appearance and then other "worldly" opportunities were to open to us. I made myself ready for them.

There was definite discipline in our home. But when the law was laid down to us, there was always a touch of humor with it. Our dad did not act in a moment of anger or resentment. He waited until he had regained control. Waiting for his edict was as much disciplining as if he had actually spanked us. As teenagers, we had the usual curfews to maintain, and our boyfriends were investigated with a parental scrutiny that, in the end, had them returning for more of Dad's unique humor. Daddy had a way with people, and he did not hesitate to use *his* way, even after we'd left home. When we married, we still went back weekly for more exposure to *his* way of things.

Just for the fun of it, for news, for family gatherings over any excuse, just for a morning coffee or a piece of Mom's chocolate cake. But then, we never left home, not in the strict sense of moving out and away.

I knew I could have been a better companion to Dee Dee. She loved being neat, being a homemaker. I didn't, and I wasn't. But we shared wonderful, close moments, some of them while singing songs together. With Kathy we became a trio. When Jan started singing along with us, a quartet. Driving in the car we sang with the whole family, doing household chores we tried out new harmonies. (In our home it was not the babies' first words that were eagerly anticipated, but whether they could mimic any musical sounds.)

Of course, thrown in among all that music, I felt it my duty to share my reading experiences with my family, granting them access to all the intellectual and spiritual information and philosophies I felt I had. (Whether they liked it or not!)

Now that we've looked at our beginnings together, I can see how odd I may have seemed to the others. To me, I was just me! I have not changed directions so much as I have grown in many directions. And I pray each day to continue growing, that I may keep an open mind in order to learn more from life. And that I can share these wonderful things, these ideals I have explored, with my husband Dick, and with our six children—whether they like it or not!

Kathy:

Growing up as a Lennon was a special experience. As third child of Bill and Sis Lennon, I had the opportunity to develop different strengths from those of my older sisters, and to explore different avenues of life. From the beginning strong values, both spiritually and emotionally, were instilled in us. This strength in body and mind and spirit enabled me to endure many crises in my life.

The Lennon family did not lead a painless life. Certainly I know I didn't, but there is always within our family a meaningful relationship that lives in us and through us. I believe it is God. Knowing that, we know what it is to love and be loved. When one is loved and knows it beyond all doubt, there is nothing to stand in the way of accomplishment. There is nothing better to heal all pain. In some ways, our parents were as young as we were, making things happen creatively, in pleasant, fun circumstances. And so we children have acted childlike throughout our days. At least, that is how I see it.

From the time we were babies Janet—just three years my junior—and I were the world's best pals. When a couple of girls can share Hoot Gibson and Tim McCoy days, and make up songs to talk to one another, their bond is unbroken. Those days passed away too quickly. Janet and I have also shared adult experiences, both of comfort and discomfort. Happy feelings, or those of emotional pain, have held us, strongly tied, through many trials.

I always found Dee Dee the quiet guide, the helpful companion and friend. With Peggy, I think a deeper friendship came as we grew older. For all of us, being together, singing together brought the true closeness, the oneness that melded us one into another. It is our public image, that oneness. It's natural. We bring it from our home!

One of the things I do best is taking everyone's inventory. My family allows me to do this because I am the Lennon girl who carries the title of counselor, listener, organizer, and advisor. Since I have no children of my own, all of my family are my strength, and I thrive on my commitments to them.

Not too long ago, my mother told me that she knew in her heart that if any of us would have branched out on her own as a singer, it would most likely have been me. When I heard this, I thought, "No, that's not so." Then, thinking about it over a period of time, I would agree with her assessment. But another part of me cannot quite imagine being a single performer. Surely, I sing solo once in a while, but the other three Lennon sisters are always there, backing me up. Their presence is my security and my stability. The *single* idea is just that. An idea. I'm comfortable for now.

When our parents bought the house on Harding Avenue in Venice, Janet and I shared a corner bedroom on the top floor. Truly, we were great roomies. We chose our own bedroom furnishings and the new materials for our curtains and bedspreads. But that was after we had been earning money and the family benefitted from our professional status as regulars on the Lawrence Welk television show. It was in that little room on the top floor, with its wonderful hardwood floors and its brightly draped windows, where we would lie in our beds for hours and talk of our deepest secrets and dreams.

When we were in our teens, a favorite time was late at night, usually after everyone had come home from their dates. Jan and I would sneak downstairs, make hot Ovaltine with just a pinch of sugar, and prepare Oroweat toasted bread, with the butter dripping heavily. We would take our feast upstairs to our room, lie in bed, and discuss our dates in great detail, making sure to embellish all the boring parts of the evening. But each time we did this, we came to the same conclusion—that our talks after those dates with boyfriends were more fun than the dates themselves.

For a time, Janet and I kept personal diaries. We promised to respect each other's privacy. This lasted a few months, until the day when Janet opened her diary and found my written comments on every page.

I laughed loudly. She didn't!

I couldn't help but tease Janet sometimes. She was completely vulnerable, and so naive. She was a sound sleeper and had a tendency to wake with a start—a jolt is more like it. One night, returning home late (after Dad's curfew, as usual), I tiptoed around our room. Jan jumped up out of her bed. "Kathy, what time is it?"

I replied with great urgency, "It's time to get up and dress for school. You'd better hurry."

She proceeded to stumble to the closet and turn on the light with the long chain that hung from the bare bulb. I watched with amusement as Janet put on her entire school uniform, all the while mumbling, "I can't believe how tired I am. It seems like I just went to sleep."

Just as she tied her final shoelace, I let her in on my little joke. I laughed loudly. She didn't!

I suppose my own naivete came in the form of being surprised that some families are not at all like the Lennon family. I could not fathom, for instance, just why some of my school friends did not want to go right home after school, or fought bitterly with their parents or siblings. Maybe we took family attachment too far. But, in growing, we found ourselves drawing enormous strength from being together. It was so natural for us to be that way, I never realized it was so special. We are open to, and experience, changes, together and separately. Sometimes the changes are abrupt and painful, other times subtle, many times joyful. But with all of this we are aware of our special bond.

One of the burdens of my life that I have to deal with on a daily basis is my concern about the harshness of the world and the suffering of its people—from the children of El Salvador to the bag ladies sitting in the park across the street from my home. I must learn to accept my limitations. I do get some satisfaction from all the charity work we do, and I do personally, because I know I can help to change a few lives for a little while.

I am glad for certain qualities beyond those of being one of a quartet of singing sisters. I am confident—I feel good about myself. I express my confidence well and nurture it in others, perhaps because I accept so much of what other people give me. I am married to a man who is confident; just the sound of his voice gives me warmth and assurance. In a comparatively short time, Jim has helped me expand my awareness and my sensitivity in relation to others. I often have to remind myself not to be so deeply disappointed when I don't live up to my own high expectations. However, I've gained from our family the ability to seriously apply a sense of humor to my attitude toward life.

I recall that, when we were small, a person was either Catholic or Public. With the exception of a few early years when our parish had no school of its own, all of our formal education came at the hands and minds of the Sisters, those dedicated and forthright women who were like second mothers.

We grew to love the nuns dearly. And dearly, we feared them. Situations and problems were good or bad—no in-between. For years we existed by the never-to-be-refuted, "Sister says . . . !" Much of the time it wasn't "sister" that fell from our mouths, but rather, "S'ter." The necessarily quick responses became, "Yes, S'ter," and "No, S'ter." Surely most nuns go *s'ter* crazy.

Their devotion was strong, their disciplines were strict. Many times we shook under the strain. I remember one instance that I had forgotten until the Book. My sisters call it a great example of Catholic-little-girl-logic of the naive 1950s.

I was nearly ten years old when our parents took us all to the Los Angeles County Museum. That fine old edifice on Exposition Boulevard housed great art and acclaimed exhibits. Our family sauntered throughout those great rooms, viewing all the famous paintings. We all appreciated the art works, mostly because it was yet another expedition with our parents into an unknown world. We thrived on such excursions. Certainly, we grew a lot, too.

Janet (who was then about seven years old) and I wandered off into a huge room that contained the statues of the gods and goddesses. Upon seeing these marble nude statues in all their glory, Janet and I blushed. We gave way to our natural impulses and began to snicker and giggle.

Later this incident weighed quite heavily on my conscience. After a few days of torment, in proper ten-year-old style, I entered the little dark space of the confessional, pulled the curtain closed, and knelt down before the screen that separated me from my confessor.

"Bless me, Father, for I have sinned," I began. "It has been a week since my last confession. These are my sins; I missed my morning prayers once, and I argued with my sisters twice; and . . . and . . . well, I committed . . . uh . . . adultery."

I distinctly remember hearing an immediate gasp from the other side of the screen. Then a stuttering voice whispered to me, "You what???"

"I said I committed adultery, Father."

Again the little choking sound. "How old are you, my child?"

I surely knew by his shaking voice that I had shocked the priest by my shameless conduct. Naturally he had not heard such a confession in months, perhaps years. "I am ten years old, Father," I replied.

"Ah, now carefully, child. Tell me, where did this, uh, ah, this transgression take place?"

"At the Los Angeles County Museum."

There was another muffled sound, then another incredulous whisper. "Of course," he said.

Then there was the longest silence I had ever known. "Now, dear young lady. In detail, tell me all of it. How did you, uh, well, ah, *do* it?"

Through my tears I blurted out the circumstances. I knew Father was very upset with me because he said nothing at all. My heart was pounding in my ears. It was quite some time before he could compose himself to speak.

"Well, my dear," he said finally. "Promise the Lord you will never do such a thing again, and say a prayer to the Blessed Mother to keep your heart and mind pure. But for your penance now, say three Our Fathers, three Hail Marys, and make a good Act of Contrition."

I made up my mind then and there never again to break the Sixth Commandment: "Though shalt not commit adultery," which, of course, I was taught meant any impure thoughts or words or deeds.

Janet:

I never wanted to make waves.

I never wanted to do anything wrong, so I never did much of anything at all. I had a precarious, even strange, position to maintain in our family. Although I was the fourth oldest of a large group at home, I was the baby of The Lennon Sisters in the eyes of a large public. "Oh, Janet!" "The little one." "Cute little Janet."

I would sit on the laps of hundreds of fans and soak in their love and attention. But at the same time I would feel guilty that it might be hurting Dee Dee, Peggy, or Kathy. After all, they were every bit as talented and important; they just weren't as small.

I have survided all that. It's strange to say it now, but I have blocked out many of the events that happened to us during those early years when, at my young age of seven, we began our professional lives as The Lennon Sisters. Oh, I can recall just about everything I did at home with the family, but not too many things that took place in the day-in, day-out activity of being a performer.

We were voices singing songs, working hard and gathering unto ourselves a large following. Our fans were supportive, loyal, and loving, encouraging us through our growing-up years. However, it took me a long time to grow up. That is, to grow up inside myself.

Though we loved our work as The Lennon Sisters, we did not live merely to go out onstage—or look into a camera lens—and sing songs. The fact is, we loved being home. I suppose that, wherever we are, whatever we are doing or thinking of doing, we throw our whole selves into it and perform to our fullest. Yes, we enjoy our work. Our work is important. Our family is more so.

Not long ago, Kathy and I stood together in the backstage wings at Caesar's Palace, Las Vegas. It was opening night, and we were not without our usual burning panic, clasping each other's shaking, clammy hands. Awaiting our musical cue, I broke the moment. "Wouldn't it be terrible if we had to do this for a living?" I said.

Kathy laughed, gave me a shove, and we were on!

During performances I feel very gregarious. I'm deeply motivated by the care and professionalism of my sisters onstage. We are charged by each other's energies. Singing with Dee Dee, Peggy, and Kathy makes me feel confident in myself, and for a time, out there onstage or before the camera, it is my world. I'm comfortable. I belong. Yet, from the moment I hit the wings of the stage after performing, I'm another Janet. Offstage, I'm shy. This thing of mine, these two parts of me, has been a source of confusion and frustration most of my life.

Once people did everything for me—my mom, my sisters, especially Daddy. When you go around with that damsel-in-distress look about you, what you receive is attention. I didn't want it, yet, somehow I must have been asking for it. I never wanted to hurt anybody, so I did everything I was told to do. I wasn't a great initiator, like Kathy, but I was a terrific follower. In any given situation, I could really take the ball and run with it.

My sisters gave me as much attention as the public did, so they too were the culprits in my uneasy development. I was so afraid that someone might think I was big-headed that I never allowed myself—not even in the deepest caverns of my inner self—to bask in the glory of being "hotshot-for-a-day."

My great escape from all this is my use of sleep. I nearly missed my debut as a singer at age seven! In the spring of 1954 our church, St. Mark, pulled together a huge fund-raising program. It was a planned musical panorama of native folk tales, ethnic songs, and dances of many nations. Aptly, the show was titled *Roamin' Holiday*.

All the people in our parish, encompassing most of the Catholic families of Venice, were to lend their talents, whatever they might be, to this program. Now Venice, California, is just a little body of land, really a corridor, that lies eastward from the Pacific beaches to the Culver City border, with Santa Monica on the north and the water-community of Marina del Rey on the south. Venice has been a haven for small businesses, beach bums, creative artisans and craftspersons, loud and quiet partisans, and roving street kids, for decades. It's expensive or it's cheap and gaudy, depending more on attitudes than economics. Parts of Venice are to be feared, but it's also a wonderful place to promenade. It's the kind of community that both suppresses and nourishes talents within its borders.

On that church program we four concentrated our talents on representing Scotland—a strange choice for girls with English-Irish-German-Spanish (and just a wee bit of Scottish) background. Our mother and Nana combined their considerable talents to sewing costumes, the kilts and tams that we wore over our white school-uniform blouses. Naturally we looked like four girls wearing authentic Highland kilts worn over white school-uniform blouses! Anyway, we chose for our songs, "Flow Gently, Sweet Afton" and the lovely "Loch Lomond."

If fortune was to give us an encore, we planned to sing "Roamin' in the Gloamin'." Fortune did smile and, using walking sticks and expelling our Scottish brogues *a la* Harry Lauder (prompted by Daddy), we were a "success."

Appropriately, the show's finale was our own country, the United States. Happily for us our uncles, Dad's brothers, were coaxed out of their "retirement" to entertain us with their New York nightclub routine, the final arrangement of which was a unique rendition of "Dry Bones." When they had sung a few choruses, four little skeletons were to join them, and the eight of us would dance and sing, "Disconnect—ahh—dem bones, dem dry bones . . . ." Again, we wore costumes that Mom and Nana had made, cutting bone-like shapes out of old white sheets and sewing them on black turtlenecks and navy blue jeans. From the audience viewpoint they were really effective, and the number stole the show.

Evidently I was not too impressed with the whole thing; just before the four of us "little bones" were to join the "big bones" onstage, I could not be located. A frantic search by my three sisters ended in my being jolted awake from behind my perch near the backstage piano. I understand that I was in a deep sleep, sucking my thumb. I know I was upset at being jarred awake. Sleep was—and is—important to me!

That event, however, was our first public appearance. From that time, though we didn't realize it then, our at-home Sunday night shows for family and friends were really preparations for greater things to come.

I always wanted to be the perfect student, to be the perfect daughter and the perfect example. I felt it *was* possible to be human and perfect at the same time. It's strange how life seems to confront you with the very problems you feel could only happen to someone else. My ideals began to crumble when, after ten years of marriage to Lee Bernhardi, I found myself facing an unbelievable reality: a failing marriage. To remember that time is to relive the most emotional and debilitating period of my life.

Family and friends had suggested that Lee and I wait a little longer before we married. We might be too young, they told us. But Lee and I had believed we could handle anything and everything together.

The years moved on, full of promise, of work, of having our

children. We began to mature. And we came to realize we lacked that deep sense of fulfillment in one another so necessary for a good marriage. We had tried for years to find the key. Instead, we found we could no longer blind ourselves to the painful truth. After much soul-searching, we decided to separate.

I could never express in words the desperate sense of failure I felt. I wanted, among the several perfects, to be the perfect wife. I hated and blamed myself. Of course, it didn't help that, from the time I was eight or nine years old, people looked to The Lennon Sisters almost as idols. How often we heard, "I want my daughters to grow up to be just like you," or, "You girls are such a beautiful example for the youth of America."

Although this flattery made me feel good inside, a part of me was screaming, "Please don't say that, because you really don't know me!" Yet that unconscious pressure to please everyone at all costs kept eating away at me relentlessly. I harbored thoughts that plagued me. What will I tell the kids? What will Mom think of me? I wondered if Lee's family would understand. I loved his parents and his family so much. Will this affect the other Lennons and their reputation? And what about the Church? And on and on and on.

I was then 27 years old, and I wanted my daddy to come back to take care of things for me the way he used to. But he was gone from us so abruptly. So tragically. For the first time, I was faced with a giant responsibility that only I should and could resolve. Always before there was someone to help me. If it wasn't Mom and the girls, it was Daddy or Lee.

I felt so alone; I wanted the wisdom and maturity to do the right thing. But what was the right thing for me?

I had spent my life allowing myself to be sheltered, leaving to others the care of everything. How could I face responsibility now? There is belief, and I had that. Deep faith in God, I had that. It led to a still small flame, a belief in myself. Choosing to enter psychoanalysis, I began to rebuild the core of the inner self to support the hearty self-confidence that I had only when I was onstage. Little by little I chipped away at my prideless exterior to find that I really do like myself, and that I am proud of my achievements.

Lee and I had been good friends throughout our marriage;

that fondness and affection will always be there. I believe it was fate that brought Lee and me together for those many years, because the results of our love are so positive—William Joseph, John Frederick, and Kristin Leigh. Everytime I look into our children's faces, I know that they were meant to be—just as they are—beautiful, wanted, and loved.

Daddy had told us often that we affect every person we come into contact with. That effect could be either positive or negative. He told us that, through the talents that God gave us, we could help others to feel as good about themselves as we feel about ourselves. Every person is as important as the next, whatever status or station. He and Mom taught us the simplicity of being a happy person. Give all the love you can, and it will come back to you in abundance. It has.

2

Long, Long Ago

Kathy:

Although most of our family's performers were not nationally famous, a tradition of performing surrounded us all through our youth. When we look honestly at our path, there were certain fortunate associations and opportunities presented to us, and we took advantage of them. We did not, in the beginning, think for a moment that we would reach the acclaim we came to enjoy. At first, we just sang songs to occupy ourselves, enjoying the discovery of tones and harmonies. It was fun to sing with the radio or television. The new medium of television was merely a new outlet for enjoying ourselves at home. But this form of mimicry pushed us outward from our home to local appearances in Venice and Santa Monica, and smoothed the pathway to fame.

This view is simple in retrospect. We could not know in our childhood how our family and social life would work to our advantage. As children we were just the Lennons, four sisters who were happy singing together around the house, then at school functions and at church events. In time we sang a song or two at the local Knights of Columbus or Kiwanis meetings. Certainly we had help from our dad and uncles, themselves singers, and from our grandfather, who first gave us the ideas of harmonizing.

We were the Lennons, that family on Garfield Avenue, just off Lincoln Boulevard in Venice, in the days before zip codes.

Our beginnings were a series of begets and begats that started with a nineteenth-century Lennon, our great-great-grandfather, James Lennon. That Lennon left Galway Bay, Ireland, and emigrated with his family to the United States. It was a few years before the American Civil War when James Lennon and his wife Mary settled in Appleton, Wisconsin, and there raised thirteen red-haired children, one of whom was John Lennon, our great-grandfather.

When John Lennon turned nineteen years of age, he married our great-grandmother, Minnie Lehman. But just two years later John died. Left alone with an infant son, Herbert, Minnie Lehman Lennon, whom we called "Amma," moved into the home of James and Mary Lennon, her husband's parents. Minnie supported and reared Herbert—called Bert—by working as a seamstress. Amma never remarried and lived to be 96. Our dad said often that from the union of John and Minnie and their two years of marriage came the one child, Grandpa Bert Lennon, his eight children and 60 grandchildren, and an incalculable number of great-grand-children.

Bert Lennon grew to be a tall, handsome, red-haired man with a great gift of gab. Before he was twenty he was a newspaper-man for the Chicago *Herald American*. Through his work he met Barbara (Betty) Heinrich, our grandmother. Betty was a lovely young dancer from Munich, Bavaria, who had come to America at sixteen. Her father, Maximillian Heinrich, had been dance master at the Koenighof Theater in Munich. He was also a shoemaker, a craftsman of some reputation. The proximity to the Koenighof instilled in Betty at an early age the desire for a career in dance. Her father, dedicated to theater work, performed and taught dancing all his life. He died at 86 years of age on the dance floor of his studio while giving a lesson.

As a member of a Gypsy dance troupe, in which she was featured as "Babette," Betty Heinrich made two tours of the United States. On the second tour, Bert Lennon was assigned by his newspaper to interview the members of the troupe. Bert was sent to New York to conduct his interviews aboard ship, so the feature articles could appear in the *Herald American* as soon as the troupe arrived in Chicago. He and Betty met on shipboard in New York Harbor. In Chicago they met again. Although they had a language barrier to overcome, Grandpa courted her in the most dashing

American fashion. We have been told that the first word Barbara mastered in English was "No." (She must have, at some point, also mastered "Yes.")

In 1909, in St. Paul, Minnesota, Bert Lennon and Betty Heinrich married. (Our grandfather had taken a job with the St. Paul *Pioneer Press*.) Within a few short years, two sons—Jack and Jim—were born to them. Soon after, the couple moved to Chicago, where William Herbert—our father—was born on April 20, 1915.

In 1917, Bert Lennon decided to move his family to southern California, having heard there were jobs to be found in the youthful and flourishing motion picture industry. Intrigued by the new business, he uprooted his wife and three sons, and with his mother, "Amma," left the Midwest to settle in Venice, the unique beach community beside the Pacific Ocean. The town was a specially designed replica of the Italian city, complete with canals and—for a short time—gondolas. A few blocks inland lay quiet residential streets of cottages and a few large Victorian houses with fancy gingerbread facades.

Four sons and a daughter were born to the Lennons after their arrival in Venice—Tom, Bob, Ted, Pat, and Mary. Today, with very few exceptions, almost all the descendants of Herbert and Betty Lennon live in Venice, Santa Monica, and the South Bay area.

Grandpa Bert Lennon found his niche in the motion picture industry, working as personal representative for Thomas Harper Ince, the great pioneering director, writer, and film producer. By 1918 Ince was settling into the sixteen-acre parcel of land that developer Harry Culver had offered free to anyone who would build a movie studio. That parcel, in the newly founded Culver City to the east of Venice, would become the site for what is now Metro-Goldwyn-Mayer/United Artists Studios.

At the new studio site on Washington Boulevard in Culver City, the film activity was heavy. "Pinky" Lennon, as Grandpa Bert would be called from then on (for his reddish hair and rosy complexion), became one of the most resourceful and respected publicists in the motion picture community. He worked with dozens of the early stars. John Gilbert, the silent screen star, rented a room at Grandpa and Grandma Lennon's house. Pinky Lennon handled all of William S. Hart's publicity. He traveled with Teddy Roosevelt during his safaris and expeditions, as well as in his last attempt to gain nomination for the presidency in 1920. As a publicist and promoter he offered the slogan for Sunmaid Raisins: "Have you had your iron today?" We are told he also coined the slogan that MGM used for many years: "More stars than there are in heaven."

One of Pinky's co-workers was a young reporter by the name of Louella Parsons. Our dad told us how much fun it was when she would come to babysit for them, but he and his brothers never got along too well with her daughter Harriet.

In an article that appeared in the Santa Monica *Evening Outlook* on March 28, 1930, Grandpa's unique flair for the dramatic is described:

"Mr. Lennon told of his experiences as publicity director for the late Thomas H. Ince (editor's note: Mr. Ince died in 1924, age 42), internationally known motion picture producer. One incident which amused Mr. Lennon's audience concerned the visit of the King and Queen of Belgium and Crown Prince Leopold.

" 'Their itinerary in Southern California called for a lot of dry speeches and dinners,' said Mr. Lennon. 'But a member of the Royal Party had written Mayor Snyder of Los Angeles and told him the honored guests wished to see the motion picture studios.

" 'By having an "escort" sign on the front of the automobile and plaster casts of the Belgian coat of arms on the car doors, the Ince machine led the royal parade to the Ince Studios, without the knowledge of the officials of the parade. Secret Service men were indignant over our act, but the Royal Family seemed to enjoy the incident immensely, incidentally having a grand time watching pictures being made.' "

Herbert Lennon had a great love for music, and he taught all of his children to sing. One of Dad's fondest memories was of his father singing "Sing Me To Sleep" while stroking his children's heads at bedtime.

During his early years, our dad sang in the choirs of the churches of St. Mark in Venice, St. Clement and St. Monica in Santa Monica. Eventually he became a soloist. One Sunday in 1929, the famous operatic tenor Tito Schipa was in the congregation at St. Monica's and was overwhelmed at hearing young Bill Lennon's voice. Fourteen-year-old Billy became Schipa's protege, singing several times for Schipa's movie friends, Douglas

Fairbanks and Mary Pickford, and the famous Irish tenor John McCormack.

Herbert Hoover was the first president elected from the State of California. In 1929, the well known composer Carrie Jacobs Bond ("When You Come To The End Of A Perfect Day," *etc.*) composed a song for the President, "Dear California." Dad, with Carrie Jacobs Bond at the piano, recorded the song and sent it as a special gift to President Hoover. The news clipping and the photograph commemorating the date are mementos we are very proud to have, as well as the letter of thanks written to Dad by President Hoover.

As a young man our dad toured up and down the Pacific Coast as a vaudeville singer with the Fanchon & Marco Circuit. He also had two solo concerts in the Hollywood Bowl.

During those years, California was separated from the rest of the nation by more than the Rocky Mountains. With the exception of motion pictures, some citrus fruits that made it to the midwest, and a growing aircraft industry, California seemed to be contained within its own borders. Any appearance in New York City was acclaimed throughout the world; but only the scandals of Hollywood made the press outside the borders of California. After the 1932 Olympics, when southern California reached world attention, Los Angeles was never again to be considered "that small town that sits out there next to the ocean."

The money that Dad earned from his appearances as a singer proved a big help to the Lennon family, because his father Bert had become ill, and he was no longer able to work full time at the studio. Dad's desire to sing professionally diminished greatly in 1931 when Grandpa Herbert Lennon died at age 45. It was a heavy blow to Betty and her eight children. Somehow our dad managed to sing at the funeral, believing it was the only gift he could give to honor his father who had encouraged his talents.

As in many homes across the nation, the Lennons struggled through the Great Depression. Amma continued to earn money as a seamstress, but the Welfare Department for the County of Los Angeles suggested that Betty separate her family and send the children off into different homes. Grandma Lennon came out of her grief fast enough to put a firm "Nein! Never!" to that idea. A family stays together and takes care of its own! Somehow!

Left, our grandmother, Barbara (Betty) Heinrich Lennon, the young dancer from Munich, whose "nein" became eight. *(The Lennon Family Collection)*

Below, our grandpa Bert Lennon and grandma, Betty, surrounded by six of their eight children. Our Dad, Bill, standing left, and (clockwise) Jim, Jack, Tom, Bob, baby Ted. *(The Lennon Family Collection)*

Right, Mom's mother, Reina Ysabel Alvarez Denning, "Nana." The young professional dancer. *(The Lennon Family Collection)*

Below, our lovely Nana with her handsome vagabond, our grandpa Danforth Denning, and their children, our uncle Dan, Jr., and our mother, Isabelle Emily, "Sis." *(The Lennon Family Collection)*

Master Bill Lennon, boy tenor, with composer Carrie Jacobs Bond, on the occasion of recording of "Dear California," for President Herbert Hoover, October 26, 1929. *(The Lennon Family Collection)*

A few years later, 1946: The Lennon Brothers (left to right) Uncle Ted, Uncle Pat, Dad, Uncle Bob. Among them they sired 39 children. *(The Lennon Family Collection)*

Our Dad, in his minstrel show makeup, for the Douglas Aircraft Show, 1943. *(The Lennon Family Collection)*

William Lennon and Isabelle Denning on their wedding day, February 19, 1939. *(The Lennon Family Collection)*

Betty Lennon's cupboard was often very nearly bare, but her ingenuity found ways of feeding her brood "pocket pleasing meals," not often "palate pleasing fare." She would, for instance, warm the milk so the children would not drink as much: "Just taking the chill off, dears." She sent her children off to school with applesauce sandwiches in their lunchbags. These were tolerable on Mondays and Tuesdays, when the applesauce was fresh, but as the week waned, so did the applesauce. Somehow this strong loving woman kept her seven sons and baby daughter in one home. As each of the boys grew older, he sought out ways to bring in money—such as paper routes, bottle collecting, even singing here and there—to help house and feed the family. Our dad and uncles told us that as boys they thought their mother to be at least six feet tall, weighing two hundred pounds. In reality all this enormous strength and energy was contained within a five-foot three-inch lady of one-hundred pounds.

Dianne:

During the autumn football season of 1935, when Dad was about twenty years old, he went back to Venice High School to watch his alma mater play University High School of Los Angeles. Our mother remembers that this was the new high school. The lovely red brick one that she had first attended had been damaged during the 1933 earthquake and had to be demolished. The new high school was square, and its facing was cold, gray stone. It would be years before it would be enlarged and painted the present bright cream color. Its sprawling building and campus now faces Venice Boulevard. (Mom spent a good portion of her high school years attending classes in tents erected on the back fields until the new building could be completed.)

At the game, Dad looked over the field and the bleachers to see if there was anyone he had known when he was in school. His eye caught the dark eyes and dark hair of a young girl who was concentrating intently on the game. Being sports minded, Dad found this pretty girl's interest in the game rare and appealing, and he finagled an introduction to Isabelle Denning. In a few minutes of conversation he realized she was the same little girl he had often teased on the beach when she was dating his younger brother Bob.

Isabelle—named "Sis" by her younger brother—captured Dad's eyes and his heart. She became the most important person in his life.

Our mother's father was Danforth Chaplin Denning, who was born June 2, 1892, one of seven children of Emily Chaplin and Frank Denning. The Denning family had moved from Missouri to Oakland, California, across the bay from San Francisco. Grandpa Denning grew up in Oakland, as a young boy delivering newspapers in the Bay Area. One experience he would recall many times was of one April morning in 1906, when he was delivering his papers and the big San Francisco earthquake hit.

Danforth Denning was forever a vagabond. His was a restless spirit, and he would yield to it throughout his life. Grandpa was a lovable man, but he was also undependable. In his youth he lived for some time in San Francisco's Chinatown, where he learned the ways and the culture of the Chinese people and became expert at Chinese cooking. In later years, when the spirit moved him, he would prepare exotic Oriental delicacies with ease. Although the rest of his family was Scottish-Irish, Grandpa was part Chinese. (That's what he told us, and grandpas never lie.) He was also a fantastic self-taught musician, able to play guitar, ukelele, and a fantastic honkytonk piano. Throughout his life Grandpa could—and would—fall back on his musical talents as a means of support. (It was a frequent falling back, as a matter of fact.)

Nana, our mom's mother, was born Reina Ysabel Alvarez, on July 8, 1894. (We grandly celebrated her ninetieth birthday in the summer of 1984.) Nana was one of five children—four girls and a boy—of Peter Paul Alvarez and Marguerita Camacho, of San Diego. Her grandparents, Lorenzo and Elena Camacho, had been one of the First Families of California. Through land grants from the United States Government, the Camacho family had owned large properties from San Diego to Los Angeles. However, as often happened in the turmoil that is California history—and the injustice that men do to one another—the Camachos lost most of the titles to these lands, largely as a result of their inability to read and write English. Nana has told us many mysterious accounts of buried treasure, stolen maps, and lost keys, which were not only part of early California history but of our family's history as well.

Peter Paul Alvarez owned the first bull ring in Tijuana, Mexico, and—not by chance—the only meat market. He did well financially, and the Alvarez home in San Diego was the scene of many fiestas, complete with pinatas, mariachi bands, and barbecued goats.

Reina Ysabel was a beautiful child and young woman. In her early years, her family moved to Santa Ana and later to Los Angeles. When she was sixteen years old, she was asked to join the large group of extras for the motion picture *Birth Of A Nation*, the D.W. Griffith spectacle that was released in 1915 and changed the course of motion picture production. Nana played the part of an angel and has related to us the agony of being tied into a harness and hoisted above the scenery. The painful hoisting, the scenes in which the angels appeared, could be filmed for only five minutes at a time.

In 1916, Nana won the Mexican Independence Day Beauty Contest held in Los Angeles. Her interest in performing began to grow, and she and her sister Eva learned Hindu dances. With the Professor Gohar dance troupe they entertained at the Orpheum in Oakland, California. Nana performed a solo snake dance in an exotic costume with curled-toed shoes and a snake made from old neckties. During the Oakland appearances, she met our grandpa Dan Denning. (So what happens when a beautiful Spanish dancing lady meets a high-spirited wanderlusting vagabond? Havoc!)

They married in Los Angeles on January 3, 1917. Three months later, when the United States entered World War I, Grandpa enlisted in the U.S. Navy, becoming an Engineer First Class in the submarine service aboard the USSH4, stationed in Seattle.

After the Armistice in 1918, the Dennings returned to Los Angeles, anxious to begin their family. But after a year and a half of marriage, their wish was still unfulfilled.

Nana resorted to the most popular remedy known to women of that time—"Lydia Pinkham." Mrs. Pinkham's syrup, according to back-fence gossip, guaranteed "a baby with every bottle." Nana's last spoonful of the thick dark syrup produced our mother, Isabelle Emily, on July 25, 1919.

A year later, son Dan, Jr., was born. As far as Nana was concerned, her family was complete.

The first taste of show business for our mother happened at age three, when she performed in one of her father's drop-of-a-hat musical variety shows, which he presented for local service clubs. Frightened to death, seated on her dad's piano, she managed to sing "Sweet Alice Benboldt" and literally shook her way through a dance routine to the tune, "Shimmy Like My Sister Kate." Little Isabelle Emily was overly shy and disliked performing onstage, but she did love to dance. She was so proficient at dance that she taught tapdance classes for small children when she was only eleven years old.

Whatever burned within Nana and Grandpa, during their few years of marriage, waned. In 1926 they agreed to cease their life together. After the divorce, Grandpa moved to Sacramento, California. Mom and her brother Danny would live with their mother but spend all their summers with him. Grandpa was a great outdoorsman. Most of his leisure time was spent fishing, hunting, and riding horseback over the wooded, hilly terrain of northern California; that wanderlust in him would not lie still.

However, at the beginning of the Depression he came upon a very profitable sport—bootlegging! Because of the Volstead Act, liquor had been outlawed in the United States. He quickly became, by 1930, the main manufacturer, distributor, and dealer in alcohol for all of northern California. When his children went to visit for the summer he had strange new chores for their little hands. Completely unaware of the true nature of his business, our mom and Uncle Danny browned the sugar to color the whiskey. Mom recalls Grandpa's huge drums of rye, corn, and alcohol that he used for his home brews.

To make his extensive deliveries less conspicuous, Grandpa Denning installed special springs in his Chrysler to accommodate the weight of the liquor cartons. Little Sis and Dan rode with him, serving as lookouts. Since they were merely children, they could not comprehend why Grandpa insisted they report any signs of police. It was, after all, just a game of "count the police cars!"

One particular incident has stood out in our mother's memory. It seems Grandpa was giving a party and had hidden some glass jugs of whiskey under the haystack by the barn, fearing it might be discovered in a raid. However, he completely forgot his hidden cache. One day months later, he became excited at seeing a huge flock of blackbirds land on the haystack. Blackbird Pie! He grabbed a shotgun and fired at them.

The birds scattered, the jugs shattered. No blackbird pie, just black market rye!

Spending those carefree vacations with their dad was always an adventure, and that made their return to school in Los Angeles, and to the quiet of Nana's home, much harder. Nana, working as a seamstress and as a candy dipper for See's Candy Company, had very little time to spend with her two children. (Nana can still open a box of chocolates and tell us what's inside each piece by identifying the squiggles on top.) The housework, cooking, and general care of her brother was left to our mom. These were difficult times financially, and Nana often found it necessary to move herself and her children from one place to another, sometimes living with relatives and sometimes spending a few weeks with friends. Our mother has the dubious honor of having attended 33 different grammar schools. Just prior to Mom's entering high school, Nana settled herself and her children in Venice. There Mom spent the remainder of her school years attending Venice High.

By the autumn of 1937, when our dad first came to call on our mother, Nana and her children were living in a very small frame house on the beach, at 24th Street and Pacific Avenue. Nana called this home her "crackerbox." Mom was somewhat embarrassed by the house, but Dad did not seem to notice the humble surroundings. Nothing bored him. He was irrepressible, and his sense of humor helped Sis to overcome her self-consciousness.

Nana, on the other hand, never quite understood Bill Lennon's peculiar sense of humor. But she knew that he loved her daughter, and he was good to her family. The wedding took place on February 19, 1939, at The Church of St. Mark in Venice. Mom was nearly twenty years old, and Dad was then 24. They began their long life together.

Dad and Mom—and Nana.

3

This Old House

Peggy:

Sis and Bill Lennon's first home was a two-room house on one of the Venice canals. After only a month of marriage, Mom had to quit her job as a dental assistant. The morning sickness she experienced resulted in the birth of Dianne Barbara, December 1, 1939. A little more than a year later, April 8, 1941, I was born and named Margaret Anne. When I began forming words I could not wrap my tongue around the name "Dianne," so my older sister became forever after "Dee Dee." I was called Peggy.

With two children, our two-room house became much too small. So the Lennons moved to a house on Boccaccio Avenue, off Venice Boulevard. It too was tiny, but there was one room upstairs for Nana. It was sufficient. Happily, Nana sat Mom and Dad down and told them how pleased she was that their little family was *complete*. (She had had two children, and she felt that constituted a complete family. The Lennons now had two children. That was that!)

However, the "completed" family expanded. Kathleen Mary was born on August 2, 1943. When Mom brought her home from the hospital, I was a two-year old, and I reacted to the new baby by declaring, "Oh, I haven't seen her for a long time!"

The expansion was to continue, and with each new baby, Nana threatened to move out. Dad swore that was why we had baby after baby. However, she never made good her threat, and I know Dad secretly was glad.

At the time Kathy was born, the country was in the midst of World War II, and Dad worked at Douglas Aircraft in Santa Monica. Soon after he was promoted to Scheduling and Spare Parts Supervisor. He took pleasure in producing and staging the minstrel shows that Douglas sponsored as community entertainment. Such shows were good promotion for Douglas and their "We build 'em, you fly them" motto.

By 1946, Mom was expecting her fourth child, so the family moved again; this time to a two-bedroom house on Garfield Avenue, off Lincoln Boulevard. In the backyard was a small one-room building that had been a real estate office. Again Nana had a private sanctuary. For awhile her threats to move lessened.

The new baby was born on June 15, 1946. Fortunately it was a girl, because Kathy had already picked the name, Janet Elizabeth. With Jan's entry into the Lennon family, Daddy gave up all hope of ever having a son. He said that, even is Mom did have a boy, he would be too old to enjoy him.

We four just grew—doing what girls do. Actually, when I learned to read, I found myself delving into books while the others played house. I joined in with Dee Dee when she hummed tunes, and even little Kathy would try out her voice, when we sang baby Janet to sleep.

Then Mom was pregnant again. There was some worry for her now, because she had suffered a miscarriage the previous year. We girls were not aware just how much concern there was, but we picked up on the concern of Dad and Nana. We knew to "be careful for Mommy." In 1950 something wonderful happened to us— a brother. William Danforth, whom we called Danny, changed Dad's life and added a new dimension to the lives of the Lennon sisters. Evidently Mom could not believe it, either. She has said that she called the nurse at least six times during the first night to be assured she wasn't being teased. "Yes, a son, Mrs. Lennon. A fine boy."

Our dad's enthusiasm caught on, and we girls—then ages four to ten—got down on our knees and bowed to the baby boy when he was carried through the front door. We were as excited and thrilled as Mom and Dad.

Just a year later, our second brother, Patrick Herbert, was born. Little Pat was a premature baby; he had no hair or fingernails and left quite a bit to be desired in the looks department. In fact, Uncle Pat Lennon, who would be the child's godfather, came over to visit his namesake. He viewed the likes of little Pat silently. Then he turned to his brother. "Bill, you should have quit while you were ahead!"

We lived on Garfield Avenue for eleven years, and it was the center of our childhood memories. At that time Dad drove a delivery truck for the Pepsi Cola Company and later for Edgemar Farms Dairy. His pay envelope just barely covered the bills for his growing family. So, of course, there was very little money left over for movies or store-bought trinkets and playthings, or the luxury appliances that were then flooding the nation. However, we never felt a lack of fun or adventure, and we used our ingenuity to create our own recreation. We continued to sing together, to make things to play with, to remake clothes.

It was a very long time before we had a television set of our own, but we were never bored. With just a little wild imagination our bunkbeds could become a covered wagon by dropping the top bedspread over the side. However, only my bunk and Dee Dee's could be used for our western treks, because Janet and Kathy's bunk set did not have enough room to sit up between the bottom bed and the top. Their beds were old sawed-off Navy bunks, the lower one of which could only be slept in on one's back or stomach, depending upon a preference at bedtime. Mom literally slipped the lower bunkee into place. "Those bunks," Dad said, "should have come equipped with an extra large pizza paddle."

The shorter bunks encouraged our daring for turning somersaults off the top; Janet was the expert at this, and we called her "Flip The Frog." Also, the beds were a favorite for Mom's go-in-your-room-and-make-up-a-game Game. Their lack of height allowed for great accuracy when dropping clothespins from the top bunk into an empty milk bottle sitting on the floor below.

When we tired of playing in our room, there were other

possibilities for fun in the Garfield Avenue house. One keen competition was the penny shining contest. Each of us had a penny that we rubbed vigorously over the living room rug. The winner with the shiniest penny had the distinction of also having the blackest, most burned fingers.

Our dining room table was our arts and crafts center. That wonderful round oak table, once belonging to Grandma Lennon, for which our parents paid her $50 (table, leaves, and ten chairs), and on time payments at that, is today worth a small fortune. But it was our playground and has served thousands of meals over the years. Today it stands in our mother's family room. Two or three generations of young people have used it as we used it—for coloring in books and on paper lace doilies that Mom would save from one Valentine's Day to the next. I would spend long hours coloring the most intricate details, long after the rest of the kids had resorted to scribbling.

At that table we cut up old Sears & Roebuck catalogs to make paper dolls. Dee Dee and I sewed doll clothes for Janet and Kathy's Betsy Wetsy dolls. Sometimes we cleared the table of all odds and ends so that Mom and Dad could use it for their "Champion of the Coast Pacific" jacks games. Both claimed handicaps. Dad's was, "Well, I'm left-handed." Mom's excuse was, "Well, I'm pregnant." We divided into two cheering sections. Dee Dee always rooted for the underdog, while the rest of us cheered for Mom. She always won, and Daddy always demanded a rematch.

Mom played hide-and-seek with us at the strangest times, and at a moment's notice. She'd call out to us to drop down below the window sill or quickly go into the back bedroom and be as quiet as we could. It was years before we realized it was no coincidence that the game began with the ring of the doorbell. Ready or not, there was the bill collector.

Dianne:

Anyone knows that belonging to a large family means a lot more than fun and games. It also means chores!

Mom did the cooking, because she loved to cook. Even when

times were difficult, she managed to serve us tasty and well-balanced meals. Each of us took her turn peeling potatoes, washing the lettuce and vegetables, and in the postwar years fighting over who got to squish the oleomargarine until the little bubble of food coloring burst and the entire contents of the plastic bag turned yellow. (There is a whole generation, several in fact, who don't know what that feels like.)

A favorite kitchen job was stirring the chocolate pudding for what seemed like hours, and staying with it until making sure the bottom of the pan wasn't sticky and burnt. The reward? The entire spoon to lick without having to share.

Peggy and I had to do the dishes each evening. I would get right into it and start washing. On the other hand, Peggy would excuse herself from the table just before the clearing began, grab a book, and disappear into the bathroom. "The queen is on her throne again," Nana would complain. Needless to say, Peggy could be found drying the dishes far into the night.

In an era when there were no disposable diapers, the laundry for nine people was probably the most difficult chore for any of us. With the first four of us Mom had only a washboard, so she was thrilled when the family finally got a wringer washer. Mom sorted and washed the clothes, and Nana would put them through the front of the wringer. One or more of us girls would pull the wet clothes out through the back. And we got to help Mom as she hung out the wet things on the line. I can still feel and hear the sound of those wooden pins clicking as I dipped my hand into her warm apron pocket to take one out and hand it to her.

If we were expert at *anything* in those days, it was carrying in the laundry and folding it, while singing at the tops of our voices, "Row, row, row your boat . . . ."

Most of the time we did our share of the house and yard work without complaint. But inevitably we had to clean our bedroom. With two sets of bunkbeds, there was only enough space for one small dresser in that room, so our clothes were kept under our beds in huge drawers that Jim the Baker gave Mom from his delivery truck. Our closet held very little. Nana stored her "fur coats" and winter wardrobe on one side. It was a great place for hide-and-seek, if you could stand the smell of moldy fox and mothballs. The clothes hanging on *our* side were a little bit too high to reach. So, after a few brief attempts to hang our clothes (they slipped off the metal hangers anyway), we just opened the door, threw them in, and slammed the door before they tumbled out again. In about a week we could finally reach the rods, but now we were standing on the clothes we needed to hang.

We didn't mind this, but Mom did. After repeating her warnings to clean the room too many times, she would send for Dad. He would set an alarm clock where we could all see it. "When the big hand gets to the twelve, this room better be clean!" Then he would smile and leave.

I tried many times to organize our housecleaning, but that always ended with Kathy and me doing the work. Janet would stay out of the way. Of course, on the top bunk, Peggy would be absorbed in a book. Somehow our organization would fall by the wayside, and we would end up playing bullfighter with a blanket. Or we would rediscover some misplaced doll clothes that demanded to be put on a doll, right then. Or we would bundle up in Nana's furs and pretend that we were caught in a snowstorm, whatever that was! It would be at the height of the "blizzard" when Daddy would walk in and haul us back to sunny Venice, reminding us that the big hand was on the twelve.

We knew what was coming when Dad would remove his belt. Kathy and I would bottom up to it. Only once, I remember, did Janet receive a spanking. Then we all cried harder than she did. But Peggy! She made such a production of trying to talk Dad out of it. She'd try to out-maneuver him, running over the beds, crawling under them, into the closet, and out again. She hadn't learned that one good swat on a soft rear was much better than five or six near misses on elbows, ankles, and knees.

We cried then, asking how he could spank us with a smile on his face. His explanation was satisfactory to us then and to this day still makes sense. "Why get mad?" he'd say. "Then you'd have the satisfaction of knowing that you made me mad. It didn't hurt my bottom. I warned you that when the big hand got to the twelve . . . ."

When illness struck, our bedroom would become an infirmary. Often, in large families, sickness can become an epidemic. It was more often sympathy for one another that felled one after the other to the sick bed. These were not totally unhappy days,

because we loved staying home from school together and com-
miserating. We had all the usual childhood diseases, but the
worst plague to hit us each year was stomach flu. Even our
mother and dad could not escape its wrath. Sometime between
Thanksgiving and Christmas, we would each fall victim. When
the first one of the family succumbed, Nana made her annual
phone call to her cousin Sue who, without hesitation, would
make the long drive from San Diego to help Nana care for us. As
sick as Dad was, he seldom failed to greet Sue with a quick
chorus of one of his infamous parodies:

> Oh Sue and Nana, Oh don't you cry for me.
> For I come from Alabama . . . .

Cousin Sue took over the washing and the cooking, which—
now that I look back on it—must have seemed endless to her.
This enabled Nana to spend her time doing what she does best.
Moving the rocking chair into our bedroom, she would hold us
on her lap and rock us each in turn. Placing cool hands on our
foreheads, she would draw the fever from our bodies. It was
almost worth being sick to be able to share those comforting
moments with Nana, the stoic but loving grandmother.

Dad was the biggest baby of all, but he never received the
attention he craved, so with each wave of nausea, he would issue
a medical bulletin on the state of his misery. Even throughout
the night we could hear him moan. "Sis . . . , oh, S-i-s . . . , I'm
gonna faint. I'm gonna die . . . ."

"Do one or the other, then," would come Mom's consoling
response. "But be quiet about it, and don't wake the kids."

Peggy:

Most little girls are aware that a grandmother's room holds
vast treasure and wealth not found anyplace else on earth. For
us, Nana's room was one big bejeweled treasure chest. One
important and lasting memory for each of us is taking turns
spending Friday nights with Nana.

After dinner, we would put on a nightie and slippers, kiss our
mom and dad goodbye, and make our way through the

backyard to arrive at Nana's tiny domain. Her room, *i.e.*, all of it her bedroom, seemed to be out of a fairy tale, with gold satin quilts and little pink satin pillows. There is no easy way to describe the soft, warm feeling of sinking into Nana's bed and experiencing her devoted attention as she would fluff the pillows around our necks, and pull the covers over us, making each of us feel that we were a princess tended by a lady-in-waiting.

The smell of that room was its own special magic—a combination of exotic perfumes, nail polish, and mothballs. Sleeping with Nana entitled us to a manicure, an embroidery or knitting lesson (after we had sorted all her multicolored needles and threads), and most exciting of all, we were able to lie in bed on Saturday morning and listen to "Let's Pretend" on her radio. Without any interruptions!

Alone with her those nights, the things that we each learned of places, of life philosophies, and common sense could never be recorded except in the practice of our own lives.

On Sunday afternoon, we would return to Nana's room and spend our time dusting all of the perfume bottles that she kept on her mirrored dressing table. There would be more radio programs, too. Nana introduced us to all the greats of radioland. We were avid fans of Charlie McCarthy, Red Ryder and Little Beaver, The Cisco Kid, Blondie, Red Skelton, and J-E-L-L-O. (Singing that commercial to Nana may have been our first solo performances.)

One drawback of spending nights out in Nana's room was that she did not have a bathroom. It was either run through the backyard (with the "Shadow" breathing down our necks) or use Nana's chamber pot in her little closet. What a choice!

"She let us choose," Dee Dee recalls, "one of her silk bedjackets from her dresser drawer of silk and satin nightwear, and wearing it, I belonged to her room."

"I experienced my first feeling of pride in my heritage," Kathy has said. "Even though I didn't speak Spanish, part of the fun and mystique of staying with Nana was listening to her Mexican programs on the radio."

Janet recalls that "Every time I opened the door to Nana's room, I had the same feeling that Dorothy must have had when she opened the door to Oz. I stepped into a land of pink, glowing color." Now, when we look back, we have come to realize that spending those times with Nana in her small house across the continent of our backyard provided each of us the special, individual pampering we needed during our growing years. And all with a touch of class.

That Garfield Avenue backyard was quite a world. We were seldom allowed in the small frontyard. So the back was our playground, with a sandbox (Myrtle, our turtle is still buried there), a garden containing a big tree with its own garden spider in it, a patio with a built-in barbecue, a clothesline, and a swing-set. It had a climbing pole, and it also had the only swimming pool in the neighborhood.

Now, before anyone gets the wrong impression and imagines a huge estate, it must be pointed out that all these recreational facilities were contained in a space 30 by 35 *feet*. The swimming pool was a rubber airplane gasoline tank that Daddy got from Douglas and cut in half. Although the tank was only three feet wide, five feet long, and six inches deep, this pool could hold at least ten kids. We all learned to swim in it, but in distance races the tallest kid always won.

There was really no room for roller-skating or coaster-riding in the back, so we were thrilled when we received permission to play in the front of the house. None of us had our own skates, but Mom had two pair of adjustable clamp-on skates. Those remained Mom's personal property, as did all the toys in the large cereal boxes—to avoid arguments. We could "borrow" them, however. For years, each of us was a one-foot skate expert: Dee Dee and I on the right foot, Janet and Kathy on the left. We skated around the block to the left, and they skated around to the right. Once in a while we got to use both skates, but because of lack of experience we had to use a broomstick to balance ourselves. We really preferred one skate rather than suffer a bruised tailbone.

When scooters and coasters became a fad in our neighborhood, our dad made the very best. He acquired an old ammunition box from the local sporting-goods store and nailed that to a two-by-four, put ball-bearing skate wheels underneath, attached a cut-off broom handle across the top, to provide us with a "perfect" coaster. (But we also had one less skater.) Our scooter was the best because it was large enough to shove Janet inside and scoot her around the corner. It beat any store-bought "Flexi" on the block.

Sports were such an important part of Daddy's life. He was always organizing relay races, kickball and softball games, and was the all-around neighborhood coach. Throughout our school years, Dad continued coaching both girls' and boys' teams in almost every sport. He was a natural athlete, a coach and a humorist (ranging from Will Rogers to Jack Benny in comment and stance), and he was also the Venice version of the Pied Piper. Kids and young people were willing to follow him and his eclectic imagination into any new activity. And it wasn't possible to play a game just to have fun! "Sure, it's important to play fair and to enjoy yourself at the same time, but let's face it, you guys, it's more fun to win!" You had to win!!! One legacy from Daddy is a love and a knowledge of sports that now has us enjoying TV sports weekends and Monday Night Football with an intensity that equals our husbands'.

Even when he worked at two or three jobs, Daddy found the time to be with us when we were growing up. His way of arranging time with us seems hard to imagine now. Our uncle Jimmy Lennon was—and still is—a local sports announcer; when he had more work than he could handle, he arranged for Dad to work weekends announcing boxing and wrestling matches. We all looked forward to our turn at being Dad's date for these evenings. Mom was glad, too, that someone was along to help Dad stay awake on the long drive to and from the San Fernando Valley Garden Arena. It was great to shake hands with *the* Baron Leone, or to catch a goldplated bobby pin from Gorgeous George's goldplated hair. At intermissions the management would have a drawing for a goldfish bowl full of money. Dad allowed us to draw the winning ticket. There was a method to his madness. The winner usually rewarded us with a dollar or two! We were allowed to keep half, but the rest of the money paid for the cheeseburger and french fries that Dad would take home to Mom.

Those drives home were moments of closeness shared with Daddy alone. He would turn the radio to classical music and drape the car blanket over our legs. We held hands; for that short time we became Daddy's *only* little girl.

Part-time, Dad restrung tennis and badminton racquets for a

local sporting goods shop and for friends. Janet and Kathy were too young to remember, but Dee Dee and I would spend hours with him in the freezing garage where he had his tools and vises. We remember the pungent smell of the shellac and the feeling of warming our cold hands in Dad's jacket pockets. For Dee Dee he made a little wooden bench to stand on because the cement floor was so cold, and after a time, she became adept at heating the awls he used for putting holes in the wood.

Dianne:

As oldest of the four girls, I became *"number one son."* When Dad headed a Cub Scout troop, I was a member in full standing. He encouraged me to play every kind of sport, particularly golf. From the time I was six years old, he would sneak me onto golf courses before and after school. Thanks to Dad, I still play better golf and win more trophies at it than any of our family members.

For eleven years our dad was a full-time milkman. Edgemar Farms required its employees to buy their own uniforms. Mom kept mending Dad's until they finally rotted. "Okay," he would say. "This is the last day I can wear this rag before it falls apart!"

The drama was set. We could invite our best friends in after school to sit on the floor and wait for his arrival. He'd enter, sit on the couch, and sadly bemoan how poor and tired he was, with nothing but rags to wear to work. "I hate this uniform and I hate that job," he'd say, as if he were reciting a Shakespearean soliloquy. "I'm sick and tired of these stupid clothes. I'm never going to wear them again." With that he would rip the sleeves off the shirt, tear at the pockets, and pull the collar right off the back, then pop the buttons onto the floor.

Our cue! We'd jump up and grab his pants legs, hanging on until they fell apart. We ripped and tore, and after a minute or two Dad would be standing in the center of the room with belt and beltloops, and his shorts. Not many kids had a dad like that. His uniform was ready for the next day's furniture dusting.

Dad managed to make shoes last longer than most. When the inevitable holes appeared, we cut cardboard shirt liners to fit the soles. Sometimes there would be a slight problem, however, because we often used the cardboard for drawing and coloring. As a result, Daddy would walk around with our masterpieces transferred to the bottoms of his socks.

At Christmas, Dad brought home the many Christmas cards and wrapped presents he had received from his milk-route. The presents were often bottles of liquor. They were considered worthless to Mom and Dad, because neither drank alcoholic beverages, so these became gifts for others. The big event was *the cards*; each one was held until Christmas Eve, when we would gather together on the living room floor for the grand openings. It was difficult to contain our excitement when Daddy would tease us, shaking each card. "What do you think, kids?" he would ask. "Should I open this one? No, you wouldn't like it. Well, maybe this one."

"Yes, yes," we would scream. "Open it Daddy, open it."

He would slit the envelope, peek inside, and ask "Do you think it's a Washington or a Lincoln?" We would cheer the message *and* the money. But if an envelope were empty of funds, we would yell, "Scrooge! Scrooge!" His only comment would be, "Oh, well, on to the fat ones, then!"

Our father made our birthdays special by taking us on his milk-route for the whole day. It was our job to carry the eggs, half-and-half, and yogurts to each house, while he carried the heavy glass bottles. Between stops Dad would time us to see how long we could stand and keep our balance without holding on, while the truck—with its open doorways—jostled, jerked, and bounced along the streets. If we tired we sat on the milk crates that were filled with ice, trying to ignore the fact that our bottoms were slowly freezing. While we sucked on rusty ice, we listened to Dad sing his songs and tell his stories of his own childhood.

The best part of our birthdays would be arriving at the local fire station just at lunchtime. There Dad would give us our very own pint of chocolate drink, something we were not allowed to have at home. The firemen would have set a place for us at their table. They would give us a small piece of cake and then challenge us to a game of ping pong. At the end of the day, we returned to the dairy to help Daddy unload the truck. And tally his delivery book. Each year the routine was the same, but when we would arrive home, all the other Lennons would eagerly sit at the big oak table and listen to us tell of the events of our special day with Dad.

Peggy:

As I write this I have a smile on my face—as all of us did whenever Grandpa Denning interrupted our lives with his visits. It was often that he showed up with little or no warning. As the years passed and the visits continued to surprise us, we would talk in the darkness of our room about him—would the visit be six minutes, or would it be six months?

Our own excitement at seeing this marvelous character was exceeded only by our mother's efforts to summon up the extra strength and supreme patience to cope with her father's always chaotic visit. "Where am I going to *put* him?" was her main problem.

We had a solution; at least, I did! "Let him sleep with Nana!" I did not understand for years why she never took that advice. I don't know which one of us Nana told one Friday night, "He *was* my husband. Now he is *not!*" We didn't even know what divorce was, or what it meant. We were Catholic!

So Grandpa slept on the living room couch or on a mattress in the garage. Once, he brought his own shelter; a large camping tent, which he strung between our garage and the back fence. It was equipped with cot, radio, lantern, and—best of all—a hole in the top through which we could watch the stars while listening to him tell us ghost stories.

Kathy vividly remembers one such visit as her first experience at camping out in the great outdoors. She was sure Grandpa would protect her from the wild beasts of Venice. She was in first grade then, eager and anxious to please. During Fire Prevention Week she brought home a long list of hidden hazards that her fire safety booklet stated should be removed from every household.

She uncovered a wealth of fire dangers, but the local fire captain seemed interested in only one, and he promised her he would come to see Grandpa the next day. When he arrived he proceeded to help Grandpa break camp. Now how many children can claim they earned their Junior Fire Inspector's badge by turning in their own grandfather?

Whenever Grandpa moved in with us, he proved to be both help and hindrance. He was our very own "Mr. Belevedere," the Clifton Webbish self-proclaimed authority on just anything at all.

He took over the kitchen completely to make homemade noodles, chorizo and eggs, chicharones, kippersnax, or pancakes. He never seemed to measure anything, nor did he resort to using a written recipe. No matter what he produced, he would use every pot and pan and utensil, then leave them all for us to clean. He claimed a topsy-turvy kitchen was the sign of a very good cook. (If that's true, I am the best cook in the world.)

Somehow Grandpa knew just the right temperature for our bath water and the proper method for drying off. He would stand us up on the toilet seat and fan us with a large towel. "To close your pores so you won't catch cold," he said. When he would wash our hair he would be very gentle and thorough, but the final rinse of cold water—"to close your pores so you won't catch cold,"—was always a shock.

His babysitting availability was welcomed by Mom and Dad. For us it was a big treat. I mean BIG! Those many hours were filled with worthy and worthless activities that Mom never quite had the time—nor perhaps the desire—to do with us. There were contests: who could shinny fastest up the kitchen doorway; who could last longest leaning against the wall on two index fingers; who could do the most push-ups, who could get ready and in bed fastest, and on and on. Grandpa believed in "little guys first," so Dee Dee and I had to work twice as hard for any victory.

With Grandpa we occasionally attempted to produce homemade taffy. The outcome never varied. We were so anxious to begin the taffy pulling that we never waited long enough for it to thicken properly, and we ended up scooping it off the kitchen floor, or off of Janet's nightie.

At times, Grandpa *and* Nana sat with us while our parents went out. Before going to bed, we dragged our pillows into the small living room and lay on the floor while Gramp played his wonderful honkytonk piano. Then Nana would sing, and both would dance together as once, years earlier, they had done in Grandpa's club, up north in Oakland. Though we did not fully realize then why these evenings were especially warm and touching, we know now that we were sharing a special friendship of two people recapturing the closeness of their early years together. He may have lacked being a good husband or even a good father, but he was a good friend; to Nana, to his daughter and son, and to us, his grandchildren.

Along with our dad, Grandpa gave us our first singing "lessons," plunking out our voice parts and giving us our first knowledge of harmonies. He played melodies and taught us lyrics we might never have known. With our separate voice registers we sang the songs that pleased him, and us.

On those rare occasions when Mom and Nana got a chance to go out shopping together, we would be left to the tender mercies of the original odd couple—Grandpa and Daddy. We were fools to beg them to play *their* favorite games with us, because we knew one or more of us would end up crying. Every game pitted the kids against the combine of Grandpa Denning and Dad. They played for real: we would have to be tough or go to bed. The main events were wrestling, boxing, squirt-gun fights, or rubber-band fights. We shied away from Dad's favorite, boxing. He took too seriously his famous fight song.

> *I know a guy, ate a piece of pie,*
> *Hum Dum Dinger, sock 'im in the eye.*
> *Poke 'im in the nose, sock 'im in the chin,*
> *I don't care if he ever gives in!*

Squirt-gun fights were more fun, but most of the time unfair. There were never enough guns to go around. Grandpa and Dad took dibs on the best two, and we girls had to share the variety of scotch-taped and plugless leftovers. It was not easy to use your thumb as a plug and pull the trigger at the same time. Eventually, the water would dribble out the handle and down our sleeves, and we would meet our Waterloo!

About the only time we went to a movie was when Grandpa took us. We would leave early and take the electric streetcar into Santa Monica, arriving in plenty of time for Grandpa to pause for a little liquid refreshment before the matinee. We never had proof that Grandpa Denning was half Scotch, but there were times that we were aware at least a fifth of old Dan was eighty proof.

Santa Monica's Elmiro Theater was located conveniently just up the street from his cronies' hangout, the Zanzi-Bar. Naturally, Grandpa could not pass by without a quick hello-on-the-rocks. He knew Mom would never allow him to leave us anywhere alone, so he just took us into the bar with him. "Just a moment, a wee respite, you might say!" He was an old showman, a showoff, and a very proud grandfather. He would sit us up on the bar, four cute little girls, and coax us to sing for his friends. He would ask for the latest song he had taught us, "just to practice before an audience," he'd say. He was such a whole-hog opportunist, he'd take advantage of the set-up to pass the hat, bewailing the fact that his poor daughter had so many children and they all needed new shoes. As a reward for our song, we would be given four glasses of cherry Coke, with souvenir plastic Zanzi-Bar monkeys hanging from the rim of the glasses. We would fill our tummies, Gramp would fill his pockets, the bar habitues would have their fill of our songs, and we would go off to the movies.

At night, lying in our beds, we would hear our mother's hurt, angry voice admonishing her father for breaking his promise and taking us into a bar again, for exploiting our talents and damaging our innocence. Could any of us have guessed that those times with Grandpa would be the first real paid performances in our long career as The Lennon Sisters?

As most children do, we enjoyed singing. Grandpa Denning may not have known the proper where or when for us to sing, but he did know the what, the how, and the why of it. Dee Dee and I sang in two-part harmony, just as a natural thing. Mom recalls Kathy's discovery of *other* notes, the third part that made up a harmonic chord. One day she ran into the kitchen. "Hey, Mom!" she yelled. "I found another part to a song."

Mom, amazed, stood and listened to Kathy harmonize with ease to the tune of the passing ice-cream truck, "Merrily We Roll Along."

But it was Grandpa who opened to us a whole new world, teaching us that there was more to every song than just the melody. Two of us sat on top of the upright piano (Kathy and Janet, of course). Dee Dee and I sat on the bench beside him, and he showed us how to pick out the chords to old barber-shop songs. "You Can't Be True, Dear," and "I Wonder Who's Kissing Her Now." It was not long before Kathy and I discovered we could find harmonies to almost any song. All of this made the four of us confident and willing to perform at the slightest provocation.

When relatives or friends came to visit the family, we recognized them as potential audiences. Before we—or they—knew it, they were! We're not sure when regular Sunday night home shows began. Certainly during and after Grandpa's visits. Our living room would fill with our uncles and their families, Nana, Amma, Grandma Lennon, a few neighbors, and friends who may have come to dinner.

On Sunday mornings we attended the earliest mass at St. Mark Church. After that we spent the whole day planning our songs and throwing together our costumes. We took time to make perfume by squeezing rose petals into little bottles of water to present to our lady guests. We wore bathing suits with our mommy's skirts over them. Nana would lend us her elbow-length gloves. (Whenever did she wear these?)

Our revues opened with "There's No Business Like Show Business"—singing the first line and humming the remainder because we didn't know the words. After that it was downhill all the way. Dee Dee, as the oldest, had to don a hat and cane and be a man so she could be master of ceremonies. It never occurred to her or to us that a lady could be an M.C. Dee Dee had a limited patter; every introduction was the same. "And now Blank Lennon will sing Blank Blank." I, Peggy, could emote nicely through "Cruising Down The River" and milk an audience's applause in grand fashion. Janet and Kathy, without the prima donna manner that I had assumed, meekly began a lullaby to their dollies, "Won't You Come Over To My House."

Each week, as if the performance were for the first time, Daddy would let himself be coaxed from the audience by Dee Dee for a romantic duet, "If You Were The Only Girl In The World." Then, as a quartet, we would rush through our most recently learned song, extremely anxious to get to our closing act.

The star of our grand finale was our brother Danny, who was usually unwilling to perform. He was not scared of the audience; he just didn't like to be forced into the grass skirt we tied over his diaper to dance the hula. Mom would allow a few moments of laughter and applause, and then she would rescue Danny, scooping him up in her arms. Wiping away his tears, *she* would announce the show was over.

We realize that the best performance of all was our mother's and father's abilities to convey the same enthusiasm for that same show, those same songs, the same acts, Sunday after Sunday.

In time, we followed those great successes by planning bigger and better programs. These shows were held in our garage for the kids of the neighborhood; Betty and Bonnie Seems, Linda and Peggy De Young, and Billy Wells auditioned every time. We told each of them they had to sit in the driveway with Bobby Esser and the Cook brothers. That made the audience look bigger!

Janet's best friend was Joni Esser, and she was the only other "star" in our shows because she looked exactly like Shirley Temple. Joni Esser took real tap-dancing lessons, and her mother made real costumes. Our backdrop and stage curtains were made by hanging old bedspreads from the rungs of the opened garage door. We were professional enough to charge admission, of course—a penny apiece. For that you got a seat and the best watered-down Kool-Aid south of Venice Boulevard. All you could drink, or two jelly glasses apiece, whichever was less. Standing room was free but no extras.

These backyard shows made hams out of us. Janet was some-what indifferent, except when she was actually singing. Dee Dee looked good, but she was usually quite nervous. Kathy seemed confident in voice and movement. And I was just perfect. All the neighborhood kids thought we were terrific, and said so. Except for Lolly Demoff. She always demanded her money back—*after* she had consumed her Kool-Aid!

Dianne:

I believe we were of one mind when we were putting on our lit-tle shows or playing our games. However, we each had different tastes when it came to our clothes. We could select our wardrobes from three sources. Nana had an old Singer sewing machine, and Mom would purchase new material whenever there was extra money. One of us would pick a pattern, and we would watch Mom or Nana create a flawless homemade original. If anyone asked me about one of these pieces, I was proud to say, "My Nana made it for me."

A second source of clothing was the imports, sent to us by Dad's cousins Bud and Joe, all the way from Oconomowoc, Wis-consin. (We could never remember if it was "Uncle Bud and Aunt Joe" or "Uncle Joe and Aunt Bud!") They had four growing daughters and were glad to pass on their elegant clothes to their California relatives.

Certainly not the least of our choices for clothes were contained in the large boxes from our church. Once or twice a year, when the carton arrived, our living room would take on the appearance of a bargain basement on dollar day. We wore whatever fit the best and needed little or no attention. It never mattered to us that these garments had been worn by someone else. For us, they were brand new. Kathy remembers, though, that one particular skirt was so stunning she could not wait to wear it to school the next day, which was free dress day. (We were given one Friday a month to have our school uniforms cleaned.) All of Kathy's fifth grade friends admired her new skirt. She felt so pretty wearing it. However, that pride turned to embarrassment when, from across the schoolyard, Marion Keller yelled at her, "Hey Kathy, that used to be my old skirt!" And right in front of Johnny Webber, too.

Janet seldom had to wear hand-me-downs. Her very best friend's mother, Kay Esser, was a seamstress, and she loved to dress Janet and Joni alike. By age three, Janet Lennon and Joni Esser had identical wardrobes from bathing suits to coats. With Joni's blond ringlets, big blue eyes, and huge dimples, and Janet's mousey brown braids with straight bangs, they looked like a couple of dolls—little Shirley Temple and Poor Pitiful Pearl.

Joni came to our house often, and stayed long. There was always something going on. She considered us "rich" since we had Nana's old fur coats, Mom's costume jewelry, a huge button box, plain-black trading cards, and lots of fabric scraps to drape ourselves in and play Hindu dancers. But we Lennon girls *knew* Joni was rich, because she had her *own* bedroom, pink satin toe shoes, dolls with rooted hair, a *genuine* Flexi, *and* a television set to watch "Kukla, Fran, and Ollie." Through the friendship of these girls—they were inseparable—Mom and Kay Esser became very close friends. During the years we worked with the Lawrence Welk Show, Kay either made or altered most of our clothes for our appearances. Later, when we had our television series, we hired Kay as our head seamstress.

When, in the summer of 1952, our mother was pregnant with her seventh child, Dad was already working at two jobs. But he and Mom needed additional income. The answer to the problem came in a strange way.

Mom and Nana had an old family recipe for enchiladas; when they made them for us it was really a treat. Dad continually bragged about Mom's cooking, and one day he was challenged by one of his milk customers to bring samples of her enchiladas. After tasting them, the man asked Dad if he might pay Mom to make a dozen enchiladas every weekend. The discovery of Mrs. Lennon's delicious specialty quickly passed from mouth to mouth throughout the neighborhood. Soon Mom was deluged with requests for weekly orders. She was in the enchilada business.

Twice weekly she stood for hours in the kitchen mixing chili, grating cheese, chopping onions and olives, frying tortillas. With Nana's help and ours, she managed to turn out at least twenty dozen a week. The list of customers grew. Dad placed the trays of enchiladas into special carrying cases he had made to hold them securely in his car. He hurried home from work so he could deliver the enchiladas to the customers in time for dinner.

Their small business continued for two years and/or two pregnancies, until the Board of Health notified our parents they needed a license to operate such a business out of their home. It would have been too expensive to comply with State regulations, so our parents gave up this mini enterprise. All the tedious work brought them little financial profit, but it was enough extra to be worthwhile. The small income certainly helped pay doctor bills for our new little sister, Mary Frances, born March 5, 1953. Fortunately this time there were no hospital expenses, because St. John's Hospital in Santa Monica had just established a policy of not charging for maternity cases after the seventh child.

Mom never had to tell us when she was expecting another baby. We learned young—or at least I did—that when she sat at the breakfast table, suddenly took a large gulp, and bolted for the bathroom, we were going to have another brother or sister.

When the time came for her to go to the hospital, we would observe the same rituals: Mom would awaken Dad in the night. "Honey, I think it's time to go." Dad would struggle out of bed and head for the bathroom to shave.

"Dear, I think we'd better go."

"Look, Sis. I've had as many kids as you've had, and I know

we've got plenty of time." Mom would laugh, admitting it was true, but the commotion would usually wake Nana, and she would start to fret and fuss about Daddy's reluctance to leave. "You know Sis always has a long labor," Dad would tell Nana calmly. "I've got to finish shaving. You wouldn't want me to look like a bum at the hospital, would you?"

When he had shaved and dressed, he would fix himself an Alka-Seltzer with lemon juice while Mom would time her pains and Nana would grow more irritated. We would sit in the kitchen with Dad, listening to his pre-hospital patter:

> *Alka-Seltzer what a blessing*
> *Fixed me up while I was dressing.*
> *My headache's gone,*
> *My head is clear;*
> *Must be Alka-Seltzer, dear . . . .*
> *Those midnight lunches knocked me flat.*
> *Say, Alka-Seltzer's good for that . . . .*

In his heart, Daddy was terrified. Each new child was difficult for Mom, but somehow Dad's exterior calm, and wacky humor, helped Mom—and even Nana—over the next trying hours.

Mom and Dad, at our favorite spot, the Santa Monica beach, 1959. *(The Lennon Family Collection)*

Great Uncle Maximillian Heinrich, "Uncle Max," the Lennon family's patriarch. *(The Lennon Family Collection)*

4

A Summer Place

Kathy:

Summer vacation meant just one thing to us. The beach. We lived only a mile east of the ocean. Since neither our car nor our money could go far, it was the most practical place for our family on Dad's day off, to our delight. Dad's enthusiasm and love for every aspect of the beach was contagious, but he could never understand why we could not just get into the car and go. "Why do we have to bring the playpen, the umbrella, picnic baskets, and thermos jugs?" he would bellow. "And dry changes of clothes for each of us and diapers for the babies, buckets and shovels, beach towels, three large blankets, two rubber balls, and a partridge in a pear tree?"

Dad would park our car at the edge of the sand, in a "no parking" zone. With the playpen balancing on his head he would lead our safari as we stumbled and complained across the hot sand to the water's edge, where several uncles, aunts, and cousins would have already set up camp for the day.

Whatever the time of day, the first thing we wanted to do was eat. We crunched our way through peanut butter and jelly sandwiches, or sand and cheese on rye. Before we could go swimming (even though most of us only waded in the shallow water), Mom made us wait that one full hour after eating, so we wouldn't get the bends. She would make up for this by taking us down to the water and helping us build sand forts and castles. When she was pregnant, which was almost every summer, she would let us help her dig a hole in dry, warm sand, so she could lie confortably for a time on her stomach to watch us play.

I have never thought of my Mom as being any particular age. But when she got down on her knees in the sand to play with us, or when she and Dad ran into the waves holding hands like young sweethearts, enjoying being together and by themselves, I think of her as being very young.

As we grew older, Dad and his brothers carried us out into deeper water and taught us how to catch a wave and ride it all the way into shore. Bodysurfing! They also taught us to play football and volleyball, and organized hop-skip-and-jump contests among all the cousins.

About the only responsibility we older kids had was to take the little kids back across the hot sand to the restrooms. (Why couldn't they go in the ocean like everybody else?)

At day's end, as the moms and the older children packed up, the dads kept the little ones occupied by tossing and catching them in big beach blankets, one by one. It was a short ride home, but even a few minutes sitting in a wet, sandy bathing suit can be miserable. We had only one bathroom at home, and Dad would save time, hot water, and first-in-line hassles by lining us up on the front lawn and squirting us with the garden hose. Though the water was freezing cold, it did not relieve the sting of our sunburns, and we could not wait for Mom to sponge down our red bodies with vinegar water. Tired and content, we would climb into bed early, smelling like freshly dyed Easter eggs.

During a period of three or four summers, all the beaches were quarantined. These were the last years of the dreaded disease polio, before the miracle of Dr. Jonas Salk's vaccine. A child's complaint of an aching neck, back, or leg struck panic into the hearts of every parent. Those summers, we looked forward to Daddy's two-week vacation, when we could get away from Venice and go to our uncle Max's (pronounced "Mox"), in the Ojai Valley near Santa Barbara.

Dad's uncle Maximillian Heinrich, our Grandma Lennon's brother, owned a fifteen-acre apricot ranch about eighty miles north of Los Angeles. He and his wife Helen eagerly welcomed our summer stays. Uncle Max was a wiry man, whose strong German physical characteristics are easily recognized throughout the entire Lennon clan. His most striking feature was his eyes. Cornflower blue they were, and young looking like a newborn baby's, to the very end.

Uncle Max—born in Munich, in Bavaria, in 1898—was a rare character. He was a philosopher, artist, adventurer, and man of nature. He grew up in Germany after the unification of the German cities and states under Chancellor Bismarck, when that nation was fast approaching the status of a world power. When he was sixteen years old, uncle Max joined the officers training school for the *Luftwaffe*, destined to take part in World War I in an aspect that revolutionized military history—aerial warfare.

He told us often of how he dropped bombs with his bare hands through small openings at the bottom of the single-engine biplanes. It did not take him long to become totally disillusioned and defiantly anti-war. Max Heinrich was one of the first German revolutionaries distributing anti-war postcards picturing a skull and crossbones under a German pilot's helmet, with the inscription: "Lives For Money." He was captured for his demonstrations, but soon escaped from the military prison and fled to Yugoslavia. When the war ended in late 1918, he returned to Germany. In the late 1920s, he emigrated to the United States to live with his sister, Barbara Lennon, our grandmother. It was not long before he found his haven in Ojai, which offered him the serenity he had been seeking.

In reality, Uncle Max's "ranch" was about five acres of apricot trees and grape vineyards, with ten acres of brushy hillsides where we hiked, ran, and played in the good clean dirt. There was the Big House, the main ranchhouse of crude stone and wood, a separate cookhouse, and a tiny stone cottage, the Little House. Nothing was ever formally planned, but after arriving and settling into the Little House, we would spend our first hours helping Dad prepare for the next morning's fishing trip. Each of us, including our younger brothers and sisters, would make our own poles from broken television antennas and hacksaw blades that we found in the old stable. No two poles were alike, but with a little nylon line and some fish hooks, Dad would manage to make them seem practical. In the evening we would sit around the kitchen table and make a dough of white bread and Velveeta cheese, which we would roll into tiny balls to augment the expensive salmon eggs we used for bait.

Mom let us sleep in our jeans and sweatshirts the first night, so that when we crawled out of our sleeping bags at 4.00 a.m., we would be ready to go fishing at once. The Si-Sar Creek, where we fished, was a mile down the road. We would hike upstream for about an hour, climbing over boulders and fallen trees, and then we would fish our way back downstream to where Dad had parked the car. We returned then to the ranch, with bruised ankles and soaked pants-legs, starving for Mom's pancakes and bacon.

Each of us would be anxious to tell the story of how she caught her trout, but we knew that as soon as breakfast was over Dad would say, "You caught it, you clean it!"

On mornings when we didn't go fishing, we would all hop into the back of Uncle Max's old green pickup truck, and he would drive us out to the orchards to pick the ripe apricots. He would divide us into two groups, the "pickers" and the "catchers." After spreading an old parachute under a tree, the catchers would shake the tree trunk, gather up the fallen fruit, and dump it into lug boxes. The pickers had a little more class. They would climb with Dad and Uncle Max into the higher branches, hang their empty buckets on a limb, select the ripest apricots, and carefully place them in the pail so as not to bruise them.

When it got too hot to work any longer, we would go back to the Big House and watch Aunt Helen slice and pit the damaged fruit and arrange it on huge wooden trays to dry in the noonday sun. In mid-afternoon, when the temperature reached well over 100 degrees, we would sprawl out on our sleeping bags in the little cool stone house, which Uncle Max had built by hand, to take a nap, read, or color. (Mommy always made sure we each had our own brand new coloring book and crayons for Daddy's vacation time.)

Because there were so many children in the Ojai Valley area, the local residents joined together to dam up part of the Si-Sar Creek for use as a community swimming hole. Our afternoons at the creek were filled with the adventures of Tom Sawyer—rubber tube riding, races from rock to rock, diving for gold, dodging poison oak, watching for rattlers and water snakes, and avoiding the skeeter bugs. (We called them Jesus bugs because they walked on the water.)

Swimming in the clean, clear pool served as our daily bath. Mom would take advantage of the little waterfalls downstream, which were perfect for washing and rinsing our hair. It seems there was no end to the number of uses for the creek. It was above all our source of drinking water. Each visit would end with the filling of glass jugs to be brought back to the ranch for cooking and drinking. Uncle Max had a well from which he obtained water for washing and feeding his horse, Pal, and his chickens, Tetrazzini and Henrietta, and his dog, Blacky; but the water was salty and oily tasting, and he never could convince us that it was "goot for da body!" There was no indoor plumbing, and the outhouse was not one of our favorite places, especially when we had to fight our way through the swarming yellow jackets and wasps, or had to accompany one of the little kids on a midnight visit.

But the shower was a different story. The water well was about five-hundred yards from the main house, so Uncle Max had taken some old pipes he picked up from his odd-job construction sites and erected a small, portable shower. Each time he could procure another piece of pipe the shower moved a few inches closer to the house. We never knew from one day to the next whether we would be taking our cold shower in the grape vineyard, apricot orchard, or in the horseshoe pit. (After we started singing on the Lawrence Welk Show one of our first projects was having a bathroom with toilet, shower, and bathtub built for Uncle Max and Aunt Helen.)

I was introduced to the world of business by helping Uncle Max sell his apricots. Funny how such a little thing can start one off on an interest that ends up being a life career. I often wonder if my taking on the business responsibilities of The Lennon Sisters—the accounting supervision, the scheduling, the production detailing, the whole operation of the organization—was partially the result of selling apricots with Uncle Max. I found myself supervising my sisters and brothers at the packing of each little carton, placing the slightly bruised apricots at the bottom, and saving the choicest (those picked by the pickers) for the top.

We set our sales stand at the end of his dirt road on the edge of Highway 150. In summer, with the peak traffic season, our expectations of profits ran high. Our luck varied, however, and when things weren't going too well Daddy prompted us to change our rather colorless selling tactics. I think this is how we first learned the true meaning of the expression "con artist." Dad would take a carton of apricots out into the highway with him and lie on the asphalt. This would start Uncle Max shouting his most often used expression. "Och by Kolly, Billy, comes it now!" When the cars would come to a screeching halt, Dad would stand up and take a big bite of a succulent apricot and say. "Um, um, um. Delicious! May I interest you in a carton or a crate?"

After dinner, Uncle Max and Dad would take us hiking in the hills in back of the houses. These hills were full of brush and tumbleweeds and ticks and dirt, but were beautiful and enjoyable to us. At the very top of the highest hill were bubbling pools of oil and tar. Unfortunately for Uncle Max, Richfield Oil Company owned all the oil rights in these hills. We would sit for long periods of time throwing pebbles and sticks into the black gas, and we would collect from the surrounding muck what we liked to pretend were prehistoric fossils. But down deep in our hearts we knew they were just the bones and feathers of birds and animals that ventured too near.

There was a mountain lion den in the side of the ravine, and Uncle Max would point out the fresh tracks that led to the mouth of the cave. I never saw the big cat, but Maxie said that many times during the cold winters the cat would creep down into the stable to try to keep warm by snuggling up to his horse Pal. Of course, the old white horse didn't take to that too well, and Max had to fire warning shots with the rifle to scare the lion away.

On these twilight walks we often came across coveys of quail, and occasionally deer would leap out of the shadows and, for one brief moment, show us their graceful forms. We marveled at their innocent beauty. But Uncle Max would just laugh and tell us that "the sneaky rascals are just on their way down to steal the apricots that Aunt Helen left to dry at the back of the house."

Later, resting from our hiking, we would sit on the knoll of a hill and with fascination listen to Uncle Max tell of his life in the Bavarian Alps and his closeness with the animals in these mountains. I recall his telling us of his friendship with the condors, now nearly extinct. There are few sanctuaries left in California where these birds can live and breed unmolested; but the Upper Ojai Valley, in particular Topa Topa Mountain, remains fairly remote and protected. When large vultures flew out into the evenings and circled the ranchlands, Uncle Max called to them again and again. Strange how they got to know his call and soon would come to him. I watched him sit and talk with them—they knew he was a friend.

All of us were intrigued by the way Uncle Max could explain the behavior of the wild creatures in every circumstance. It was as if he could communicate with each of them on its own level. He loved all animals and creatures; we believe he was enchanted, much in the same way as the grandfather in the story, *Heidi*: Uncle Max was a leftover, in our own time, from one of Grimm's *Fairy Tales*.

It was here we once again caught a glimpse of Mom and Dad, not as our parents, but as husband and wife. Holding hands they climbed the hill together to drink in the peace and warmth of the day, in the remnants of the dying light.

It was on one of these warm evenings, in the summer of 1953, that we all witnessed an event that is still unexplained.

The sunset was beautiful, and we were sitting on the steps of the Big House watching the changing colors on the sheer face of Topa Topa Mountain about fifty miles across the valley. Suddenly a huge brilliant light appeared on the top ridge, and it seemed to be round in shape and burning. At first we decided it was a reflection of the sun bouncing off a butane tank somewhere below. However, as the sun went down behind the hills and the sky became quite dark, the object did not change in appearance. We called Uncle Max out to see it and asked him if it could be a brush fire. He was one of the few men who had ever climbed the treacherous mountain, and he assured us that the light was coming from above the timberline and was much too large and the wrong size for a campfire. It was a fascinating and exciting sight. Just when we began to calm down a little, the object lifted into the air and moved to the extreme side of the ridge. It then changed color from red to green to orange and back to the brilliant silver. There was no mistaking it for a plane or helicopter, because at that distance the lights on the more familiar craft would be almost invisible. And this thing was huge! Stunned, we watched the massive light move back and forth. Soon neighbors from other ranches began to converge on Uncle Max, seeking his opinion. They knew he was very familiar with Topa. Around 10:00 p.m., the Highway Patrol came up too, and they were as baffled as the rest of us, figuring if anyone had an answer it would be Max Heinrich. But all he could do was shake his head in wonder. Completely amazed and bewildered, all of us watched in silence until around 11:00 p.m., when our UFO just blinked out. We never saw it again, nor did anyone else in the area. But every night we would watch the sunset with a little more interest and a slight touch of expectation.

When Uncle Max Heinrich died in January 1971, no one in the family was in a position to live on—or take care of—the ranch. It was sold, and our cousins, our brothers and sisters, and several friends went up to Ojai for a last visit. We spent many hours that day sharing our collective memories of the many summers we had spent with him at the ranch.

Together, we gathered the treasured belongings of our grand patriarch. When we had completed the packing and sorting and had exchanged the many mementos of his lifetime, we climbed the golden hill behind his home one more time. At the setting sun we all looked out over the ranch, the vineyards and orchard, over the valley to Topa Topa Mountain. It was a moment of family unity; the group, numbering more than a score of us, clasped hands. In a prayerful farewell tribute we yelled out, "WE LOVE YOU UNCLE MAX . . ." And it echoed back, "Max . . . Max . . ., Max . . ."

With tears spilling from our eyes, we all ran down the hill to our cars and drove down the little dirt road to the highway—never to return, except in memories and dreams.

Janet:

Summer holidays meant the beach or Uncle Max's ranch, but Christmas holidays meant home. For us, Christmas was a time of sharing and fun and impatience. It was a time of sacrifice for Mom and Dad, particularly when they didn't have the money to fulfill our long lists of desires. But we kids never felt deprivation, nor did we ever fully realize the problems Mom and Dad went through to finance their gifts. We were always satisfied with the homemade presents even more than with the hard-earned, store-bought ones.

At this time of year Daddy was at his wittiest, and that enlivened the household quite a bit. His sense of humor was forever active, and he seemed to delight in deflating dignity. Mom's worst time came each Christmas when the dignity Daddy delighted in deflating came to visit—Nana's relatives! We looked forward to their coming, even though Mom warned us to be on our best behavior and begged Dad, "Please don't do anything silly to embarrass Nana." I really think Daddy wanted to do as she asked; but when Nana's relatives walked through the front door, something snapped, and he would somersault downstairs, landing upright with his hand extended for a handshake. He was met with polite little chuckles from them and gales of laughter from us. He never let us down.

Our Christmas table always held an extra-large ham, given us by Nana's sister, Aunt Sally, and her husband, George Hearst. Uncle George was the oldest son of publisher William Randolph Hearst, and a very kind and gentle man. They sent lovely gifts every holiday. More exciting to us were the gifts they sent on just plain old everyday days. Several times a year, a large carton would arrive, containing *new* clothes, gold charms, dolls with lifelike skin, and scented soaps in every shape and color.

One summer day, Aunt Sally and Uncle Georgie invited us to spend the day with them at Marion Davies' beach house (now a Santa Monica beach club), a huge mansion; and it was fabulous! We were served our luncheon on the terrace by real servants, and helped into our bathing suits by real maids with black and white uniforms. The swimming pool was beautifully decorated with large fountains and statues. I thought it funny that people would have a pool right on the beach. But after our swim, Uncle George took us by the hand and led us down to the ocean so we could feel the familiar sand in our toes. It was a perfect day, marred only by poor Peggy's mishap. She had gone off alone to the bathroom (the house had fifteen or twenty bathrooms), which was a big mistake. Although her screams echoed throughout the house, it took Mom nearly ten minutes to follow the sound and find her in one of the upstairs hallways.

Sally and George Hearst loved to hear us sing. They called us their "miracle kids," long before we thought a career remotely possible. They were convinced we were headed for stardom. And so it was with great excitement, but not necessarily surprise, that we received a Webcor recorder from them—not a tape or wire recorder, but a machine that made celluloid record discs. With this gift they demanded we make them records of our songs so that they could be the first to have our voices saved for posterity. It was fun to sit with the microphone and record our harmonies, tell stories, and talk to them by this remote method. Today, these recordings are among our most prized possessions, and our children and sisters and brothers love to hear our "little girl voices."

Our Nana spent several summer vacations at the famous William Randolph Hearst Castle at San Simeon. She has treasured black-and-white photos of her and Aunt Sally swimming in the Grand Roman Bath Pool. Because Kathy is an antique collector, Aunt Sally has given her many beautiful *objets d'art*—crystal, china, furniture, and gorgeous oriental rugs—that once belonged to the Hearst Family.

Many times our Grandma Lennon's Victoria Avenue home was the center of Lennon family gatherings. This old-fashioned, brown shingled, two-story house was what I term "very Venice."

On Sundays everyone came for dinner, including the fast-growing number of grandchildren. Gramma cooked the meat herself, and all the aunts helped with the salads, the vegetables, and desserts. In the afternoons the uncles played football with neighborhood kids, and we would put some records on the old wind-up Victrola and watch the younger ones sing and dance. We would take turns cranking the record machine, giggling when we heard the music slow down. Then one or another would have the opportunity to show off our strong muscles by cranking up the machine to proper speed. We can still sing those very few songs that were Gramma's record collection—"When My Irene Was About Sixteen," or "How Are You Gonna Wet Your Whistle When The Whole Darn World Goes Dry?"

Dee Dee and our cousin Michael were the two oldest grandchildren, and they had the job of reading the Sunday funnies to the younger children, keeping them quiet and out of the kitchen. Michael became the voice of Dagwood, Jiggs, Sluggo, The Phantom, or Prince Valiant, and Dee Dee was Blondie, Maggie, Nancy, Little Lulu, or Iodine. They also taught us how to crackle chewing gum, how to sweet-talk Gramma Lennon out of a "kookie" or lemon drop from her big amber jar, and how to show bravery while spending five minutes alone with the light off in Gramma's broom closet. Our dads considered this a major accomplishment.

It was hard to resist a sneak out onto the big laundry porch to catch a peek at the dessert. If it was Gramm's lopsided cupcakes, we would let out squeals. Due to the incompetence of the old oven, these cupcakes took on the strangest shapes, but due to Gramm's "chocolate thumb," none ever tasted better. With only one bathroom downstairs, the scramble to wash hands for dinner was something to behold. It was everyone for himself, and many accidental trips were taken over the giant bar of Fels Naphtha soap which was propped up against the bathroom door to keep it from slamming shut.

The older cousins got to eat in the dining room at the big oak table and participate in the grownup conversations, while the smaller ones ate in the kitchen, giggling and exchanging "knock-knock" jokes.

Our Dad's only sister, Aunt Mary, was a young teenager and seemed "not too old" to all of us. She could manage to slip us an extra piece of dessert or help us get out of clearing the table. Though she was our aunt, she was more like a big sister. If we were well-behaved during dinner, she would let us go upstairs to her room to play with the special doll and cradle she had won at the church bazaar.

Occasionally the aunts and uncles went out together, and we cousins, after piling into beds in threes and fours, waited for our babysitter, Aunt Mary, to come and read to us or make us up in Gramm's face powder and lipstick. She was our friend, confidante, all-around great makebeliever, and most importantly, the perfect liaison between our world in Gramma's room and the grownups' world, which began at the bottom of the stairs.

Dee Dee and Peggy tell me that Gramma's house was not always the scene of happy get-togethers. During World War II, it was the meeting place for all of the family that remained at home. They recall the strange wailing of the air raid sirens filling the air and Mom hurrying them into coats and hats to rush to Gramma's, just a few blocks away. There they watched and they prayed in the darkness until the all-clear siren.

Christmas Eve found many wide-eyed anxious faces in the upstairs windows eagerly searching for a glimpse of Santa and his sleigh. As soon as we heard the jingle of bells and a loud "Ho, Ho, Ho" downstairs, we raced down to get a quick look at Santa's boots and big toy bag dashing through the front door. While we little kids were busily opening our gifts, Amma played Christmas carols on the piano, and our uncles provided the singing. This was our first appreciation of a family musical blend. The harmony, though simple and improvised, had a sound like no other. Gramma managed to have a little gift for each of us, usually a pocket comb or a handkerchief, for which she would apologize, as grandmas will, for not being able to give more.

We continue to have our family reunions at Christmastime. There are approximately two-hundred aunts, uncles, cousins, and grandchildren, all residing in California—and most of them in the vicinity of Venice.

The younger kids like to run up to one or more of the relatives and say something like, "I know who you are. You are my mom's Aunt Peg's youngest son, Mark." We see one another during the year, but at Christmas the Lennon get-together is in toto!

We have ceased exchanging gifts; each person brings food and clothing for underprivileged families. After the initial first hour or so of enthusiastic greetings and eatings, we all move on to the living room to make ourselves comfortable. There we share our Lennon family Christmas traditions. We begin by singing "Silent Night," and then Uncle Jack, the oldest, dressed in his German lederhosen, announces the changes that have taken place within the family throughout the year. He leads us in welcoming new in-laws, presenting new babies, and remembering those who are not able to be with us. After Uncle Jimmy briefly recounts our family history, he invites all to ask questions regarding our heritage. Stories of their childhoods are recalled by our aunts and uncles. We coax them to tell our favorites, and once in a while we hear a new one to add to our legacy. Uncle Jack draws the stories to a close with his patriarchal pleas, "If I may be so bold, I implore you younger kiddies to continue this tradition and keep this feeling alive long after we older folk are gone. There is nothing more important than family, and in all humility I do believe we have the best." The focus of the evening then turns to music. Our uncles and Aunt Mary sing the same nostalgic songs each year.

Within the family, Uncle Jack and Uncle Tom are the only two who cannot carry a tune. Uncle Jack is diplomatic enough to narrate or lip-synch all the songs. But Uncle Tommy proudly rehearses to get ready for his vocal solo of "O Holy Night." A la Al Jolson, he dramatically falls to his knees to sing, "Fall on your knees; O, hear the angel voices . . . ." And the applause for his courage drowns out his questionable vocal sounds. The four of us Lennon sisters sing our favorite Christmas medley, "Chestnuts roasting on an open fire . . ." and "Have yourself a merry little Christmas . . . ." Each family in turn entertains the rest with its own unique musical contribution. Finally, the younger members bring out their guitars and a fiddle, and with the music of their generation bring new sounds that add to the family traditions. Our festive singing and dancing continues far into the night.

Grandpa Dan Denning and our baby sister, Mary Frances, June 1954. Within a few weeks both would be taken from us. *(The Lennon Family Collection)*

Our great grandmother, Minnie Lehman Lennon, "Amma," not too long before she died, at age 94. *(The Lennon Family Collection)*

A happy time: Nana's ninetieth birthday, July 1984. The Los Angeles Dodgers' jacket was a gift from team manager Tom Lasorda. *(The Lennon Sisters Collection)*

5

Some Things That Happen
For The First Time

Kathy:

1954 . . .

We came to know and we had to accept a side of life we never had to face before. That July was particularly hot, temperatures high each day, and we were very uncomfortable. Mom was expecting her eighth child at any time, and the days were really difficult for her. Our little sister Mary, sixteen-months old, suffered from eczema, and the heat irritated her skin rashes and made her fussy most of the time. It was due to this restlessness that one afternoon Mom allowed us to play in the frontyard where the breeze from the ocean cooled us a little. We sat on the front porch to wait for Daddy to come home from work, and the little kids rolled on the grass with balloons that Mom had tucked away for just such a day.

Perhaps the only unpleasantness of the afternoon would occur when, every fifteen minutes or so, a test car from the automobile agency down the street would come screeching around the corner. For years, we and the neighbors had been petitioning to have the agency stop this dangerous testing of brakes on our street. Unfortunately, to no avail.

The events of that hot summer day remain indelible. I was performing cartwheels on the front lawn when, out of the corner of my eye, a flash. I saw Mary toddle out into the street after her runaway balloon. I rushed toward her, then heard the roar of the test car coming up the street. I had almost reached her when Mom pulled me back. I was saved from being hit by the car. Mary wasn't.

The next moments are somewhat blurred, but I recall the ambulance coming and Mom leaving with Mary for the hospital. A dear neighbor, Virginia Inglehart, came over at once to take charge of the family. Nana was crying hysterically. Virginia put us all in the back room of the house and told us to pray. My mind raced through so many fears and guilts that I was unaware of where anyone else was, or what they were doing. In my terror I resorted to what almost any Catholic girl might do when facing a family tragedy. I made a promise to God in my prayers that, if Mary lived, I would become a Carmelite nun, living in seclusion the remainder of my life.

The telephone rang. In a few minutes Virginia came to us. "That was your mom calling, and she said to tell you that your little sister Mary is now in heaven with God, and we have our own special angel."

Then we huddled together in need of comfort. I wanted desperately not to believe it.

Not long after, Daddy arrived from work. He saw the commotion in the neighborhood. He looked at Nana's face, and he knew something terrible had happened. "Is it Sis?" he asked.

Nana shook her head.

"Don't tell me which one it is," he said. "Just bring them in and line them up."

Dee Dee was at work in downtown L.A. at the *Tidings* office, a Catholic newspaper. So, Peggy, Janet, Danny, little Pat, and I lined up. I will carry forever the look that came over my dad's face when he realized Mary was absent. It was only that very week that she had said her first sentence. Two words: "Bye, Dada."

Dad left immediately for the hospital to be with Mom. Soon they returned home together, but there was the sad task of telling Dee Dee. He drove down to the bus stop at the end of the street and waited for her.

She was surprised to see the car, she told us later. She climbed in while Dad put out his hand for hers and held it tightly. "I have something to tell you." She could see he had been crying, and her first thought was that Mom had had the new baby, and that she had died. "Something terrible has happened," Dad told her.

"Is it Mom?" she asked.

"No. It's Mary-poo." At first Dee Dee was relieved. It wasn't Mom. But then the frightful shock set in. Mary had been her special little girl. Her crib sat next to Dee Dee's bed. And because Mary had not learned to say "Mama," it was to "Dee Dee" she called in the night.

In a few minutes Dee Dee and Dad arrived home, and—without saying anything—Dad walked into his bedroom and went into the closet. We could hear his sobbing through the closed door. It was the first time any of us had ever heard Daddy cry, but it would not be the last. For months afterward, he would suddenly retreat to his room. In the dark space of the small closet he shed tears of grief.

We girls went into our bedroom and looked at Mary's crib. It was a new emotion for me; I remember it so well. Emptiness. We sat there and cried together until Mommy had us get into our beds. Amidst all the chaos, she had managed to cook some dinner, and she insisted we eat. "I don't want any of you to make yourselves sick," she said. "We all need each other very specially now, and we need our strength."

Our mother was the essence of strength. She may have been torn apart inside, her eyes were always filling with tears over the loss of her baby girl, but she controlled her grief in front of us. We remember her moving forward, leaving to God the provisions of the future. Hers was an example to follow when, en masse, friends and neighbors began to arrive. And they did arrive in droves, with their compassion and their food, and all the love we needed then and came to depend upon.

Kay Esser, Mom's friend, had been vacationing in the Fresno area when the accident had happened, and she returned to Venice immediately. I believe that Kay was a great source of support for Mom. I can recall these two women sitting together on the living room couch—Kay giving Mom the reassurance and comfort that anyone needs at a time like that. The health of the expected baby was more important now, Kay said. She helped Mom to reaffirm that the mental and physical state of the rest of us was dependent upon her reactions.

Dressed in bright colors, we celebrated the "Mass of the Angels" for Mary Frances. One of the most beautiful expressions of that funeral day was hearing the entire St. Mark's Grammar School sing the happy, affirming songs of the innocent soul reunited with God.

Then, on July 29, God's gift for rejoicing was the birth of William Paul, a darling baby with a little round face. Such a face: it reminded us of the Campbell Soup Kids. We were grateful that he was a boy, so that the recent memories were not constantly brought to our minds. His presence consumed every waking minute, and all of us fought to be the one to rock him and hold him.

Janet:

In early September our family suffered still another loss with the death of our best pal, Grampa Denning. Again our faith was tested, and with his passing we were forced one more step away from childhood. (It wasn't until years later, in therapy, that I realized it was at this point in my life that I began to shy away from those I loved most for fear of losing them.)

Within a few weeks, another change was on the horizon. Dad was promoted to outside field salesman for Edgemar Dairy. This meant he would wear a suit and tie to work and drive his own car to appointments with various restaurants and large eating facilities. It also meant a raise in his pay, which made possible another change—a new car, the first brand new car we had ever had.

Dad took the entire family down to the automobile showroom, and we decided on a white and red station wagon. Oh, the smell of that new car! Driving home we felt like we were the spiffiest family in the world! And another first for us was that we didn't have to stop along the way for repairs, only hamburgers.

It was a new season, the autumn of 1954, and Dad's new job, the new car, and the new baby found us settling into the comfort of new patterns. We accepted the events of the summer as an expression of God's Will. And progress, new adventure, was in the air—something good would happen.

In October, Dad's boss at Edgemar Farms telephoned with a

surprising request. He was president of our local Lions Club. He offered us, the Lennon girls, twenty dollars to entertain the club members at a luncheon. He had been one of the singers in *Roamin' Holiday*, and he had enjoyed our performance. He thought the members of the Lions Club would also enjoy us. We were flabbergasted. To be paid for just standing and singing. We were excited about it; if that's all they wanted, we would give them our all.

We had a problem. Our Scottish medley—at its best—lasted about four minutes. Daddy asked his former accompanist, Don Shaw, to help us build our repertoire, using some of our uncles' old arrangements and tunes. There had been The Lennon Brothers before The Lennon Sisters. After the war, Dad and his brothers Bob, Ted, and Pat began singing for service groups and local radio and TV shows. As winners of talent contests, they had appeared with the Freddy Martin and Paul Whiteman orchestras. Their rehearsals were held at night at our house on Garfield Avenue, because we were the only family that had a piano. And so the Lennon-Sisters-to-be watched with great admiration and absorption as the Lennon Brothers practiced. They signed a record contract with Mercury Records. With their career on the rise, they started receiving promising offers. However, they could not all take time off from their regular jobs to audition, nor would they travel and leave their growing families, already numbering twelve children. So The Lennon Brothers abandoned their professional singing.

It was great fun to sit at the piano with Don Shaw just as he had with our dad and his brothers. He helped us learn harmonies to the old songs. Dad taught us some of his favorite songs, too; he did not know harmonies, but he did know what he wanted to hear. Peggy and Kathy tried different notes until it sounded right to him, and Dee Dee and I doubled on the lead together. We did not fully understand the words we were singing when we sang the very old love songs and sad refrains, but Dad's memory of them motivated us to express the emotions and learn the phrasing. The people for whom we sang, particularly the older people, loved to hear the old songs. As we grew up, we realized their meaning and beauty. These songs—"Among My Souvenirs," "My Rosary," "The Old Refrain." They gave us insight into bygone days.

Now we needed an accompanist. We found her, and much more, in a high-school friend of our parents. With Virginia Lovil and six new songs (old ones, really) added to our Scottish medley, we performed our first paying job. We left our amateur world behind. When we sang from then on, we received some compensation, even if it was only a free meal, or a free ticket to the event in which we were appearing.

From the Lions Club appearance came many more offers: service clubs, church groups, school events. At $20 a show we were soon earning $80, maybe $100 a month. Dad acted as our musical coach, our chauffeur, and our critic. Mom took up the role of dresser, and gave us lots of encouragement. Our parents decided to use the money we earned to build a dormitory addition to our two-bedroom house, for the four of us. Dad even drew up plans that included a single bed and a chest of drawers and a mirror for each one of us. This dream room was now our main goal, so we accepted every job with the idea that it meant another piece of linoleum, a wooden beam, or a window frame for our new room. A chest *and* a mirror for *each* of us!

When we think of those first days as The Lennon Sisters, we all remember one particular night. It was our first performance for *all* of $25, from the Oddfellows Club of the South Bay Area. Their high officer introduced us and thanked us for drawing the largest crowd they'd ever had. We could hardly keep a straight face as we sang through our program. Imagine receiving $25 for 25 minutes of singing for 25 people!

Our uncle Jimmy Lennon arranged many appearances for us. He had been singing in the Santa Monica area for years and was quite active in several civic projects and community groups. He was Master of Ceremonies for the Venice Beach Beauty Pageant for most Independence Day celebrations. Those Fourth of July events, for which he always supplied the entertainment, were part of the several contests held annually throughout the State to select a "Miss California" for the "Miss Universe" event. We were excited when Uncle Jimmy asked us to perform, because we really looked forward each year to seeing the parade of bathing beauties.

Any girl over age eighteen could enter. There were the inevitable leopard-skin suits and gold lame spiked heels and girls whose heavy buildup of makeup could not make up for their heavy builds. But among all the assorted shapes and sizes we usually found three or four girls whom we thought were truly pretty, and we rooted them on to their eventual defeat, since judges never choose the ones you want anyway.

Kathy:

One of the judges of the 1955 Venice Beauty Pageant was singer Joe Graydon. He hosted his own local television show on KABC-TV. An afternoon program of music and talk, always interesting and informative, it was ahead of its time. When we had finished singing our songs for the pageant, he asked us to appear on his television program. We were thrilled.

I'm sure the first time we arrived at the ABC Studios, they didn't know quite what to do with us. We had no costumes, but our school uniforms were alike, so we wore those. In complete awe, we were taken into a little room and powderpuffed until our noses didn't shine. The makeup man was Rudy Horvatich, who helped us understand our first little bit about television activity.

We were ushered onto the program's set, and although it was just a small corner of a huge barn-like building, we were fascinated by it—and by Joe Graydon, who awaited us. He put us at ease by introducing us to the stagehands, showing us the camera, the props, and the lights. The crew members were aware of our fear, so when it was time to sing we took comfort in their friendly presence. It really wasn't as terrifying as we thought it would be. By the time we sang our second song we were old pros.

Joe Graydon received a good response from his television audience for our appearance. We were asked to return again for two more programs. We began to form what would become lasting friendships with many of the staff and crew at ABC. Shortly, though, the Graydon show was cancelled, and we said goodbye to everyone, not knowing that for the next fourteen years the American Broadcasting Company would be our second home.

In the autumn, on October 16, another little sister was born. We named her Miriam, the lovely Hebrew form of the name, Mary, and called her Mimi. With her big black eyes and round moon face, she was our real live doll. A few days later, Dee Dee, a student of St. Monica High School, Santa Monica, had what proved to be a memorable date.

Dianne:

Lawrence Welk, Jr., a classmate of mine, was having a party at his home in Brentwood, and he asked me if I would be his date for the evening. My sisters and I were going to sing for a Halloween dance that same night, so I told Larry it wasn't possible to go with him to his party. Larry persisted and told me he would pick me up at the Club when I was finished singing. He assumed I would be singing with a choral group at the Elks Club that night.

He arrived just after we began to sing, and he was surprised to see me singing with my sisters. He apparently enjoyed what he heard. When we had concluded our songs, he said he was going to tell his father about us. We didn't really think too much about his offer. And evidently, Mr. Welk didn't either, because it wasn't until five or six weeks later that we received a telephone call from Larry. It was early one Sunday morning in December.

"My dad is sick in bed with a cold," Larry told me. "And he can't leave the house. Come over right now and sing for him! I mean right now!"

What a surprise.

Janet:

That rainy Sunday morning, still dressed in our church clothes, Mom and Dad and the four of us girls drove to the Brentwood home of Lawrence Welk. I was at an impressionable age, and I certainly was impressed with the wide, beautiful lawn and the red-tiled roof of the old Spanish house. We were all excited when Larry opened the massive front door to us.

We entered those portals and were immediately introduced to Fern Welk, Lawrence Welk's wife. Larry took us into the spacious living room, and we were introduced to Ed Spaulding, Mr. Welk's close friend and business manager. I gazed around the large room and wondered how a small family could live in such a large space. Kathy and I stroked the velvet covered chairs, and our heads turned upward to see the crystal chandeliers. In one part of the house, wrought-iron gates led to—of all things—a bedroom. The central hallway had a nook that was lighted in blue, and in the center, surrounded by flowers, was a lovely statue of the Blessed Mother.

When Mr. Welk came into the room, he was wearing a purple satin smoking jacket and velvet slippers with gold embroidery. I know each of us had a fluttery, burning sensation in our stomachs and limbs, but he charmed us with his smile, and we relaxed. Once Daddy and Mr. Welk began speaking, they discovered that they had mutual friends in the music business. Mr. Welk carried on a normal conversation, like a real person. "My, my, my," Mr. Welk said finally. "Let's see what my son has found for me."

Kathy:

Over the years since that December day, each of us vividly remembers moving to the piano and standing next to it—against it really. We felt the need of its massive support, although we did not use it for the audition. I blew the starting note on a pitch pipe, and we sang the spiritual, "He," *a cappella*. As frightened as we were, our voices were clear. We watched with relief as a smile spread across Mr. Welk's face. Then we saw that everyone else was smiling, too.

When we finished, Lawrence Welk asked to hear one or two more songs. Each time we began to sing, he had the same pleasant look on his face, and he followed our singing with applause. Then he asked us if we would sing over the telephone for his producer, Ed Sobel, and also for his musical director, George Cates.

Mr. Welk congratulated us and then spoke more casually. "I'd like you girls to sing on my television show sometime." That was all. He thanked us, and when the warm goodbyes were spoken, we left his beautiful home on Tigertail Road.

On the drive back home to Venice, we were suddenly thrust back into our real world. Daddy said that he was proud of us and that, if Mr. Welk really wanted us, he would call. But Dad also said that it would not be the end of the world if he did not call. We felt that way, too. Just the experience itself was great. It had been fun, and it had also been scary; if we never had to audition again it would be just fine.

Mr. Welk meant what he said. Two weeks later he telephoned and asked if we would sing for a luncheon benefit for the Daughters of Mary and Joseph, in Santa Monica. Each year he appeared at this Christmas affair, and the nuns were thrilled to have him (and his accordion). He wanted to observe the response we would receive from the general public. Mom purchased pink corduroy coats for us, and we wore Christmas corsages of bells and holly.

We were warmly received. Right then and there Mr. Welk asked us to appear on his Christmas Eve telecast. Live from Hollywood.

Peggy:

Christmas Eve, 1955. The day of that national television debut arrived much too soon. And not soon enough.

Apprehensive, yet strangely elated, we walked into the studio and made our way to the dressing room assigned to us—the ladies room at the back of the makeup room. (ABC was still a far cry from the studios of today, and they were having a difficult time accommodating the personnel of a weekly network show.)

Mom began to set out our new outfits with motherly pride and care, hanging them from every available doorknob and window lock. They consisted of navy blue linen suits and blouses with large collars and red satin bows, which gave a choirboy effect. One can imagine Mom's horror when the producer, Ed Sobel, came in and said, "You're not going to wear those, are you?"

Completely unaware of television requirements, we couldn't figure out why the suits were so objectionable. Then he pointed to the white collars and said gruffly, "These things will throw a glare that will knock us off the air. Wear something else!"

At that moment he was the personification of the producer seen in every movie, lacking only the megaphone and the whip.

It was Rudy Horvatich, the makeup artist, whom we had met on the Graydon Show, who came to our rescue. There was no real wardrobe department for the show then, so Rudy was in charge of Mr. Welk's clothes, and he attempted to coordinate the costumes and apparel for the entire show. Noticing the tears forming in our eyes, he said, "I'll just send the blouses out and have them dyed light blue. Don't worry, Mrs. Lennon. Ed will love them."

We rehearsed onstage in the afternoon, and I remember how quiet it was as all the band members listened to our *a cappella* song. Here we were, four little girls who couldn't even read music, singing for trained musicians. And yet, when we finished, they all applauded. What a beautiful feeling. They liked us!

Kathy:

That night, as we were standing backstage trying not to be nervous, the representative for the advertising agency and sponsor of the show came up to us. "Now listen, girls. Don't be nervous. There are only thirty-million people watching you out there." That did it!

The stage manager walked us to our marks on the stage, and before we could catch our breath, the little red light came on. Mr. Welk was introducing us. "This is the oldest, Dianne," he said. I must have been frightened to death because—as Dee Dee smiled—I took a little step forward and bowed. "And this is Peggy." Again I nodded and continued to bob my head throughout each introduction.

Maybe I was caught up in all my bowing, but I couldn't find my starting note and had to sort of slide into the song on the fourth word. I can still see the panic in Peggy's eyes as her silent glare told me I was wrong. During our song, I allowed my eyes to dart to the side of the stage where Daddy stood. I needed some sign that I was doing all right. (Years later, as we watched the old kinescope film of that first appearance, I was surprised to see that my sisters' eyes also darted off-camera toward Daddy, for his approval.)

The public response to our national television debut was overwhelming. Letters came from every part of the United States, most of them commenting that we reminded them of their nieces or granddaughters. Heaven knows we were not beauties, but we sang well and in good harmony. Mr. Welk thought well enough of that evening to invite us back on the show again and again. Our parents were proud, but we admit now that we had conflicting emotions. Our pride was mixed with a touch of humility, and also some embarrassment.

"My friends will tease me, embarrass me," I told Mom, longing not to return to school for fear of ridicule.

"If they tease and embarrass you," she replied wisely, "they are not really your friends."

We appeared twice during the Christmas vacation and guested several more times during the next three months. Just as spring was upon us, near Eastertime, Mr. Welk invited us to join his musical family.

It was then that Mom and Dad sat us down and made some promises. We could continue to go to our regular schools with our same friends, and we would never have to attend the Hollywood Professional School. They were sure that the hours of work could be minimized to allow time for our homework and normal day-to-day living. Mom and Dad singled out Dee Dee and Peggy and reminded them that several of their friends were working in dime-stores or restaurants to help their family finances. We agreed that this was our way to help our family.

"But most important of all,"Dad said, "God has given you a very specal gift that He wants you to share with others. At times, it will seem a difficult thing to do, but there are reasons why we are given certain talents."

Mom added, "Through television you can reach many lonely, unhappy people. Maybe you can make their days brighter."

And so we accepted Mr. Welk's offer and began our dozen years of association with the Lawrence Welk organization.

6

Curtain Up! Light The Lights!

Janet:

Our first encounter with producer Ed Sobel that Christmas Eve was rather uncomfortable. It took a few weeks to see through his gruffness and what I thought were his harsh manners. In time, I found him a deeply kind and loving man. Perhaps because I was the youngest of the group, I got to him first. Ed Sobel's elfin-like demeanor could, at a moment's notice, become the *Little Caesar* of Edward G. Robinson, or swing the other way and, with a twinkle in his eye, assume the Kris Kringle-Edmund Gwenn stance. I was the apple of his eye, although he could not remember my name. He often called me Janice, his wife's name. When he tried to be practical, he would call me "Vuntz," rather than "hey you." And always tenderly. I never knew what it meant, but having heard such strange words pour from Uncle Max's mouth, I assumed it to be a German term of endearment. (Years later I found out *Vuntz* was a yiddish word meaning "bedbug.") I loved this man—for us, he was a teacher and mentor—and I know he loved us. He once told Daddy, "Bill, if only your girls were orphans. I'd take one of them home for keeps."

In those early days of our association with Mr. Welk, we were able to attend school five days a week. The show's director, Jim Hobson, was thoughtful in arranging our rehearsals around our school schedules. During the early part of each week we rehearsed with Dad in our converted garage-den. We would listen to recordings and decide together which songs were suited to our age and style of singing. I admit, being youngest, I went along with whatever was decided by my older sisters, although sometimes I asked, or begged, to have one of my favorites included in our growing repertoire. We couldn't read music, but Kathy and Peggy picked out harmonies to suit the melody lines that Dee Dee and I sang together. We memorized tunes almost instantly. Dee Dee would type five copies of lyrics to songs, labeling "solo" or "unison" or "harmony" where appropriate. Then Daddy would listen to us and work on our diction, phrasing, and "feeling." We would sing a song through three or four times for polishing, and that was that! It did not occur to any of us until much later that some singers take days to learn a song.

In later years Daddy asked Uncle Pat Lennon to help me find a fourth part to a song. My voice was growing stronger as I grew older, and it seemed time for me to begin singing harmony. Uncle Pat could read and write music and play the piano a bit, so his talents helped us to enhance our sound. We didn't sing four parts all the time, only when they would create the right sound at the right time.

Each Thursday we went to the Aragon Ballroom in Ocean Park, to rehearse with the Welk orchestra. It was an old dance hall at the end of Lick Pier, but we felt the romance of that place. Our nostalgia was based on the fact that it had been an active part of our parents' and our grandparents' youth.

Kathy and I would run across the highly waxed dance floor and slide to the back of the ballroom, pretending to be famous ballroom dancers of the 1930s and '40s. It reminded us of the times we watched the Lawrence Welk Show before we were The Lennon Sisters. At home, Kathy and I would jump around to his music in front of our old second-hand Kaye Halbert TV set. In fact, one night we were so great at this that we invented a new dance. We showed it to our parents with a feeling of superior accomplishment. To our surprise and disappointment as well, we were informed that we had "invented" the thousand-year-old polka.

At the Aragon though, we were dazzled by our own gliding and sliding expertise, what we thought was real professional ballroom dancing, while the band rehearsed their arrangement for the next television show. It was inevitable that Dee Dee and Peg would spoil our fun, reminding us that we were in the Aragon to sing, not dance. Still we always took a final slide directly into the rehearsal room assigned to us—the ladies room. With those great old tiles on the walls, the acoustics were flawless, and we never sounded better. For six years, Mr. Welk heard each new song we had prepared in the ridiculous atmosphere of the ladies' restroom. (Sadly, the Lick Pier, along with the Aragon Ballroom, burned to the ground in the early 1970s.)

Each Friday after school, we went to the ABC Studios for a production rehearsal. At this rehearsal the producer and director set the performers on their stage marks, timed the several sequences of the show, and decided on appropriate camera shots.

The first song we ever did in production was "Shifting, Whispering Sands." The set was an old, broken-down log cabin, where the four of us little girls sat on a braided rug. We were clustered around an old prospector in his rocking chair. With our eyes gazing toward his weathered and tired face, we sang, "Won't you tell us the story of the shifting, whispering sands?" The old prospector sitting in that chair was "Aladdin." Laddie, as we came to call him, captivated us. He could have sat there for an eternity telling stories, making us believe with his magic gift of drama and theatrics all the words that flowed from his lips so profusely. We were taken in by him from the first. He was an old song-and-dance man, violin master, cornball, and ham. His full name, he told us, was Aladdin Achmed Abdullah Anthony Pallante, and he was born in "old New York."

Of course, as we grew older, we realized that he was Tony Pallante from Plainfield, New Jersey, but his Barrymore style and flair made his exotic name more believable than his real one. From his eyebrow-penciled mustache to his teeny size-five shoes to his rounded middle, we loved him. And it didn't hurt either that he seemed a younger version of our Grampa Denning, whom we so recently had lost.

Every week there were many routines that had to be staged for the various acts. Consequently, on Friday afternoons, there were hours of sitting around and waiting our turn. Although we brought our homework, we knew we would procrastinate until Sunday night anyway. In the early months we took these opportunities to get acquainted with the studio crew. There were a few we had met when we had appeared with Joe Graydon, but there were many new faces. They were all warm and eager to show us what parts they played in getting the show on the air.

Bill Dahl was the head electrician on the show. He and his co-workers were really the first to become our friends. In fact, one of them, Bobby Kuykendahl, branded us "the Katzenjammer Kids." Bill, Bobby, Hector, and Ernie worked upstairs in an old lighting booth, where they soon taught us to read their cue sheets with great accuracy. After they adjusted their headsets to fit us, we would move the dimmer handles on the switchboards like real pros.

That small booth became a little hideaway for us. We had many card games, lunches, and surprise birthday cakes with these great guys. The only person who objected to our frequent trips to and from the dimmer board was Ed Sobel. He was so afraid we would trip and fall and hurt ourselves that he told us very strongly that he "preferred" that we didn't go up there at all. So good old Bob Smith, head of the electric department, who remained on the stage floor during rehearsals, became our lookout man. At the slightest sight of Mr. Sobel coming our way, he would grab an available headset, call Bill Dahl, and say, "Tell the Katzenjammers to duck."

Bill Dahl remembers that Peggy was the first to venture into the switchboard room, that Dee Dee was a champ at gin rummy with a compulsion for saving small cards, and that the boardroom birthday celebrations—Dee Dee initiating the ritual on her seventeenth—included his fiftieth birthday. We presented him with a cake and 100 candles.

Kathy learned to drive using Bill Dahl's '51 Dodge. At fifteen years of age, she steered it onto Stage "E," causing minor scratches to the bumper and a broken bridge to the building.

One day when I was ten years old, I was playing with the headset in the boardroom and accidentally connected with Jim Hobson, our director. I could hear him swearing into his microphone at the camera crew. Frightened, I dropped the set like a hot potato, never to touch it again.

Jim Hobson was Ed Sobel's number one fan, sidekick, companion, and buffer. He was very tall and handsome and soft-spoken, and it was only natural that all four of us Lennon sisters would fall in love . . . .

Kathy:

He really was *my* first love, because I savored every pat on my head, and I tried so hard to please him, to be just perfect. All his directorial commands were, for me, gently given and received.

Janet:

It was through Ed Sobel and Jim Hobson that we took a first professional step, taking direction promptly and seriously, and respecting ourselves and others in the rehearsal situation.

Jim's assistant director was Maurie Orr. "Doodie," as we called her, was an important member of the production team. In the early years of television it was seldom that one saw a woman in any capacity, except as secretary or script girl. We idolized her and would hang around her worktable and ask what we might do to help. She found very important things for Kathy and me to do—straighten the clip box, sharpen her pencils, walk to the commissary and fetch her a lemonade. A favorite task was to unpin the big braid from the top of her head and brush out her waist-length blond hair. Her upper echelon status did not stop her from taking part in the tomfoolery that went on backstage. But the head of Backstage Tomfoolery was Eddie Holland.

Eddie was head of props and completely in charge of the production set-up. How he could spend so much time planning and carrying out the zany antics around that studio and still have all his props in order is beyond my comprehension. His sense of humor was limitless, though a bit warped. His idea of offering sympathy was to needle somebody. Dee Dee and Eddie became great friends and engaged themselves in competitive nonsense whenever possible. But Ed took advantage when we were onstage and in front of the cameras. He'd take his squirt gun and run up onto the fly floor, which held the overhead lights and curtain pulleys. Then he'd zap Dee Dee behind the head or shoot down to her ankles and even water-spot her dress. When his aim was off, I'd get it on me. Either of us would have to stand unflinching, trying to keep a straight face. One night when we'd finished singing before the camera, Dee Dee rushed offstage, grabbed her squirt gun, and ran to find Eddie, who was busily moving sets. When he saw Dee Dee, he attempted a getaway, and became entangled in the side curtain. "You wouldn't shoot an unarmed man, would you?" he pleaded.

"You bet I would," Dee Dee laughed, as she emptied her entire water gun into his shocked face.

There were two lighting directors on the Lawrence Welk Show in those first years. Vince Cilurzo, our first LD, had an exotic waxed mustache, extending six inches on either side of his face. He took the time to teach us the names of the many different kinds of lights—peanuts and spots, 2-Ks, and Kleigs with barn doors.

Truck Krone, who later replaced Vince, taught us a few things, too. "The Lawrence Welk Show had been on the air quite successfully for awhile," Truck has said. "At age 35, not believing myself a Geritol type, I was thinking of moving on to other shows as a lighting director. I met the Lennons and stayed on the show another eight years. Because of Janet, Kathy, Peggy, and Dee Dee, the Welk Show became one of the fun shows to do. Now, what makes a guy who has been in show biz all his life turn on to four giggly, Catholic girls who sing?"

For one thing, I was a challenge to his expert and technical professionalism. During rehearsals, he said, we looked just great, but then when we were on the air, my face went almost black. He checked his lights, shouted at his video control man, the technical director, and the makeup man. It was simple, and I could have told him, but he didn't ask. It was because I was shy, and I would turn a deep shade of red when we were before the audience. In black-and-white telecasting, such redness of skin comes out black. To remedy the situation, I wore clown white makeup and Truck gave me my own peanut spotlight.

According to Truck, "Kathy stares at the floor during camera rehearsals. Or, at least, she did in those years. As if she were out of it. But in any year she has never missed a cue. Now Peg; I always believed she had a little Chinese heritage. Her eyes kind of slanted. But as she grew and became the only 'C' cup in the group, her eyes got rounder." Truck told me that *his* eyes got rounder, especially when he thought Peg was developing some kind of puppy love crush for her buddy, lighting director Trucker Krone. "I was a little squirrelly about this," he said. "Finally the day came when I had to confront this. I had a new car, and she wanted a ride in it, so we drove to the Santa Inez mission and had dinner.

"On the way back she said she had something to talk about. We pulled over to the Malibu pier and took a walk all the way out to the end. She explained that she thought she was in love with an older man. I interrupted right quick and told her that I was going with someone and that she was just infatuated. Peggy laughed. Two months later she married Dick Cathcart, the guy she was talking about all along."

Trucker admits that—while he may have seemed to be brother, uncle, surrogate father, and Protestant confessor to three of us—he knew Dee Dee least of all. "I don't know why. I've thought about it and concluded nothing. She was so damned beautiful, perhaps aloof. Probably she was smarter than me."

Peggy:

Each Saturday morning, when other families did those things that families do on a Saturday morning, our family was geared to "getting the girls off to the studio." It began early, because we had to be in place and ready for the day's rehearsal and "live" telecast at 6:00 p.m.

During the first six or seven years, 48 weeks a year, the Lawrence Welk broadcasts were live. The order of the day was cooperation and dependability. If our call was 8:00 a.m., we had to be on our tape marks onstage and have our mouths open to sing when the sweep second-hand of the clock reached the "12." Discipline was absolute; Mr. Welk's organization was strict, and we absorbed his teaching—self control, responsibility, professionalism. They were good lessons, and we were never late for a stage call, although we had a few near misses. Of course, they were not our fault. Daddy believed in never being late, but he also believed in never being early. Everything he did, or we did with him, was timed. He didn't guess; he had a stopwatch, and it went everywhere with him. *We* had to be timing experts, too. Our time tests might come when we were in the bathroom getting ready for a date, or running down the stairs and out the door. Then he'd punch the stop-watch and yell, "Okay, tell me when thirty seconds are up."

"Dad, I can't. I'm late now."

"That's tough! The watch is running . . . thirty seconds."

And so, totally irritated, we'd try to count in our heads exactly thirty seconds, minus the few we took arguing. But if we missed by more than two seconds, we'd get a whack on the back of the head. Couldn't help but laugh!

Saturday mornings were timed. Dad knew just how long it took for him to plaster down his disheveled hair with brilliantine hair tonic. He knew how long to took to walk down the four stairs to the first landing, nine stairs to the next landing, two stairs to the floor. He made a science of eating a bowl of Puffed Wheat with half-and-half and lots of sugar. He knew the exact time it took to go from the front door to the car and how much time it took for the motor to warm; he knew the exact seconds between every signal that stood on Venice Boulevard all the way into Los Angeles to Vermont Avenue. He made it possible to drive non-stop the whole fifteen miles to the studio. There was one flaw in all this. If you stubbed your toe, you were dead.

In any event, we made those trips to work with only seconds to spare; that is, if we ran from the car to the studio.

We began our routine by pre-recording vocals. Most often a song would be part of a production number, with lots of movement and dancing. Since the microphones could not follow all the people and the sounds, the song was recorded ahead of time. This happened with about ten songs each show. Absolute quiet was necessary onstage during the recording "take." Never a Saturday went by but that there was some irritating or jarring sound whistling through the air. Either the air conditioner blowers were left on or a telephone was not unplugged or someone failed to heed the flashing red light outside the studio and burst in, yelling the latest football score. Frequently, it was an unsuspecting carpenter, unaware of what was going on onstage. The stage manager would yell, "Hold it. Quiet, please! Pre-recording."

"What? We can't hear you up here. We're hammering!"

The four of us pre-recorded almost every song we ever sang on the Welk show, because our different heights and voice levels made it difficult to get a good blend through one microphone. Most performers didn't like to pre-record. It was fine singing and having it finished, but when it came to mouthing the words, panic set it. Mr.

Welk would not tolerate anyone missing a word; he usually stood about two feet away and watched. But we didn't mind it a bit. It just wasn't hard for us. We did a song the same way every time, because with four people we had to know exactly what we were doing. So after setting our routine on a song, it never varied. The habit carried over to our solo performing, too. Although we ad-libbed various parts of the song, we made sure it was the same part each time. That made our lip-synchronization easier. So the actual show became a cinch for us, because the difficult work was done. We relaxed and enjoyed it. And that is what audiences saw.

At ten years of age, Janet pre-recorded a recitation of the poem "Lovely Lady Dressed in Blue." On the show she sat in a little wooden rocker, holding her doll, and lip-synched to her recorded recitation. When she came to the middle of the poem, the speaker box onstage began to buzz loudly, completely drowning out her recorded voice. The sound of the pre-recording was going out over the air, but Janet herself could not hear anything onstage. She did not panic, realizing by then that it was just the stage speaker that was blank. She kept on reciting her poem at the same pace and with the same inflection as always. When, after about fifteen seconds, the sound came back, she was in perfect synchronization as if it had never happened. She was perfect.

Those onstage were completely surprised, and those in the control booth, glassed in as they were, were unaware that anything had gone wrong. Unwittingly, Janet had, with great ease and calm, saved an otherwise embarrassing situation.

As calm as Janet was on the show, she dreaded pre-recording time, whether she sang a whole song by herself or had only one word. It was not because she felt she did not have the ability; she was just flustered at being the focus of attention. Even today, she breaks out in a rash whenever she sings solo. When Janet was very young and her turn came to sing, Mr. Welk would come downstairs from the control booth, bringing her a glass of water. Then he would adjust the microphone, pull over a chair, put her on his lap, and hold her hand. Thoughtful as this was, it did not help much. You could detect the tear in her voice. Years later, she admitted to us she would have to go into the bathroom and be sick before a pre-recording session. Then she had to muster all of her courage and step out of the dressing room and onto the stage. When the singing was over, she was a different person and did not mind doing the show at all. She really loved performing and dancing in the production numbers. Of all of us, Janet has the most natural abilities, and we are still amazed at each of her routines.

Janet:

I confess that the time when I was able to go through the "lovely Lady" poem and overcome those seconds when the speaker box buzzed was due to the fact that I just didn't know any better. I had been trained by that time to just continue on with whatever I was doing, no matter what.

I *can* recall a problem we had lip-synching "Santa Lucia," a song everyone at some time or another sings in school. For us it seemed that the words were impossible to remember. The lyrics just aren't written in everyday conversational language; they do not easily fit into a pattern for memorizing. We surely did try. Honestly, we did:

> *Now 'neath the silver moon, ocean is glowing*
> *O'er the calm billow, soft winds are blowing.*
> *Hear balmy breezes blow, pure joys invite us.*
> *And as we gently row, all things delight us.*
> *Hark, how the sailor's cry, joyously echoes nigh,*
> *Santa Lucia, Santa Lucia.*

We were so baffled by it we copied the words on a piece of paper and glued it to the bottom of the gondola in which we were sitting. I was scared that Mr. Welk would find out. Our stage manager, Woody, kept threatening to tell him. So, throughout the whole song, in a pretense of being carried away with emotion, we glanced up to the camera and then languidly back down to the floor of the boat, hoping no one would notice.

On other occasions the recording machine went haywire, and when it happened during the show, everyone held their breath. One night Larry Hooper, the tall, lanky bass, was singing "Wake the Town and Tell the People." As he began the second chorus, he had to resort to "Wake the town and tell the . . . Wake the town and tell the . . . Wake the town and tell the . . ."

Peggy:

Studio E, the stage from which we televised the Welk show in those years, has a wonderful history. It was the only building on the lot of the old Norma Talmadge Studios. The stagehands mesmerized us with the stories about the movies made there. Most exciting to us was that part of *The Phantom of The Opéra*, starring Lon Chaney, was done there. (Other parts of it were done at Universal Studio's Stage 27.) We gazed up into the rafters and imagined Chaney's horrible visage, ranting and raving in shrieking madness. Once, Pat Donaroma, a stagehand working from a little cubicle at the very top of the ceiling, asked me to climb the catwalk. I climbed all the way to the top and carved my name in the main support column of the stage. I was honored, because only the guys who had worked way up there were allowed the privilege of engraving their initials. It was perhaps the scariest trip I ever made. But I was really in heaven when I looked down on the miniaturized stage with nearly invisible people.

Everyone, in time, came up with ideas to make lunch breaks more interesting. It was always a relief to have the pre-recording finished, and the guys who had brown-bagged their lunches set up a net between two light poles on the dirt lot adjacent to the studio. We would choose up teams and play volleyball until the last moment before our call. Often we lined up trash cans and, using the volleyball, would see who could make the most baskets in a certain amount of time. Even Mr. Welk played those games with us.

In later years the band members began to hold jam sessions. It was unusual because some would play instruments they did not normally play. Bob Lido, violin, or Pete Lofthouse, trombone, would grab a bass fiddle. Neal Levang, guitarist, played hoedown fiddle. Jack Imel, dancer, played the drums, and Pete Fountain would treat us all with his jazz clarinet. It was Orie Amadeo, clarinetist, who taught us to jitterbug. Those dancing and laughing musical sessions were happy times. And this camaraderie with the band members lasted through all our years of working together. Trombone player Barney Liddell has said that, as we grew, it was not easy for the band guys to keep from falling in love with us. "There were good vibes between the orchestra and the girls, and it possibly made them feel more secure so they could just sing as they did, and do so well."

When the lunch break was over, we headed for the makeup room. We spent several hours getting our hair done, or trying to. During our first years on the Welk show we did our own hair. Mom twisted and curled and braided as best she could, but then the hairdos held up only as long as did *Kay's Wave Goo*. Harry Blake, the show's makeup assistant, decided we needed help. Along with his makeup chores, he was also hairdresser each week for Alice Lon, the "Champagne Lady." Perhaps it was his professional pride that eventually forced him to ask, "Wouldn't you like to have your hair cut and shaped a little?"

I was scared; the others seemed thrilled by the prospect. What would we do if we didn't look exactly like ourselves when he was finished? I guess I was too dumb to realize that that's exactly what he wanted to accomplish. Now Dee Dee's hairdo was not too bad; she had really beautiful hair, and she liked to wear it in a long ponytail, quite fashionable at that time. All Harry did was fluff it out a little. Kathy's hair was quite thick, and it wasn't too difficult for Harry to comb it a little differently and trim here and there and cause it to bounce softly. Of course, Janet just had to wear braids, and did until she was fourteen years old. Poor thing.

I was a different matter. He really changed my hair completely. I had been wearing my skinny bangs to the side and the rest of my hair drawn back into a slick ponytail. He cut my bangs and made them curl on both sides. He trimmed the sides of my hair and tapered them to the back. My hair was still skinny, but it was quite an improvement, and I was impressed. In fact, this was a real turning point in my life—from little girl to young woman. I guess anyone who has ever had a fresh hairstyle knows the uplifting feeling it can give . . . except Janet. She just had to wear braids.

As a child, Janet seldom showed any display of ego, but made her discomfort known when it came to hairdos and makeup. From her first appearance on TV at nine years of age until she entered high school, braids were her trademark. As her hair was being braided for the show, she would despairingly sigh that she knew she would "never get to wear my hair like the other guys." But to our TV audience, Janet Lennon was braids, and braids she stayed until she was almost fourteen.

Four of us plus Alice were a little too much for Harry every week, so he hired extra help. We had a series of hairdressers, but then came Roselle Friedland. She is a charming German lady and very European. When we started calling her "Rosey," she was shaken a little. Nobody had ever called her Rosey, not even her MaMa (Mutty). She was our best critic because she was so "truteful." It didn't bother her a bit to tell us a certain song was "not so goot!" She gave us style, however, because she introduced us to the then fashionable hairpieces and wigs; and to girls with the thinnest, scraggliest hair in the world, they were a godsend. No more hours under the hair dryer with unsatisfactory results. Rosey just brought our hairdos to work with her. Hooray for "Rosey's lib!"

Janet:

When I think of the makeup room and its mirrored wall, I can't help but think of all the other girls on the show with whom we shared its reflections. First of all, Alice Lon, a naturally beautiful lady who never put on airs. We admired her self-confidence and respected her genuine honesty.

Subsequently, Norma Zimmer joined us. Everyone who has seen Norma on television imagines her personality to be sweet and kind and quiet. Well, in part that is true. She is sweet and kind. But quiet? Never! She has a laugh that sounds like a hen cackle. It just kind of explodes out of that tiny lady and starts everyone else laughing. She is a terrific sport and not above singing rock and roll. She could "mash potato" with the best of them. She is a consummate sharer of secrets, and many afternoons in our dressing room we got the real lowdown on things from Norm. She helped us grow, and grow up.

In the early 1960s, Mr. Welk hired a young dance team, Bobby Burgess and Barbara Boylan. They could dance anything from the "Black Bottom to the Boogaloo." They were our ages, and it was a change for us to have other teenagers to work with. Bobby was a former Mouseketeer from Walt Disney's Mickey Mouse Club, and we had worked together on that show. So it was with much enthusiasm that we renewed our acquaintance. Bobby laughed when he recalled that he had had a crush on Dee Dee since he was a little boy and always knew he was going to marry her. Barbara was particularly fun for Kathy and me. Now we had someone else to giggle with and confide in. But she was just as naive as we were, and the three of us blindly and innocently made fools of ourselves at every opportunity. She would spend the night with us when we were on the road, just so we could share any new lessons of life we had experienced. A couple of times Kathy and I felt positively adult when we discovered we could tell Barbara a few things she didn't know yet. Looking back on those days, we really hadn't experienced that much of life, but being with adults and professionals made us feel old and very knowledgable.

Then there was Jo Ann Castle. I should say there *is* Jo Ann Castle. If anyone "is," she *is*! Growing up with her, we were alternately shocked and convulsed with laughter. She played honkytonk piano in a style all her own. We loved being around her because we were never sure what she was going to do or say. She was unpredictable. For the four naive Lennons, she was an enticing personality, and we were as moths to her flame. She was completely honest, and if her forthright explanations of things shocked us then, at least they were always done in good taste (except for the few whoppers that weren't). She was earthy, with a touch of class. She loved wholeheartedly, and we are fortunate to have been on the receiving end. We see her frequently; for a time she was a neighbor of mine and we exchanged babysitting chores. And she never turned us down whenever we asked her to play for us at some hospital or a benefit, and she still shares with all of us her enormous zest for living.

For a year or two, we had to handle our own wardrobe. Then ABC Studios had the good fortune to acquire Rose Weiss. And their good fortune was our salvation. She exploded onto the ABC lot and literally *made* the wardrobe department. We were fascinated by her. She took over the place. With her salt and pepper hair and designer's dream figure, she was a strikingly attractive woman, and what style! I don't think we ever saw her wear the

same thing twice. She had more hats and antique jewelry and shoes and coats than we had ever seen in our lifetime. And, boy, did she know how to wear them! She showed us how, too. You see, Rosie was aware of our lack of knowledge in the fashion department. But with her special care and patience, and a flouncing scarf here and there, she gave us style.

One evening she took me from the stage and said she thought I needed a jabot. I turned to Kathy and whispered "What the heck is a jabot?" But, sure enough, right there in front of everybody, she took a length of ribbon, and with many ruffles and flourishes, she tied it round my neck. It was a jabot, all right, what else!

Rosie went to bat for us with our producer and director, too. She wasn't afraid to tell them that we little girls were now getting to be young ladies and didn't need all the sweet, sticky, "cutesy" clothes. She managed to get us into jeans and skirts and pants and sweaters. She even raised our skirt hems to knee length. And I never heard anyone tell her she was overstepping her bounds or being too pushy. After all, no one was going to hassle the one person who could stand outside Mr. Welk's dressing-room door every week, and in her inimitable Jewish-mother style, yell, "Okay, Lawrence. Hand me out your pants!"

Because of our age differences, we had conflicts when it came to clothing. We never really argued about clothes, but embarrassing situations did arise for one or more of us at different times. During our first years with the Welk group, each of us had to sacrifice pride for the good of the group. Dee Dee and Peggy suffered a little more than Kathy and I did. We often needed three costume changes a show, so Ed Sobel gave Dad approval to search for a clothing store that might furnish our clothes in exchange for a televised credit. Henshey's Department Store in Santa Monica was more than willing to supply us with clothing. The big problem was that Dee Dee, Peg, and Kathy could wear clothes from the teen department, but I was still wearing children's attire. It was impossible to find matching outfits. Then, Pauline Steutzle, Henshey's coordinator, solved our dilemma. In clothes-designer Trude of California, she found a willing ally to create dresses for me that matched my sisters from the regular junior line of designs. But then we did not agree on styles.

"That dress is too young for me."

"Couldn't my waist be a little tighter?"

"Don't take the hem up too much. My legs are too short."

That color really is ugly on me."

It was a losing battle for Dee Dee and Peggy. During 1957-58 they were eighteen and sixteen, respectively, and they felt they should not have to garb themselves in full skirts and bows. On the other hand, if Peg and Dee Dee were indulged, Kathy and I would look out of place. (That season we were ages fourteen and eleven.) Our television image was still "little girl America," and so the older Lennon sisters had to give in most often.

Kathy and I had our pride, too, and we did not agree to everything. Once Kathy had to fight her way through a dress fitting, to overcome girl-woman embarrassment and humiliation. Miss Steutzle frequently said Kathy should be "eating more Wheaties" and hinted that perhaps she should start wearing a slightly padded bra. She was a skinny fourteen-year-old then, and blushed when told it might be best to help nature fill out her clothes. "I'm not as well endowed as Peggy," she mumbled. She burst into tears. "I can't wear a padded bra, no matter how many pink hearts and blue bows it has," she said.

In the end, she regained her self-esteem, and her feelings were respected. She was allowed to blossom naturally.

Peggy:

The times Dee Dee and I suffered most were Christmas and holiday television shows. Picture Dee Dee and me hanging Christmas stockings on a mantel while vocalizing to the song, "I Saw Mommy Kissing Santa Claus." *That* is suffering—at least when you are seventeen, or eighteen, or nineteen years old. At Easter we had to don bonnets and frilly dresses. Those outfits were embarrassing enough, but Dee Dee, a senior in high school and Homecoming Queen, had to carry an Easter basket and skip around toadstools singing, "Here Comes Peter Cottontail."

Many of the young people today working in television cannot possibly know the pressures of performing on live TV. Our dress rehearsals on Saturday afternoons were run-throughs for the purpose of timing the various parts of the show and for rehearsing camera and other technical movements. No one could stop to correct an error; if we didn't know what we were doing by those last hours before air time, it was too late. There were always the feelings of anxiety and excitement, unmatched by today's programs that are taped and then edited. If a mistake occurred during the live TV days, it was noted by thirty to fifty-million viewers. We had to learn to compensate and go on; we could not quit. Because Mr. Welk was such a perfectionist and demanded the same from all of his organization, we had very few slip-ups on the air. But those we had were unforgettable.

One of the show's young tapdancers forgot his dress shirt one evening. He borrowed one from one of the other men on the show; in his panic he borrowed a shirt twice as large as he was. Luckily he had his own cufflinks with him. Running out onto the stage, he stuffed the extra long sleeves into the arms of his jacket just in the nick of time. His dance routine went smoothly enough until his left cufflink popped, and the sleeve began to slide down his arm. Slowly, the cuff oozed over his hand, over his fingers, down below his jacket hem. That long arm just kept moving downward until he looked half-man, half-gorilla. It stopped slipping, finally, just below his kneecap. He continued doing his buck and wing, dancing away until the final move, a huge spinning turn—and he kept smiling. He made the spin all right, but nearly flogged himself to death in the process. It was an event that, in the end, the viewers may have thought was just part of a comic tapdance routine.

When we had a theme show, a whole program built around one idea, we often had to contend with animals. Professional animals, trained to act and do the necessary movements or cute things that, for relief, added "dimension" to the theme. For instance, for the "County Fair Show," the whole stage was set up with booths and games and balloons, and we sang on top of the Ferris Wheel and on all the fair rides. Now, no county fair is complete without animals. It wasn't too bad to dodge flying chickens on occasion, nor too awful to listen to—and compete with—squealing pigs and bleating goats. But for one show they really got fancy and brought in a huge dairy cow. As she was led onto the midway scene, she slipped on the slick stage surface, and it

At the Harding Avenue home, our first musical rehearsals with Dad, for Lawrence Welk's TV Show. *(The Lennon Sisters Collection)*

Singing a new arrangement for Lawrence Welk in the best sound room of the Aragon Ballroom, the ladies' restroom. *(The Lennon Sisters Collection)*

Lunch break on show day, ABC Studios, Hollywood, 1956.
Left to right: Kathy, Peggy, Bill Dahl, Dee Dee, Dad, Rocky
Rockwell, Janet, Larry Welk, Jr., Lawrence Welk. *(The Lennon Sisters Collection)*

A proud Mom and Dad Lennon, with their rising young television stars. *(The Lennon Family Collection)*

Young star, Janet, with her peers, Cubby O'Brien (Mickey Mouse Club), Paul Peterson (Donna Reed Show), and Johnny Crawford (The Rifleman). *(The Lennon Sisters Collection)*

Right, early 1955. The Lennon Sisters' first publicity photograph. *(The Lennon Sisters Collection)*

Mars Company "Milky Way Awards," with Lauren Chapin (Father Knows Best), Johnny Provost (Lassie), Brenda Lee at piano, Rusty Hamer (Make Room For Daddy), Tommy Rettig (Lassie). *(The Lennon Sisters Collection)*

literally scared the - - - - out of her. "It" was all over our dresses and our legs and shoes; udderly disgusting. And the smell was atrocious. We gagged our way through that number, during which our bass player, a health food nut, loudly insisted, "It's only hay."

We did live commercials, too. One evening, I was doing a Polaroid camera commercial with a well-known actor, who shall remain nameless. He told me how easy it was to load and take a Polaroid picture. After having me pose, he snapped the shutter, and to my horror (live, on camera, on the air), instead of pulling out the negative on which the picture was being processed, he nervously pulled out two negatives. Knowing full well that the second picture was a complete blank, I hesitantly counted to ten. The poor guy whipped the picture off the negative, and with great aplomb lifted it to the camera with, "Now, isn't she beautiful?" There was *no* picture. Dead silence. He panicked; he stood there staring. He would still be standing there today if I hadn't turned to the camera and said, "Well, maybe I counted wrong. Let's do it again."

With perspiration dripping down his forehead, our nameless actor managed to lift the camera again and haltingly finished the exposure. It was the longest commercial on record, and I'm sure it was the longest night of his life. We never saw him again— except when this clip was shown on Dick Clark's "Bloopers" television show.

One night, January 24, 1959, we received a telephone call while the show was in progress. When the time came for our song, we boldly called Mr. Welk to our side and announced coast-to-coast the birth of our new sister, Anne Madolin. Our parents had no choice but to name her that; you can't easily change a name already known to millions.

Most Saturday night shows ended with a medley of old songs. They were usually arranged and played in typical Welk-champagne style, with a touch of Dixieland thrown in. Waiting in the wings to sing the good-night song, we were often grabbed by the hand and swung into an impromptu dance with some of the stagehands. Even Lawrence Welk would get into the act. How exhilarating it was to whirl so fast that it took our breaths away. How difficult it was then to puff and pant our way through the closing "Good Night Ladies . . . ."

After the show was completed, it took only a few moments to pack up and say good-night to everyone, particularly since bandmembers had to hurry off to the Aragon Ballroom to play for dancing until 2:00 a.m. But we always made it a point to run to the production booth and say thanks to the staff and the engineers.

Tired as we might be, we looked forward to what was awaiting us at home—a hot bath, Pond's Cold Cream, the little kids, and the best meal of the week, prepared by Mom. Feast night, after a hard week's work, consisted of baked potatoes, small sirloin steaks, creamed corn, green salad, and buttered, grilled hamburger buns.

Sunday meant church, a little rest. And put-off homework.

By 1958, Lawrence Welk's shows enjoyed such high ratings for the ABC network that Mr. Welk proposed the idea of having two national shows each week. His concept was based on his belief that the country's youth should have an opportunity to express themselves. He suggested to his sponsors a showcase program whereby youngsters would be brought from all parts of America to show their talents as instrumentalists, singers, and dancers.

In contrast to Welk's Saturday show, most of the featured music would be contemporary; thus, the possibility of expanding his television audience. The idea was accepted favorably by his staff, the Dodge Division of the Chrysler Corporation, and ABC. The "Top Tunes and New Talent Show" came together in a relatively short period of time. Mr. Welk made the final selection of musicians for his "junior band." It was decided these boys would be weekly regulars with us. The boys, most in mid-teens, made it more fun for us, and it was nice to have new friends our own ages. Then there were singers and dancers, who would appear on a "featured guest this week only" basis.

When the Tuesday night show was added, The Lennon Sisters' weekly routine changed drastically. For the first time since we began television appearances, we were unable to attend our regular schools five days weekly. Dee Dee had graduated from high school by then. Janet, Kathy, and I, traumatized at the task of telling our

teachers we would have to be absent Tuesdays because of the taping, did not take into account that the nuns could be compassionate.
They sensed our anxiety and went to special lengths assuring us
there would be little problem in supplying us with appropriate
assignments to take to the studio. Those nuns at St. Mark's and St.
Monica's were as concerned as our parents that we lead a normal
school life.

It was then that Lois Lamont, Mr. Welk's secretary, was
notified that the show was responsible for supplying us—and
any young person of school age—with a welfare worker. The
California laws require that children under age eighteen be super-
vised every working hour by appointed representatives who
would see to it that they were not overworked, that they study
lessons, and that they eat properly and on schedule.

Consequently, on Tuesdays our makeshift classroom was set
up behind the audience seats at the back of the studio.; long con-
ference tables for the high schoolers, old prop department antique
desks for the younger set. It was very hard for any of us to settle
down to schoolwork on that erratic schedule. It was less than
ideal, since we were on call at all times to rehearse vocals, to
camera-block and pre-record. However, Kathy, Janet, and I were
the *only* girls in that class of twelve students, so we looked forward
to those Tuesdays with some enthusiasm. And just the thought of
having private tutoring had us feeling like rich little poor kids.

Our first welfare lady—of the many that were to follow—was
really very nice, but she took her job too seriously. "During school
hours we study. At rest period, we rest. At mealtime we eat." On
her first day we were, by 4:00 p.m., so well-rested and well-fed that
we could not stand the thought of the impending mid-afternoon
snack break.

"But you have to have your afternoon nutrition, girls."

"Gee, we're not hungry," we pleaded.

She compromised by buying one small carton of milk and
sticking three straws in it. She was so serious, and we didn't want
to be rude. So to control our laughter, we lowered our heads and
pretended to drink. But bubbles coming out of the top of the milk
carton gave us away. (Daddy later branded this type of over-
conscientous teacher, "Letter of the Law Ladies.")

These tutors came and went with great frequency. We preferred some over others, of course; and it didn't take our crafty minds long to separate the good guys from the bad guys. Being typical schoolkids, we would make up nicknames for the teachers, write them on slips of paper, and pass them from desk to desk, until everyone was giggling. We may not have advanced so much in the three "Rs," but we could get straight "As" in quick-study character analysis.

Those days at the studio meant more to us than just sitting on props and moving to the rhythm of a song. What part did each of us play within our singing group during those Welk years?

Janet—everyone loved her; her eyes carried her feelings out to millions of people. It hardly seemed possible a child could hold so many in the palm of her hand. She had no idea how she touched people. Dee Dee, Kathy, and I would stand and watch her, captivated by her sweetness.

Dee Dee was happy to play the ingenue. Never afraid to sing, she was perfectly matched to any of the young singers on the show; she was the epitome of the bobbysocks-ponytailed teen of the 1950s.

"And me?" Kathy says. "Well, I wanted to sing as well as Dee Dee someday. She gave me something to strive toward. I wanted to be as smart and as articulate as Peggy—although now I pride myself in not putting my foot in my mouth as much as she does! I had no chance to be as cute or as talented as Janet, but she was my pal, so it didn't matter. I was me, and the only thing I cared about was that Daddy thought I was great. And he did!"

When I think of those times, I, Peggy, was perfectly content to sail along in the middle of the group, achieving whatever I could and not having to do too many solos. Although the main thing I remember is that I had to play all the oriental roles, because my eyes are slanted.

In looking back, our feelings were not of jealousy, but of pride in one another. They were days of friendships, days of accomplishment. Before we had completed high school, we were famous, recognized if we just went down to the grocery store to buy bread and milk. We were proud, yes, but we were also aware that we had to protect our privacy. I believe I was continually surprised at being recognized. I liked it, but I was a bit in awe of it.

Just a few months ago, Janet and I entered an elevator to go to the top floor of a building in Westwood for dinner. Just as the doors were closing, a scruffy young man entered, pushed a button, and then looked around at us and stared. He had punched a button for a floor lower than the top, and as the doors opened for his floor he turned and said, "You've just made my day. Gosh, you're still beautiful." And with that he left.

"Now," I said, turning to Janet, "how is it that a teenager knows who the heck we are?" It still baffles me.

Kathy:

Me too!

Because, over the years, the image of "The Lennon Sisters" has been an underlying cause of periodic frustration for us. We appear to be all-American, apple pie, girls-next-door. And in many ways, that is exactly what we are. But four 8-by-10 glossies, wearing crinoline skirts, singing with an accordion, we are not!

We have felt an honest respect from our peers, but from other levels of the entertainment world we have felt otherwise. I believe many in the executive branch of the industry have placed us into a category that limits our marketability. And they seem to be afraid to suggest using us, for fear of being termed square by association. A preconceived reputation always precedes us into the corridors of the decision-makers—and frequently, it has been a stumbling block. I know we're not alone in our frustration. This is, however, an unfortunate part of success; this is, too, a part of life.

It has only been in the last few years that we have been able to rise above this attitude. We are comfortable in what we do and proud of who we are.

We have known that, for many years, our names have been the answers for crossword puzzles and TV game shows. However, we knew we had reached the pinnacle of fame when, in 1984, the Trivial Pursuit Game asked: *"What Lawrence Welk quartet answered to Diane* [sic]*, Peggy, Kathy, and Janet?"*

7

A Few Of My Favorite Things

Dianne:

I'm going to take up the pen here and fill in some of the pieces that have been left out. I will try to connect events and people, places and things of early years and later times.

In other words, I'm going to fill in some blanks.

In the autumn of 1956, our Garfield Avenue house was bursting at the seams. It was inevitable that our ever growing family must find larger quarters. (We were five girls and three boys, Mom and Dad, and Nana.)

"I was walking to the grocery store one morning," Mom recalls, "worrying about how we would house and feed one more child in the coming spring. I began to talk to God, 'I know this is a funny time to pray, but what am I going to do? Okay God, I tried to do what you wanted me to do, the very best I know how. Now we're having another baby. The kids are hanging from the rafters. You've got to find us a new house. I'm leaving it in your hands.' "

When she arrived home from the store, one of our neighbors was sitting in our small living room. "Sis," she said. "There's this big old two-story house for sale just two blocks away."

Mom explained to her that we didn't have the money to buy a larger home right now. "But just go and look at it, Sis," the neighbor said. "It would be so great for your family."

Later in the day, our mom and dad walked over to the house,

"just to look at it." They fell in love with that house on Harding Avenue.

"It was such a homey house," she told us when they had returned home. "The kitchen is newly decorated, and there are six bedrooms. *Six* bedrooms! It had been an old boarding house, and the couple who now own it have only two sons. So some of the rooms upstairs are closed up. The owners tell us that they make their living buying old homes, then rebuilding, redecorating and selling at a profit, and they've asked to see our Garfield house."

They saw it, liked it, and the trade was made.

The four of us girls lay in bed late that night talking about all the things we would miss: our delayed light switch that gave us time to jump into bed before it pinged off; the big mirror over the fireplace, too high for us to see into, unless we used the couch as a trampoline (without Mom seeing us); our linen closet, which oftentimes housed a little mouse family; the blue linoleum on the bathroom floor that turned our hands blue each time we scrubbed it (Peggy never knew that); the "kachang" sound of our back door slamming shut; our ironing board that unfolded from the wall. It would never be the same again. All we knew of the Harding Avenue house was that it had all those rooms.

On moving day we dressed for school, knowing these were the final hours at *home*. Kathy wandered the house, looking into the small rooms as though they were shrines. We ran our hands over the walls; Janet spent several moments next to the rounded walls by the front door where she had played so often with her dolls.

Kathy picked up our five-year-old brother Danny, and sat him on her lap.

"We'll never be here again. Let's kiss the walls goodbye." She said they tasted cold, and like *Spic and Span*. Leaving Garfield Avenue ended an important era of our lives. But how could we know then of all the years of closeness our family would share together on Harding Avenue.

We could hardly wait for three o'clock that afternoon. When the school bell rang for dismissal, we ran to our new home. The first thing each of us did was to gallop upstairs, just because there was an upstairs. We ran from room to room, squealing and gawking. I found one of the smaller bedrooms and shouted, "Oh,

Peggy, this is our room. We can decorate it so neat."

"The boys," Kathy shouted, "will have so much room to play with their little rubber cowboy and army guys on their own bedroom floor." Then she called to us, "Hey, just look at our closet!" Janet and Kathy had hung their clothes in their closet, which took up only a small part of it.

Janet suggested they might use the rest of the closet to play with their dolls. "Nobody will even know we're in there," she said.

"Hooray, the house has two bathrooms! We'll make the little boys use the downstairs one so that the one up here will stay dry, and the toilet seat will stay down."

Meanwhile, friends and relatives kept bringing in our furnishings and other familiar objects. Slowly, the new place was becoming home.

That moving day is when I remember meeting Betty Sanford. I watched a mattress slowly make its way up the stairs. When it reached the top landing I saw a smiling face emerge from underneath. "Hello," the face said, "which way to your room, dear?"

It took a moment for me to answer, I was so surprised by such a feat of strength and coordination from a woman. But then, Betty Sanford would be a source of wonder for years to come. We could and would call on her for anything and everything, and she would never fail "to give her all."

In the midst of moving, our professional lives took on a new dimension—recording. It was easier for us than live television. No camera and no audience, and all mistakes could be corrected. I don't believe any of us was particularly impressed with the idea of "cutting a record," because, after all, it was just another facet of our job.

George Cates, musical director for the Welk Show, produced our early recordings. He selected our songs, arranged, and conducted our recording sessions. Our first single was "Mickey Mouse Mambo" and "Hi To You." We were invited to sing both songs on the Mickey Mouse Club TV show. Janet and Kathy were beside themselves in anticipation of this appearance. On the other hand, Peggy and I didn't want our friends to hear us sing those childish songs. Some of Peg's ninth-grade pals brought a record player to school and played her "big hit" in front of the class. Agony!

For our second session, we recorded "Toy Tiger," the title song for a new motion picture. As a result of this, we were invited to attend the movie premiere. So far, recording was not too bad.

We were pleased with our first Christmas album, because we were given more choice in the selection of material. We chose traditional songs, and we were allowed to sound like young ladies. In may of 1957, we recorded "Let's Get Acquainted," an album with some contemporary songs. During the photo session for the album cover, another brother was born. Dad had driven us to the photography studio that afternoon. We were excited and nervous, because Mom had started having labor pains just before we left home. Knowing that Mom always had a long labor, Dad felt that he had plenty of time to sort through a box of fan mail during the time we were being photographed.

But we girls were not relaxed. "Dad?" I asked. "Please call home to see if Mom is ready."

"Now listen, you guys. I've been through this thing nine times before, and she won't go for at least another six hours."

Enduring another ninety minutes of continued nagging, Daddy relented and called home. "What . . . ? When . . . ? Who took her . . . ? Is she all right . . . ? You're sure . . . ? That much, huh . . . ?"

All those questions didn't tell us much. "Thank God! Boy, she surprised me, too! I'll drop the girls off as soon as they're finished and go right to the hospital. This is the easiest baby I've ever had!"

Dad then announced to us, "You have a new brother. He weighs seven pounds, six ounces. Mom is fine. She did this without me. I can't believe it!"

That album cover will always remind us of Dad's easy delivery of our black-haired, almond-eyed brother Joseph Lawrence—Joey.

One album, "Best Loved Catholic Hymns," was produced under unusual circumstances. Dad had wanted to record an album of this kind for quite some time. But he could not get anyone to share his enthusiasm. So our German-stubborn father virtually did it on his own. We made a list of our favorite choir hymns. Dad did the rest. He paid a young boy organist one-hundred dollars to accompany us to St. Gregory's Catholic Church in Los Angeles, where there was a beautiful pipe organ. Using a borrowed tape recorder, we taped twelve songs in two hours. George Cates was astounded by the quality and the sound. Dad, self-satisfied, gloated. That album sold better than any other we have made.

Another aspect of being in the public eye was the promotional offer from Whitman Publishing Company to produce coloring books, magic slates, comic books, novels, and paper dolls of The Lennon Sisters. We signed an agreement with Whitman and were quickly surprised that our items sold so well. For several years, we were told, our products were top-selling items for the company. We did laugh, looking at these coloring book caricatures of us. "My nose is too big." "Just look what they did to my hair. It's slicked back!" Imagine a comic book story of us—who have such fear of flying—calming passengers on an airliner at the height of a great thunderstorm!

We enjoyed our paper dolls as much as the public did. We eagerly awaited each new line of dolls and clothes so that we could compare outfits and see who had the cutest wardrobe. And we couldn't wait to see if the dolls' faces looked like ours. Jan's usually did, except for the added freckles. And Peggy never stopped wishing that her legs could be that long and skinny.

We appreciate having these souvenirs for our families now. But recently Kathy was dealt a great blow when she saw in her monthly antique magazine, Lennon Sisters Paper Doll Kits, $25.00, under the heading "Old Collectibles."

During our early years in show business, we were exposed to a host of new experiences, one of which was the press interview. The publicity we received was extraordinary. Interviews did not seem foreign to us, perhaps because we liked to talk about our family and our life and work. We had been allowed to take part in conversations with adults since early childhood, so we had little or no inhibitions. I doubt we'll ever forget the first question-and-answer encounter, however.

After school one day, Dad drove us to the famous Polo

Lounge of the Beverly Hills Hotel. The ABC publicity people had set up an interview with a well-known lady I will call Miss C., the writer of a syndicated beauty column who desired to discover the beauty secrets of The Lennon Sisters.

Miss C. arrived dressed fit to kill, with feathered hat, fur stole, and baubles, bangles, and beads. It became obvious to us that our school uniforms weren't the most appropriate attire we could have chosen. Miss C. sat down at the table and ordered "weak tea and crisp pumpernickel cinnamon toast—paper thin."

"Mr. Lennon," she began. "You don't mind if the girls speak at the table, do you?"

"No," Daddy said. "The fact is the only time when all the family gets to visit and talk with one another is at the dinner table."

"Oh?" she nodded. Her reply rang with overtones of disapproval. "Do you girls like jewelry?" she asked.

Janet, Kathy, and Peg seemed to draw a blank, remaining silent. To fill this void, I piped in bravely. "Well, I kinda do."

"Of course," said Miss C. "You being the oldest, you would. What kind of jewelry do you wear?"

"Oh," I said quickly, "I like anything that isn't too gaudy— small dainty things like this bracelet." I showed Miss C. a small gold disc with the initials, D.L., hanging from a tiny gold chain. "I don't like big, flashy jewelry."

No one had to tell me to bite my tongue, because my sisters sat in a deafening silence. The cold stare of Peggy alerted me to look more closely at our interviewer, and I felt the blood rush to my face. Miss C. was one solid mass of bracelets from wrists to elbows.

"But . . . but . . . sometimes," I stammered in faded voice. "Sometimes, I wear more than this . . . . It's just a matter of personal opinion and taste. I mean . . . some people look good in gobs of jewelry."

Miss C. let that pass, asking what we did for recreation.

"We go to the beach," we responded in unison.

"I might have guessed that. You all have such nice tans. Do you time yourselves in the sun each day?"

"Oh, no," Janet answered. "We just stay out all day. We love the sun."

"Heavens," Miss C. exclaimed. "Don't you get sunburned?"

"Sometimes, but we know it will turn into a tan right away."

"What kind of suntan lotion do you use, then?" she asked me.

"Oh, we don't use lotions. Mom usually rubs us with vinegar."

"With what?" Miss C. asked, incredulously.

"Vinegar," I replied.

"Oh, my dear!" Miss C. said, and once again changed the subject. "Do you cream your faces?"

"No," we responded.

"Well, do any of you girls use cream at all?" she asked.

Desperate to say something that might please her, I spoke quickly. "*I* do."

Miss C., with great relief, turned to me. "Yes?"

"Well, sometimes, I cream my elbows."

Miss C. was elated. " Wouldn't the world be a better place if everybody creamed their elbows?"

This kind of conversation became too much for Daddy, and he excused himself from the table, leaving us to fend for ourselves. Just in time, too, for the waiter returned with Miss C.'s tea and toast. "Sir," she commanded. "I ordered my toast paper thin, and this is not paper thin. Return it to the chef and tell him, paper thin."

We girls could not look at one another, for fear of losing all composure. Miss C., adjusting her hat, her fur stole, her napkin and notebook and pencil (upon which she had written nothing at all), attacked again.

"Now Janet, what do you use to brush your teeth?"

"A toothbrush," she answered innocently.

"No dear, what I mean is, do you use paste or powder?"

"Oh, toothpaste," Janet responded. "Colgate, or whatever is there. Something like that."

"Don't you know that powder is much better for you? Do you mind if I say that you use tooth powder?"

"No, I don't care," said Janet. Her glance said, why-did-you-ask-me-in-the-first-place?

For an hour and a half, we continued to frustrate Miss C. with

The Lennon Cowgirls on a 1956 Lawrence Welk TV Show, singing "Wayward Wind." *(The Lennon Sisters Collection)*

The finale of a Garry Moore Show, Spring 1960. Allen Funt, Andy Griffith, Carol Burnett, Moore, one bride, and three maids. *(Photo by J. Peter Happel: The Lennon Sisters Collection)*

Yes, there was such a TV Quiz Show! *(Photo by Russell Schweizer: The Lennon Sisters Collection)*

With Ralph Edwards, celebrating Lawrence Welk's "This Is Your Life." Lawrence Welk, Larry, Jr., and Donna Welk, right. *(The Lennon Sisters Collection)*

our unsophisticated answers. We never realized how many *bad* habits we had in beauty and health care.

"White bread is bad for you," she said.

"Zest is a detergent soap and will ruin your complexions."

"Peanut butter is oily, and grape jelly is sugary, and one or both will cause blemishes."

"You don't spray your throats? My, my, my!"

"Desserts every night? Oh, my!"

When Miss C.'s article appeared, our beauty secrets were completely unrecognizable to us. Either that or our memories were as paper thin as her toast.

Most of the interviews followed an identical line of questioning: Are you really sisters? How did you meet Mr. Welk? How do you like working with him? When do you get your schoolwork done? Do you girls ever fight?

In the first years of our increasing national recognition, people were curious about those four little girls from Venice who sang on the Lawrence Welk Show. And there was always the speculation about our large family. Movie magazine articles stated: We never had a problem . . . Our mother was peacemaker . . . Our brothers were jealous . . . Our sisters were bothersome . . . We always went to church together . . . We never went to church at all, except in a crisis . . . .

We thought perhaps once their curiosity was satisfied, the magazines would stop writing about us. But we underestimated their fascination with us. During the first five or six years, those magazines contributed a great deal to our popularity. We were cover stories for years along with Elizabeth Taylor and Jacqueline Kennedy. We made it a practice to be cooperative with magazine interviewers. Our parents advised that, if we didn't, we might suffer some derogatory articles about us.

Our lives were not as glamorous or as exciting as, say, Bobby Darin or Sandra Dee, Connie Stevens or Frankie Avalon. We were in school, at work, at home—that was that! Whether we cooperated or not, it made no difference in the end. The magazine writers began to stretch and pull and make up their own stories. Entirely untrue, these fantasies appeared month after month in almost all the magazines. We were somewhat bewildered by this, but we found we could do nothing about it. Even when we tried to set the record straight with new stories, the truth eluded the typist.

For instance, when my engagement was announced, magazine interviewers clamored for my impressions and plans. I was happy and looking forward to marriage; I was in love and anticipated raising a family. I agreed, finally, to talk with several writers, in the hope of avoiding ridiculous, speculative articles that might be written about Dick Gass and me.

"POOR BOY TO MARRY RICH GIRL"—the magazine cover proclaimed. Within the text of the story, it was claimed that Dick and I would never marry because of the disparity of our incomes; a telephone-cable splicer marrying a star!

Magazines grabbed at anything for a headline in order to sell their journals. When Janet's sixteenth birthday approached in 1962, a photographer, posing her for a picture, handed her a gift-wrapped box and threw confetti on her. "Smile," he said. That photo was used to accompany an article entitled "The Night I Became A Woman, by Janet Lennon." Many fans reading only the title and not the article itself, wrote to ask Janet how she could exploit herself that way. About all the article said was that Janet had reached an age that, in some states, is considered attaining majority.

With Kathy, it was publicity dates. They were like those dates any other girl in her late teens might have. Except for one thing: a photographer went along with her, and the boy was usually a young actor or singer she had never met. "She is beautiful, and he is handsome, and together they take a great picture." It was good copy.

One of Kathy's dates was Fabian, all the rage with teenagers at the time. He and a photographer picked her up one afternoon at St. Monica High School. Together they bought a pizza and drove to the beach. Kathy and Fabian posed in front of our family's Malibu Beach guest house while eating their pizza. "Now let's get a shot of you two running in the surf, holding hands," the photographer said. There was Kathy running down the beach with America's heart-throb, and all she could think of was how embarrassed she was to be holding hands with a boy she had just met.

Then they returned to our family's home and were photographed drinking hot chocolate in front of the fireplace in the den. "Now, Fabian and Kathy," the photographer directed, "just gaze into each other's eyes."

Under her breath, Kathy muttered to Fabian, "Nothing against you, but isn't this horrible?"

"I'm embarrassed by this, too," he whispered. They laughed and were finally able to relax together. She never saw him again.

Another of Kathy's publicity dates was Bill Bixby. One of the magazines wanted a picture layout of them frolicking in the snow. Kathy and Bill left at 6:00 a.m. for the mountains. Bill was half asleep, because he had been to a party the night before, so she did the driving. Bill had a great sense of humor, and that made the day tolerable. It was, in fact, almost fun, and they posed throwing snowballs, riding toboggans, and staring at snow. The next weekend, the same magazine requested another layout of them. So Bill and Kathy hit golf balls at our dad's driving range, raced slot cars at an arcade, and did the inevitable running on the beach. That publicity date for the two of them never became anything more—much to the disappointment of one of them!

When Janet began dating, she went through much the same routine for layouts. The boys were Don Grady (*My Three Sons*), Cubby O'Brien (*Mouseketeers*), and Johnny Crawford (*The Rifleman*).

We went along with the magazines in those early years and even allowed them to host bridal and baby showers. But it embarrasses each of us now to realize how naive we were then. We trusted their motives and what they told us would be the basis of their articles and photo layouts. We never suspected we were being used, each time thinking something redeeming might come out of it. Eventually we discovered such favors carried a price. The nature of the magazines began to change; bolder statements were being printed. Sweetness-and-light did not sell at the newsstand.

In the sixties, fan magazines moved to adopt the techniques of *Confidential*, splashing shocking headlines across their covers. Any article on its pages had only a sentence or two to support the headline. We watched our name and reputation move into bizarre forms:

Monty Hall, The Other Man In Peggy Lennon's Life

What Kathy Lennon Could Teach Liz And Jackie About Love

Three Sisters, All After The Same Man

Kathy And Fabian—
"We Should Have Known Better But We Didn't"

The Lennon Sisters Leave Home

The last one was a nasty one. It claimed the four of us had decided to move into a beach house at Malibu because we were tired of having peanut butter and jelly dropped on our good clothes by our seven brothers and sisters, and were rebelling against Daddy running our careers. Such lies hurt us deeply, but they were nothing compared to what would come later.

However, I have to admit this constant exposure helped to bring about offers for guest appearances on other television programs. Our first departure from the comfort and familiarity of the Welk Show was our appearance on Jack Benny's "Shower of Stars." Fred MacMurray, Carol Channing, and Jimmie Rodgers also guested on the show. As children, we were in awe of these stars, but after working with them for a few days we realized they were just people. With few exceptions, this particular fact was reaffirmed over and over again throughout all the years of working with celebrities.

Choreographer Miriam Nelson aided us in our debut as dancers. The song we were assigned was "Getting To Know You," from the musical hit, *The King and I*. We each had a young boy dancer as partner, and we hung on for dear life as they whirled us around the huge oak tree, the centerpiece of our plantation production set. We had such pride in this first attempt and could not wait for our friends to see us dancing. All our partners were cute; but Kathy, being twelve years old, was not satisfied with hers, a rather pudgy boy. She was so afraid her friends would think she *liked* him.

Soon after that we were off to another studio for Walt Disney's Mickey Mouse Club. Janet and Kathy were in their glory when we four sang and danced with Bobby, Annette, Darlene, Cubby, Karen, Tommy, *etc.* We girls were presented with our own Mickey Mouse ears—for Jan and Kath, much better than receiving payment.

Within the year, other big events included an appearance on Eddie Fisher's Christmas Show, and our first performance on Perry Como's Show, an absolute favorite. Our guest shot with Eddie

Fisher came at a time when he was in the headlines almost every day. He and Debbie Reynolds, America's sweethearts, had separated, and rumor had it that Eddie and Elizabeth Taylor were more than friends. We were sure that, after six days of rehearsals, we would know the inside story. But, as nice as he was to us, we were never taken into his confidence about Liz or Debbie.

Janet, age eleven, was madly in love with Eddie and secretly hoped he would give up both ladies for her. She settled for a token of his attention. He gave us the beautiful pink organdy dresses with charcoal-gray velvet ribbons that we wore on the show. Janet became a fanatic over Eddie, and she never missed watching his weekly show. In the diary she kept during those years, she described how she felt when she missed one program. "Dear Diary, had to miss Eddie tonight. Sob. Sob." At the bottom of the diary's page were scribblings, in various handwritings or printed styles: "Janet Fisher. J. L. Fisher. Janet Lennon Fisher. Mrs. Eddie Fisher."

It would be an understatement to say we were thrilled when asked to appear with Perry Como. He was exactly as we had hoped he would be—gorgeous! Nothing seemed to upset him, and his relaxed attitude permeated all aspects of the rehearsals. If a musical arrangement was difficult to learn, he would simply disregard it and sing it in his own informal style. Nobody minded, of course, because Perry Como could not make any song sound bad. He once asked us to be regulars on his television show. If anyone could have persuaded us to move home and family to New York, Perry Como would have been the one. But Venice was home.

For almost three decades we have busied ourselves with television guest appearances on such series as The George Burns Show, The Bell Telephone Hour, The Hollywood Palace, The Garry Moore Show, Jimmie Rodgers, Roy Rogers and Dale Evans, The Everly Brothers, Glen Campbell, Dick Clark's American Bandstand, Jerry Lewis, Jerry Reed, The Jackie Gleason Show, and many specials. Among these television specials and series were The Mac Davis Show, The Cher Show, NBC Follies with Sammy Davis, Jr., The Andy Williams Show, The Don Knotts Show, Pat Boone, John Davidson, Dinah Shore, The Tonight Show, Hollywood Squares, Family Feud, The Newlywed Game, The Joey Bishop Show, Dick Cavett, Mike Douglas, and Merv Griffin—and many local and syndicated shows, including the all time great "Quiz-A-Catholic."

Early on, the most prestigious show on which we performed was The Ed Sullivan Show, televised over CBS on Sunday evenings, live from New York. The excitement we first felt was quickly transformed into disappointment by the businesslike "do-your-thing-and-then-sit-down" atmosphere. By the very nature of its vaudeville format, with top entertainers performing in act after act, no one had time to get to know anyone else. On our first of several guest appearances, we never even saw Ed Sullivan until after we had finished our songs and he called us over to shake hands on camera. "Are you two sets of twins?" he asked. Evidently, it was the first time he had ever seen us, too.

Our first summer tour, with Lawrence Welk, 1956. Kathy, Dee Dee, Janet, L.W., and Peggy. *(The Lennon Sisters Collection)*

1957. Our first professional trip to New York City, to appear on The Perry Como TV Show. Nana instructed us to wear proper hats and gloves to The Big Apple. *(The Lennon Sisters Collection)*

8

We'll Travel The Road,
Sharing Our Load

Janet:

From the beginning, touring was a different way of life: we ate in real restaurants, traveled on airplanes, and slept in hotels.

Our first out-of-state personal appearance was in Kansas. The date was June 30, 1956. We had been semi-regulars on the Lawrence Welk Show for about five months when we were asked to help open the First National Bank in Wichita. We were both excited and fearful about going—excited because it meant a great adventure in our young lives, yet fearful because it also meant leaving the security that we had always known in our home. We couldn't imagine what it would be like. The only hotels we had ever seen were those in television westerns where Hopalong Cassidy or Roy Rogers stayed. We pictured ourselves carrying our luggage through the saloon and up the stairs to our room, while dancehall girls giggled and an old man played a honkytonk piano in the corner.

Because this was to be our first time away from home, both Mom and Dad accompanied us. It was one of the few times Mom went with us, because she felt her place was at home with the younger children. None of us had ever flown, so Dad arranged for us to arrive in Wichita a day before our scheduled performance, so that, if we were tired from our long flight, we could rest overnight. We were surprised to discover that our hotel did not resemble the Long Branch Saloon. In fact, it was plush and modern and had a TV set in every room.

We were greeted warmly by Mr. Sullivan, president of the First National Bank of Wichita, who immediately offered us an invitation to dine with his family and close friends in a private banquet room at the hotel. Daddy advised him that our religion did not permit us to eat meat on Fridays, and he hoped it would not cause Mr. Sullivan too much inconvenience. "Oh, don't worry," retorted Mr. Sullivan. "We have great Kansas City flounder here."

When we were seated at the lavish dinner table, we found ourselves facing thick, large, juicy steaks. "That's what we call K.C. flounder out here," Mr. Sullivan laughed, unable to control his exuberance at putting one over on us. Shocked because we had never in our Roman Catholic lives eaten meat on Friday, we all four turned as one to Daddy. Looking as if it were his move in a championship chess game, he shrugged his shoulders and said, "Well, if that's all there is to eat, then that's what we shall eat." So we did, amazed that steak tasted so good on Friday.

The following day we performed on a bandstand that had been set up in the parking lot next to the bank building. It was extremely hot and humid, but the audience was warm and responsive. After each show we signed autographs and shook hands with the people. It was all new and overwhelming. Eating every meal in restaurants and not having to make our own beds added to our astonishment.

On Sunday we were taken to the country club for breakfast and a swim before our last performance. During the meal, we learned that the plane we had originally been scheduled to take to Kansas had collided with another plane in mid-air over the Grand Canyon, and everyone had perished. We were young and impressionable, and the thought of getting onto an airplane and flying home terrified us. As the Kansas sky blackened and there were reports of tornadoes expected by afternoon, our fears grew worse. When it began to rain in torrents, we were panic-stricken.

Dee Dee wanted to rent a car and drive back to California; Mom suggested we take a train; Kathy said she was ready to make a new life for herself in Wichita; Peggy buried her head in a book; I wanted to take a nap. But Dad decided we would fly.

When we reached the airport that evening, we learned that it had been shut down because of the storms. Dee Dee, Peg, and Dad spent four hours in the car, listening to weather reports, as if that would calm their nerves; Mom sat with Kathy and me in the ice-cold airport bathroom, while we threw up our nerves. And when the plane finally left at midnight, the flight was horrible. We were jostled up and down, as we flew through tremendous thunderstorms. We looked to Dad for comfort, but he had put on a big, black blindfold and fallen asleep. I followed my sisters' course, pulling out my rosary. The next morning, the newspapers were filled with pictures and articles about the tornadoes that had skipped through Kansas and flattened a large section of Wichita, just about midnight.

Only a few days later, Mr. Welk told Dad of an approaching tour he was planning—two weeks of one-nighters—and he wanted us to go along. Most of the cities were hundreds of miles apart, so all we could think about was flying fourteen times.

Kathy:

I considered running away from home. It would be better to run away than to die. I packed a few things and sadly but quietly made my way to the door—of the linen closet. I climbed onto the bottom shelf and hid away among the towels and sheets. I must have been there for hours, but nobody missed me. I never heard a single "Where's Kathy?" There had been so much noise and confusion around the house that they hadn't even known I was gone. After a while I just got out, unpacked my bag, and that was that. I figured better to die than live forever in the linen closet!

Janet:

The day we left on that tour was highly emotional, partly because Mom stayed behind. At the height of our traveling days, from 1957 to 1963, leaving home was never a matter of packing, kissing the kids goodbye, and going out the door. We dreaded the sight of our desk calendar. It was an unwritten law not to mention the coming tour until the day we packed, which was the day we had to leave. It never was a "you'll get used to it" thing.

The Welk troupe gathered at the airport. All the band members knew of our fears of flying, and they tried to keep our spirits up. But one of the guys, Dick Dale, had heard enough crying out of Kathy and said to her, "For Pete's sake. We haven't even stepped on the plane yet!" That only caused her to cry even more. After take-off from Los Angeles International Airport, in a four-engine, prop-driven aircraft, we flew directly over our house and then headed eastward to another world.

Touring had its problems—fast meals, quick changes, going to bed late, arising early, catching the plane or bus, glum faces, *etc.* Home for a week, out for two, home for three weeks, out for four. It was a difficult way of life for us, but we benefitted from these experiences. We learned to work and live with all kinds of people, how to conduct ourselves in public, and how to be tolerant of the idiosyncracies of others. We took a hard look at our own actions and reactions, accepting the responsibility for them. We felt we were accountable in some way for every heart we touched and every hand we shook. Our job and our reason for singing was to give of ourselves. In that giving, we in turn received so much.

We played a town or city in every State in the Union. Most look the same, at least from the point of view of airports, hotels, and auditoriums. We couldn't spend very much time sightseeing, particularly when we were with the Welk band on those one-nighters. But when there was a little time, we tried to see as much of America as we could. From the air we could see the changing terrain; in the days before jet airplane flights, pilots flew at lower altitudes and on occasion went off course to circle some national monument so that everyone aboard could get a better view.

We remember certain sights: the glowing colors of the Grand Canyon and Zion National Park, the sparkling snow crowning Mt. Hood, clouds of spray floating up at us from Niagara Falls, the tiny Statue of Liberty way down in New York Harbor, the Aurora Borealis from 30,000 feet in the Montana sky, the Mississippi River twisting and turning and cutting the country in two, the gray-blue haze over the Smoky Mountains, bridges that floated for miles straight out from Florida's shores, the golden sunset on the bayous of Louisiana, whitecaps on Lake Michigan, the patchwork farms quilting the Missouri countryside, the Golden Gate Bridge, Mt. Rushmore so close you could almost touch the faces, the miles of wheatfields across the plains, the clouds circling the mossy cliffs of Hawaii. But the most beautiful of all, as we climbed that final ridge of the San Bernadino Mountains, was the splash of light spreading out in every direction as far as the eye could see—the glory of Los Angeles, the great city that men and women had crafted out of desert sands—home.

There were, too, the pungent smells: the ginger flowers that filled every inch of space in Hawaii, the cooking grain from the Quaker Oat Company in Cedar Rapids, Iowa, and caramel corn and peanuts from the Planters' shop on the boardwalk in Atlantic City. I can remember the steamy smell of room service even when you ordered a cold sandwich, hot roasted pheasant in the hills of South Dakota, the green smell of grass after an Indiana rainstorm, chestnuts smelling like baked potatoes in the winter in New York City, or the stockyard smelling just like a stockyard in the Chicago summer, any kitchen backstage at any casino in Las Vegas, and the icy smell of new snow at Christmastime at Lake Tahoe. But most refreshing was the smell of the Pacific when the door of the airplane opened in L.A.—home!

And sounds: the trains that nearly tore through our hotel room next door to the station in Albuquerque, New Mexico, cabdrivers yelling at us in New York City when we crossed on the green light, trumpets, clarinets, and trombones warming up before a show, the street musicians of New York, the Ferris-Wheel screamers when we were in the middle of singing "Ave Maria" at any state fair, airplane motors humming and changing pitch and humming again, suitcases being snapped shut, microphones too loud, microphones too soft, thunder through the Dubuque, Iowa, sky in midsummer, the wind whistling down the Redrock Amphitheater in Denver, the hotel operator in Eau Claire, Wisconsin, saying "Good morning, it's six a.m. and six below." And the best sound of all was that of the little kids when we opened our front door and heard, "What did you bring me?" We were home.

Distances between concerts, and limits on time between those appearances, gave us no alternative but to fly. The band members didn't mind flying—until we came along. Our long green faces and glances of impending doom soon had them squirming. Whenever a bump or jiggle set our adrenalin pumping, we would grab the nearest available hand and squeeze for dear life. Often the band members walked off the airplane with rosary marks embedded in their palms; they called them battle scars. Most of the plane trips were uneventful and pleasant, but a few were real beauties. And those are the ones we remember.

We have been hit with air turbulence outside of Washington D.C., resulting in galley doors flying open and silverware and dishes rolling up and down the aisles, and pillows, coats, and hats falling from above the seats. A window popped out on landing in Seattle, falling into my lap. We've lost an engine over Kansas City and landed on foam. One aircraft fell through the runway in Great Falls, Montana. We've been in downdrafts over Texarkana and tossed about in a tornado on approach to Dallas, just as the control tower was being evacuated.

Sometimes we could relax and play cards, or help stewardesses pass out fruit and sandwiches. Once, on a chartered aircraft, the pilots invited each of us to sit forward in the cockpit during takeoffs and landings. What an awesome feeling to see the world and sky from a pilot's window and feel the delicious shiver as the ground comes up to meet the wheels of the plane with a great "thunk."

Kathy:

When we joined the Welk show, Alice Lon was the only girl in the band. On those trips she was like a big sister and helped keep our spirits up. She was homesick for her three little boys, and we missed our brothers and sisters, and sometimes we would sit together and cry about it. We needed and loved each other. I believe I was Alice's favorite. I really don't know why, but perhaps she could discern that I was shy and needed more attention. Anyway, she asked me if I would come to her dressing room every night and help her zip up her dresses, see that her hair was right, and talk with her a little bit before the show. Her thoughtfulness did much for my morale.

One evening we were playing at the new Twins Stadium in Minneapolis. We were seated on a bandstand in the middle of the baseball field, right on the pitcher's mound. The mosquitoes were out in force, attracted by the bright lights, green grass, and the smell of new blood. They attacked, and with our bare shoulders and semi-short skirts, Alice and the four of us were primary targets. At intermission we went down to the locker rooms to dress and bandage our wounds. That was only the first night of a two-week trip of one-nighters. The five of us, swollen and bitten, hugged each other and cried.

It is hard to explain the relationship we had with the guys in the band. They were fathers and brothers and friends and teachers. And though in today's society it is probably hard to believe, throughout our many, many years of growing up in the midst of some thirty men, we were always treated with respect. It could have been different. When we first joined the show, we could do no wrong in Mr. Welk's eyes. He never missed a chance to tell the band members how much we practiced, how talented we were, how perfect we were in every way. He constantly held us up as the image of what they should be, or try to be. And that could have easily turned the guys against us. But there was no professional jealousy. Somehow they realized and recognized the difference between what Mr. Welk said and what we actually were.

To a man they protected us. We loved each and every one of them, and they in turn cared for us and watched over us. In that respect we were a family. We did not have a casual working relationship. We teased, kidded, laughed. danced, worked, and played together. They never overstepped the bounds of propriety, and they saw to it that we were never placed in any situation that could harm us.

As we look at it now, perhaps this overprotection was in some ways detrimental to our growth. They never let us hear so much as a "hell" or a "damn." We were living in a dream of make-believe as far as the real world was concerned. Yet they were an exceptional group of men to have been able to take four little girls and guide them through to womanhood unscathed.

Not that they were angels. Many mornings we'd have to tiptoe up the aisle in the plane so that those with hangovers wouldn't scream with pain. A lot of the guys had relatives, too. It was amazing how many beautiful cousins many of them had in every city. We rubbed sore shoulders and handed out a lot of Alka-Seltzer. We sewed buttons on jackets and pressed wrinkled coats. When we landed at our destinations, we took care to awaken the last man asleep on the plane before it departed for parts unknown. We made early morning wake-up calls to some of the guys who were sure they would sleep through any and all alarms, and sometimes did. We helped make excuses when they were late on the bandstand, and generally tried to protect them as much as they protected us.

California State Law required that a teacher-welfare worker accompany us on each tour, even in the summertime. We tried to select our favorite teachers for these trips. Eleanor Petrie was one of the first. An excellent tutor but, more important to us, a good sport. We knew Dad liked "Petey," because he never stopped teasing her. We studied hard in dimly-lit hotel rooms, often at sunrise. Once in awhile Dad would peek his head into the room. "Hey, everybody," he would announce. "It's a beautiful day. Let's go to the park."

"Now, Bill, you know these girls must get three hours of schooling each day," Miss Petrie would say. "It's a California State Law."

"But Petey," he would say. "We're in Ohio."

She often would relent, rationalizing that a picnic would be like a field trip.

Dad nicknamed our tutors. Peggy Cobb was "Corn-on-the," Mrs. Gonzalez became "Mrs. Gomez," later just "Gomez," because it was easier to say.

Eve Baxter, another favorite, became nurse, teacher, and mother-on-the-road. She had a deep interest in the arts and cultures of the world and helped us mature during those awkward teenage years. Eve was actively involved in teaching the deaf, and we asked her many questions about her work. One afternoon, Eve, Peggy, Jan, and I found ourselves locked out of our rooms, so we sat down in the hotel hallway and talked until Dad came with his key. Eve began to teach us the alphabet in sign language. We did not get up until we had memorized all 26 signs. Later this became our secret form of communication with Eve; to the point that even while onstage we could signal to her how we felt. "B-o-r-e-d" or "W-h-a-t-a-b-o-m-b" or "I-m-s-t-a-r-v-e-d!"

On one promotional tour, we were handed a note by three pretty teenage girls. "Hello, Lennon Sisters," it read. "We're from the School for the Deaf, and we enjoy watching you sing. Thank you for your autographed pictures." We confidently spelled out "Thank you very much" in sign language. That mutual communication touched us all.

Many cities we played rarely hosted celebrities. There were often thousands of citizens jamming the airport awaiting the arrival of Mr. Welk and company. To sounds of neighborhood hundred-piece accordion bands, we would deplane and sign autographs for the fans. We would pose for pictures, give out a few local TV or radio interviews in an airplane hangar, then get our luggage (everyone carried his or her own) and pile into the waiting cars. The Dodge Division of Chrysler Corporation sponsored our TV show, so local Dodge dealers of each city would drive us in a caravan through town, advertising Dodge and the concert that night. These were always days of celebration for the Dodge people, and many times their happy hour began long before our arrival. On numerous occasions we were saved from calamity only by quick thinking and expert driving of our own band members.

Reaching our hotel, we usually stood in a long line to register. Too often there were mix-ups about who roomed with whom—it is difficult to conceive that a group of forty people traveled without a road manager.

Myron Floren tried his best to keep us together, but he encountered constant problems. Once, in Indianapolis for the Indiana State Fair, one of the largest in America, arrangements were not made for us until two weeks before we were to arrive. Every hotel in town was packed, and we ended up at a place that bordered on Skid Row.

The rooms were so small that the toilet barely fit into the bathroom, and the washbasins hung out over the beds. We stayed there for a year one week. Janet and I thought that it was really great to look out our window and see the red lights in the rooming house across the street. The girls who lived there were standing in the doorway, and they seemed friendly, too!

When we received room keys, we went upstairs and unpacked our costumes, sometimes as many as ten different sets. Out came the travel iron, and we ironed what dresses we could on the floor. Good carpeting made for good pressing. It was interesting to look at the bottom of our iron after each trip to see how many colors of burned rugs we had collected. We hung chiffon dresses in the bathroom and turned on the hot shower. Steaming was wonderful, although we couldn't use the bathroom for about thirty minutes afterward. And sometimes our dresses slipped off hangers and fell into the tub. Many evenings we went to work with soggy hems.

We would order room service and set our hair—again. If we went into the steamy bathroom too early, our hair became limp once more. Half past a cold sandwich, it was time to go to the arena or auditorium. Some were new, modern concrete buildings, with glass doors and acoustical ceilings. Many, like Carnegie Hall, were gilded, with maroon velvet curtains that smelled of mold and dust. Then there were those bandstands placed right in the midst of a racetrack, no covering, no backdrop. There were show rings at state fairs, where animals were also judged, with sawdust floors, road apples, and the lingering scent of barnyard. Dressing rooms matched accordingly. If we happened to manage an assignment to a men's gym locker room, we were lucky. Those had large mirrors and plenty of space for hanging costumes. There would even be ten toilets. (Of course, the first time we saw one of those "things" hanging on the wall, Janet and I couldn't figure out how to use it.)

Dressing rooms could also be just little wooden cubicles with a couple of folding chairs and a mirror contributed by a thoughtful neighbor. Our costume changes have taken place in the backs of trailers, in the cabs of milk trucks, in underground hovels, beneath the seats of stadiums (where we knew people could peek through the cracks in the grandstands and see us dress). Several times, there were no doors, so the four of us took turns in pairs, holding up a sheet.

The most horrible dressing experiences were the tents. When I say "tents," I mean the ones they set up on an infield of a racetrack. Under the canvas, it was sticky and humid and filled with mud and gook that naturally followed a midsummer storm. Mosquitoes loved these perfect breeding conditions and the red blood of western-raised girls.

Having no mirrors or places to hang clothes was bad enough, but the final blow was that these same tents were used during the night to house the donkeys and goats from the sideshows. It was impossible to dress without getting skirts and high-heeled satin shoes soiled with what we hoped was only mud.

Mr. Welk arranged the format of our concerts before we left home, so we never had to rehearse our shows on the road. There wasn't time, because as soon as we would arrive at the auditorium or stadium and dress, the show would begin. Mr. Welk started every one of his shows on time! It mattered little if someone was in the bathroom, or off in the next county, the show began precisely on schedule. There was no excuse for being late; either you were there or you were not. One was "on trial" if not on time. Sure enough, you got the hot seat on the plane the next day. Everyone called it the confessional box, and if Mr. Welk gave you "that look," you were sure to be his seat partner on the next flight. Even if you admitted you were wrong and had no excuse, Mr. Welk would still come back with, "That's no excuse."

The concerts were fun. Really they were. For the first years, we sat on the bandstand with the other singers during all of the show. After a few nights of a tour, it would get a little boring listening to the same songs and same people saying the same things over and over again. So we played games; no one could tell, especially Mr. Welk. He had repeated his philosophy again and again: "Boys and girls, look like you're having fun. But don't have any."

We would whisper riddles or make up knock-knock jokes, while keeping an eye on Mr. Welk, just in case. When I think of sitting on those bandstands, I can remember the way I felt looking out at all those people. I wondered if they thought I was real. Did they know I ate toast for breakfast? That I cried frequently? Did anyone realize I had a mom and she had me make beds and do dishes? The people weren't real. I wasn't real. Then I tried thinking of them eating toast in the morning, making beds, and crying. Often I felt in a state of suspended animation. It's funny how a young girl can stand apart and look at life like that. And remember it so many years later.

I would be brought back to reality when it was my turn to sing. I was glad my sisters were with me. It wasn't difficult to sing to those people when I had my sisters shoulder to shoulder. And we loved to watch Janet polka with Mr. Welk—so, too, did America. She was so little and quite unaware of her most charming dance mannerism. When she put her arm around Mr. Welk, her little hand, never able to reach his waist, ended firmly attached to his bottom. What a whirling pair they were, and when he would lift her off the floor, it was not difficult to see why Janet was his favorite, and a favorite of his fans.

We had our share of autograph requests and praise, although on occasion something a little different would happen. Such as the time in Des Moines when a little old lady came up to us on the bandstand. The dancing portion of the show was ending, and the concert portion was beginning. The little old lady tapped me on the shoulder and said, in a not so little voice, "Would you mind autographing my book for me?"

Our tenor, Jim Roberts, had just begun to sing, "Faith Unlocks the Door." Mr. Welk looked around to see where the disturbance was, so I leaned over and said politely, "Ma'am, we'll gladly sign your book after this show segment. You see, Mr. Welk doesn't want us to sign autographs during the performances, because it's not fair to the other performers."

"Oh, but you are my very favorites. I've watched you grow up, and you are so sweet. Please sign it now."

"But Ma'am, we're not supposed to right now."

"But you are so sweet! Sign it now!"

"I'm sorry," I whispered. "We just can't!"

Grudgingly, the little old lady turned away, then yelled back at us. "Aw, I knew you were brats, anyway!"

After the concerts, we usually went back to the hotel, hoping against hope that the coffee shop would still be open. In some parts of the Midwest and South, everything closes by 10:00 p.m., and since we never could eat a full meal before the show, we were starved by midnight. Sometimes the restaurants would stay open just for the band members, but not often enough. Then we would have to go looking for an "after hours" food joint. Sometimes I felt as if we were breaking the law, being hungry at that time of night. Occasionally, we would find a special restaurant, but most often we had to settle for a White Castle or Howard Johnson's— but I can't tell you what ambrosia their hamburgers were to a famished "down-on-her-luck" singer.

Our tours varied little over those twelve years, with the exception of some new faces and voices and new songs and dances now and then. Great times, great friendships. Not too many outstanding incidents, perhaps, because our routine was so structured that it left little time for anything out of the ordinary. The years have melded into one another now, with only a specific dining place, or a particularly great fair ride, or a sad farewell etched firmly in the mind.

There were frustrations, of course. At eighteen years of age, perhaps the most important event is one's high-school graduation day. Five months ahead of time, I had written on our calendar, "SUNDAY, JUNE 11, NOTHING, PLEASE! KATHY'S GRADUATION—FINALLY!" The day was to come, but not at all the way I had planned it. The Lawrence Welk tour was scheduled for June 4 through 14 that year. June 11 would be spent in Washington, D.C.

When Mr. Welk announced that trip, my tears choked me. I felt so alone; I knew no one else would understand, and so I could cry about it only to Janet. "This is the worst thing that could happen to me. There is nothing I can do about it, but it is so unfair! It's the only day I ever asked for. Why do we have to go?"

Janet's consoling could not undo the injustice I felt. All through morning classes at school, I sat and cried with Bonnie and Nancy, my best girlfriends. We discussed my obligations to my boss and the group and to my sisters, and I fluctuated between thinking I was merely feeling sorry for myself and thinking this is the worst trauma I could experience. Although school friends gave me an early surprise graduation party before our departure, which did lift my spirits, I still felt robbed of the pomp and glory of the graduation ceremonies of the Class of Sixty-One-derfuls.

On June 11, 1961, in Washington D.C., I sat onstage watching the other performances and pictured in my mind the event and excitement over 2,000 miles to the west. I tried to picture myself in a cap and gown, when my thoughts were interrupted by Mr. Welk's voice. "Ladies and gentlemen, we have a special announcement to make. Our little Kathy was supposed to have graduated with her high-school class tonight. To take the place of her high-school superiors, we are happy to bring to the stage her Uncle Jack Lennon, who is with the American Embassy here in Washington. Kathy, would you please come to the front of the stage?"

Uncle Jack and I approached the microphone together, and we hugged each other. "Honey," he said, looking at me. "As your godfather, I have not been able to be with you on very many special occasions in your life. I was traveling all over the world. My heart breaks for you because you cannot be where you most want to be tonight, but my heart is full because I am where I want to be. I am honored to be the one to present to you, Kathleen Lennon, your St. Monica High School diploma."

I kissed Uncle Jack and felt honored at having such a special commencement exercise.

When I entered my Sheraton Park hotel suite, I was shocked to see the whole band there. "Surprise!" After their applause, my pal Dick Dale stood up. "Kathy, we want to help fill your loneliness tonight. We do have a little gift for you. Hope you like it." More applause as I opened the gift, an engraved gold disc charm with the masks of comedy and tragedy; so appropriate, for it paralleled my feelings.

When everyone had left that night, Jan, Peg, and I climbed into our beds. (Dianne was now a homebody and back in Venice.) We talked over the excitement of the evening's events. About 12:30 a.m., the telephone rang. "Hello," I answered.

All I heard was a bunch of screaming girls with an operator trying to interrupt. "Is this Kathy Lennon?"

"Yes, it's she. It's her. Well, yes, it's me!"

"Go ahead, please."

"Kath, this is Bon and Nance and Shirl and Wendy and . . ." The names kept rolling on. "We want you to know we all made it and thought of you the whole time. The Dean sends her love, and so do all the boys, especially Sal and Tom and Manuel (giggle, giggle). Well, we have to get ready for Grad Nite. We'll see you next week. A big party at your house. Ha ha! Bye-Bye!"

Certainly we noted changes in our country in the 1960s, not the least of which was a young couple in the White House who were not unlike stars. Our new heroes were young astronauts. Television programs were now bringing the world into our living rooms in living color.

Although our lives were sheltered within the family structure, by reason of our profession we had to go out and experience a broader world. We recognize that we were given opportunities that other young people would never receive.

After Peggy married, Janet and I were road roomies; we finally had the freedom to do whatever the two of us pleased. Only, since we didn't know what to do, we didn't do anything. About the raciest we could get was to go down to the lobby of our hotel to buy a movie magazine, or collect hotel matchbooks and light each match, one by one. If we got really bored, we would take out the local telephone book and count the number of Lennons. We could get somewhat destructive. One night after dinner, we dropped our peas, one at a time, out of our tenth story window at unsuspecting passersby.

From 1962 to 1967, the Lawrence Welk Orchestra spent its three-week summer vacations performing at Harrah's Club at Lake Tahoe. We considered working there the highlight of our work year, even though the running joke among the band members was, "We're so lucky .... How many organizations get to spend weeks rehearsing for their vacations?"

Janet:

Mr. Bill Harrah was a generous man. He gave us a house on the lake every year, affording us the opportunity to bring Mom, Dad, and the family for an annual vacation. After Dee Dee and Peg married, they used the Harrah homes on the lake, and Kathy and I elected to take a room at Harrah's North Lodge. Most of the single guys and girls stayed there. Another step towards independence. Reading excerpts from my diary recaptures those carefree days!

Monday: *Opening night. Had butterflies. Show went great. Exhausted after rehearsing for two days.*

Tuesday: *Kath and I ordered bagels, cream cheese, and coffee brought to our room this morning. Just relaxed all day in bed reading movie magazines and doing our nails. It's so great not to have any responsibilities.*

Thursday: *Laid out by pool. Tried to get tan all in one day. So sunburned. Wrapped our red-and-white bodies in wet bed-sheets.*

Friday: *Waterskiing today with Bobby Burgess. Kathy stood up first time. Took me two tries. Skimmed half the lake with my rear end.*

Sunday: *Walked with Kath up to church behind our hotel this morning. So beautiful. Situated among tall pines. Pews and altar set up in clearing, with only blue Tahoe sky for a roof. Surely makes you feel close to God.*

Tuesday: *A lot of guys brought their kids to pool today. Kath jumped in and saved little Gina Amadeo from drowning. What a hero! Heroine?*

Wednesday: *Out by pool again. Little Gina A. was running around crying and throwing tantrums all afternoon. Someone yelled, "Hey, Kathy. Throw her back in."*

Thursday: *Hoopie (Larry Hooper) took me fishing. Had pancakes at a Japanese restaurant.*

Saturday: *Took Heavenly Valley Tram up mountain with Bobby and Barbara. Chipmunks around everywhere, even ate nuts out of our hands. I wonder if Bobby and Barbara will get married.*

Monday: *Kathy and I went cruising between shows tonight looking for parties. Found two, but were too chicken to go in. Came back to dressing room. Kathy was in such a hurry to curl her bangs for second show, she wet them, rolled them in her new metal roller, and used the hand dryer. She blew the hot air on that curler until she knew it would be dry. When roller came out, so did her hair. Called her "crewcut" all night. I laughed. She didn't.*

Thursday: *Kathy keeps getting letters from R.K.L. He's a kook from Colorado. He calls her his "Beautiful Sunshine." We laugh at his letters, but he's scary.*

Friday: *Been eating Black Forest chocolate cake. Been working it off, though. Tonight chef took us on tour of Harrah's bakery. Like touring heaven . . . .*

Saturday: *Group from show went on breakfast trail ride this morning. Had to get up at 6:00 a.m. Ugh! Horses sluggish, so were we. Food tasted great. On return, Patty Trimble's horse got too close to a tree, and her beehive hairdo got tangled in big branch. Kath and I tried not to laugh . . . . Walked bowlegged rest of day and through both shows tonight.*

Monday: *Kath got another letter from R.K.L. today. Postmarked Lake Tahoe. Said he watched his "Beautiful Sunshine" walk home from club last night. Got scared and finally called the sheriff!*

So much for our unchaperoned, carefree days . . .

Kathy:

. . . for we gained too quickly insight into the hazardous side of being well-known performers. It seems that R.K.L. had been a fan of mine for years. I received frequent love letters, and at this time they were arriving almost weekly. His messages rambled on about watching moons rising over mountains and about dreams of his "Beautiful Sunshine." Since these statements seemed the extent of his first communication, I felt no great concern. It did not bother me when letters began showing up at Tahoe, since we knew how closely he followed our careers. But when the postmark on the envelope read Lake Tahoe, and he inferred in his letter that he had watched me walk home each night, we informed the local sheriff.

Sheriff Bradovich was deeply concerned. It had not been too many years since he had been through the Frank Sinatra, Jr., kidnapping at Harrah's. He wasn't about to let anything like that happen again. He read through the letters, quickly ordered deputies to walk us to and from the club, stationed several other deputies atop the casino roof, and even had more staked out atop our hotel roof. We were well protected because the men in the band, alerted to the situation, took turns accompanying us whether we were walking, dining, or shopping. I can look back now, especially in the light of events that happened several years later, and comprehend their concern. But at that time, for Jan and me, the whole thing was like a Nancy Drew adventure.

Deputies searched our room each night before we locked ourselves in. Bobby Burgess was rooming just below us and made a heroic promise: "If you need anything, just stomp on the floor, and I'll come up and save you."

Letters from R.K.L. continued for three or four more days, and Sheriff Bradovich did not let us out of sight. Then the letters stopped. We all breathed a little easier. After a few days, Jan and I had almost forgotten about the ordeal, when I was awakened very early one morning by a loud clanging at our window. Quietly, I elbowed Janet awake. "I think someone is trying to get into our room," I said.

"Oh, no!" she whispered. "What should we do?"

"I don't know," I said. "But follow me."

The sun was just rising, and I saw the shadow of a man silhouetted against our rather thin drapes. We crept out of bed and sneaked under the window ledge toward the closet. The only weapons we could find were two large wooden coathangers.

The shadow at the window continued to move and make noises, and I felt a sudden surge of bravery. With my weapon in one hand and the drapery pull in the other, I stood in front of Janet and courageously flung open the draperies to expose the mysterious intruder. We stood there dressed in our shorty pajamas, with rollers in our hair, staring aghast at—a window washer.

He was as startled as we were. Sheepishly, we waved our coat hangers at him, and he waved his wiper blade back at us.

Janet:

Mr. Welk had hired his son Larry to work as band boy, bag boy, or just "hey boy" on all of our summer tours. Larry had a great preoccupation with racehorses, and the band members were glad he came along. He served as the local bookie in almost every town. Hence, his long-standing underground nickname, "Cookie The Bookie."

Larry might as well have been employed to entertain The Lennon Sisters. We all thought him the funniest guy that ever lived, and we were perfect stooges for his jokes. For awhile, Larry was put in charge of an infernal machine called the applause meter. He sat each night and monitored our concerts and the audience reaction to each song. On a prepared sheet of paper, he would write the rating (from 1 to 100), reflecting the intensity that the applause registered. Mr. Welk would study these sheets after the concerts and give lectures when he felt they were necessary. However, the applause meter was not a true record of the audience's appreciation. A violin solo certainly did not demand foot-stomping and cheering, although people might be moved to tears by it. A guitar solo of "San Antonio Rose" could bring down the house.

At times like this, we were glad that Larry was our pal. He would cheat for us. "Listen, you guys," he would say. "I gave you an eighty-five instead of a seventy-five, because Bob Havens got one-hundred by lying on his back playing "Tiger Rag" on his trombone with one foot. Now, I know that kind of audience-rousing choreography just doesn't go with 'Ave Maria.' So I helped you a little."

Larry Welk was full of fun, but he also had great depth. He could reveal his deepest thoughts and express his truest feelings, and then turn right around and do the goofiest things. But that is what made us love him. He was so much a part of our own family. He would arrive at our home unexpectedly, bringing along his tenor saxophone. He didn't know how to play it at all, but he swore he could play the "One Note Polka." And he did. To the screeches and howls of the kids and that stupid horn, Mom would set an extra place at our table, and in her heart as well.

Larry's mom loved having us in her home, too, and she always had a freshly-baked cake in a round glass container waiting for us.

We headquartered in Larry's bedroom. What a place! His bathroom had a tub that was entered by stepping through a five foot keyhole. He had a beautiful hi-fi system and the first stereo set we ever heard. We would lie on his bed and listen to his great Dixieland albums. It didn't matter if one of us were there or ten. It was Larry's room, and, as such, it belonged to us, too. Sometimes we might go into the backyard, which was really an estate with beautiful grass and well-tended gardens. We would chase their two peacocks around the grounds; or Larry would sneak us into his dad's bedroom and open the massive closet to show us the hundreds of suits and shoes that belonged to his dad. It even had the smell of a clothing store. A far cry from Mr. Welk's simple beginnings in a small German community in South Dakota.

When we lived within the intimate circle of Mr. Welk's band and staff, there were many occasions when we would be taken by surprise by his slight misuse of language or words uniquely phrased. At times, he too would laugh and ask what the true proverb was, compared to his mangled version.

We would like to share some of these "Welkisms," because they have long been a source of lighthearted fun for all of us and for his audiences. They are a part of his enduring charm.

> "Well, Myron, the people seem to be coming here in groves."

> "Fellows, let's be honest with each other. Let's put all our tables on the floor."

"Boy, those programs are selling like wildcakes."

"She sure is my cup of dish."

"They're trying to pull the wool over my head."

"Just because I'm mad at you doesn't mean I'm mad at you."

"And remember folks, wherever you go . . . there you are!"

There were times when Mr. Welk just used the wrong word. One night, immediately following an outdoor concert, there was to be a gigantic fireworks display. Mr. Welk was asked to make an announcement to the audience. "Ladies and gentlemen," he said. "We would like to ask you to stay seated for the beautiful flashlight display."

Mr. Welk loved golf and managed to play even while on the road. One day, we were scheduled to perform for a Shriner's Convention. Mr. Welk's secretary informed him that he couldn't play golf because he was to have lunch with the Imperial Potentate of the Shriner's organization. When we arrived in the hotel lobby, Mr. Welk was asked once again if he could play a few holes of golf. "Not today. You see, I'm having lunch with the Imperial Totem Pole."

When onstage, Mr. Welk captivates his audience. He is casual and makes the audience feel that they are an integral part of the show. But on television, he rarely gets the chance to do anything but read cue cards. His show contained twenty songs or routines in one hour, with five commercials interspersed. No time left for expanded introductions. It is unfortunate for his audience, and very unfair to him, that he may present a stilted image of himself on camera. The pressures can be tremendous, and at times he read the intros without thinking. "Take the 'A' Train" came out as "Take thee a train"; "A song from World War I" came out as "A song from World War 'i' "; "Can't Take My Eyes Off Of You" came out, "Can't take my eyes off to you"; and "We'd like to bring Barbara and Bobby back" came out as "Barbara and backy Bob."

His *faux pas* were not limited strictly to television. During a press interview, he called to one of his singers to join in the conversation. "Alvin Ashby from Evansville, Indiana, come on over here and tell everyone who you are and where you are from."

One night at the Hollywood Palladium, where the band played on weekends, Mr. Welk was called to the side of the stage. Standing there was a young man whom we all knew and who had sung a number of times on the television show. "Why Elmer," said Mr. Welk. "So nice to see you again. Won't you come up and sing with us tonight?"

"Of course, Mr. Welk," said Elmer. "But you know I've changed my name now. I'm not Elmer Gooley any more. My name is Dick Hudson."

"Sure Elmer, I'll remember."

"No, it's Dick, sir. Dick Hudson."

"Right."

A few minutes later, Mr. Welk went to the microphone. "Folks," he said. "Tonight we have a young friend with us whom I'm sure you have seen on our show." At this point he looked toward Elmer, and Elmer took the opportunity to mouth the name "Dick Hudson"—as largely as possible.

"Will you welcome Mr. Dick Hudson!!!" And turning to the side of the stage Mr. Welk yelled, "Oh ELLLLLMMMMM-EEEEERRRRR!"

One time Mr. Welk bumped into an old friend. "My, my," he exclaimed. "Isn't it a long world?"

And our favorite: "Since The Lennon Sisters left me, they've been digging their own funerals."

The four Lennon Sisters, with Dad, offstage in Atlantic City. *(The Lennon Sisters Collection)*

Father's Day, 1960. Finally, the Compleat Family Lennon! The four oldest, top, need no introduction. Surrounding a proud papa are left, Patrick, little Anne, Joseph, Danny, newborn Christopher, Miriam, and William. *(The Lennon Family Collection)*

9

Oh, Mein Papa!

Peggy:

There is no equating the traveling we did for the Welk organization with the kinds of traveling we did alone with Daddy. All the precise planning that went into a Welk tour just never materialized when we hit the road with Dad.

Daddy timed things. Never early, never late. And he was right! We never missed a plane. But, oh, the near misses and the shattered nerves that went with his split-second timing. I am sure that much of our aggravation on any of those tours was due to that clock-like quirk of Dad's. We would pace up and down, waiting for Dad to finish shaving. It made us fidgety and irritable. Finally he would languidly stride out of the bathroom, soap still in his ears. "Why are you so worried?" he would say. "We have thirteen-and-a-half minutes to get to the airport, and it's only five minutes away. Relax!"

Janet:

But how could we relax?

When we were on the road, the one thing we always wanted was to lie around in our bathrobes, order room service, and let it all hang out. But, no! Daddy wouldn't hear of it. How could we possibly want to put that hotel food into our stomachs? He would make us get up and get dressed, and then we would head for the nearest restaurant that boasted of homestyle food. And those cafes (they were *never* restaurants) all looked alike: black-and-white tiled linoleum floors, menus types in blue ink covered in plastic, dirty window sills, Coke signs blinking on and off, and those scratched plastic octagonal water glasses containing no ice. Mostly, the food was pretty good, but it never matched those lost moments of lazy living in a hotel room. However, this was not the worst way to dine. At least we were alone. But Daddy had other, more exhausting ways.

He wanted us to have a home environment on the road, and hotel living was not home, to his way of thinking. So he would latch on to the first likely person who might ask us over for dinner. Daddy was continually looking for good food like Mom's. And he felt we needed fresh food to keep up our strength.

Dianne:

Now, we will admit that, because of Dad's environmental demands, we met some pretty terrific people. Not only the hoi polloi who invited us to their posh country clubs, but the fairgrounds keeper and the deputy sheriff and the farmer who owned the prize hog. Boy, could their wives cook!

Daddy didn't realize that this was tiring for us, because he was proud of us and concerned that the people who were so kind to us should know his daughters were not snobbish. It was his great interest in people—and perhaps a kind of reverse snobbishness on his part—that kept us hopping from farm to farm and from kitchen to kitchen. Although we sorely missed the leisure time, we couldn't help but love Dad for being the way he was.

We seldom got to eat at a hotel dining room, except during interviews. And never were we allowed to stop for fast foods. "Nothing but grease, pure grease!" he would shout.

Except once!

Janet:

And that one time made up for all the missed ones. We were playing a fair in Seymour, Wisconsin. As there was no suitable hotel near the fairgrounds, we had to stay in Appleton, a distance of about thirty miles. But they were dark, backroad miles, and it seemed far longer. After the Fair one night, we piled into our rented car and headed for the hotel. About halfway there we came upon a roadside drive-in that we had noticed on all of the previous nights. Once again, we begged Daddy to stop for hamburgers. "Please, Dad, we're starved, and there won't be any place open when we get back to the hotel. Please! Please!"

"Nope," he said. "I told you girls that drive-ins have rotten food. I know. I used to deliver milk to them, and besides, you guys always order things and then you never eat them."

"Oh, please, Daddy. At least if we stopped you could have a chocolate milkshake, and we promise we'll eat every bit of our hamburgers. Please!"

At the mention of the ice cream, suddenly we could see a little light turn on somewhere in Daddy's brain. He pulled into the parking area, then turned to us. "Okay," he said. "But you can't eat in the car. You'll just get the stuff all over you. It never fails. Eat in a drive-in and you spill everything. You'll have to sit at that little counter over there."

We all voiced our horror at once. Here we were, still in our costumes, all alike in black skirts, red blazer jackets, and black ties—in the middle of Nowhere, Wisconsin. Boy, did we look dumb. Starving or not, we could not conceive of leaving the confines of that car. "Please, Daddy," I whimpered. "We'll be so careful, and we'll just die if we have to go out there dressed alike."

It's Friday night," Kathy whined. "And all the kids our age will laugh at us."

Just at that moment a waiter came over and asked if he could take our order. We looked longingly at Daddy, and he finally gave in. "Okay. Give us four hamburgers and one chocolate milkshake made with your best chocolate ice cream."

"But, sir" the carhop said. "We don't make our milkshakes with ice cream. We make them with a prepared milkshake mix."

Of all the terrible crimes in the entire world, none was more horrendous for an ex-milkman than making milkshakes without *real* ice cream! Dad gave each of us a look that could kill.

"I don't care how you *usually* make your milkshakes," he

said politely, and with controlled firmness. "I will gladly pay for ice cream to put into it. You do have a milkshake machine? Just put about three scoops of your best chocolate ice cream into it with some cold, real milk. Okay?"

The poor carhop departed with the order, and Dad presented us with another stony glance. "I told you guys it was going to be rotten. You'd better eat every bite of those burgers, too!"

Dianne:

Now, as for those hamburgers! The meat was raw, the buns were stale, there was no mustard, and the catsup came in those little plastic packages that make it taste like little plastic packages. As the carhop placed Dad's tray on the car window he said, "Oh, excuse me, sir. Your door is not shut completely." And with the innocence of teenage inexperience he snapped the door closed with his foot, thereby tossing the chocolate milkshake, with real ice cream, all over Daddy's new white sportcoat.

We were a little bit mortified, a great deal gratified, and a whole lot grounded!

Kathy:

Daddy's most outstanding characteristic was his ability to make us laugh. Not only at jokes, but at situations that, without this gift of his, might have affected us adversely. He could find humor in anything, particularly our own human frailties. That's why we laughed when he did things that aggravated us to no end.

For instance, my hair! While growing up, we loved the hairstyles that were "in"—the Sandra Dee look, or the Connie Francis look, or the Annette Funicello look. When I was fourteen, I combed my hair to the side and styled my bangs into a little curl over my eyebrow. Daddy hated it.

"Why do you comb your bangs that way?" he would shout.

"They just hang in your eyes, and then nobody can see your face!"

"But Daddy, everybody wears their hair this way!"

Dad could never just give a "yes" or a "no" answer. He always seemed to have an exaggerated little "warmup story" that killed our point, but left us laughing. "Well *'everybody'* doesn't have a good old dad like me who really cares how his daughter looks. You should be terribly *proud* that I take such a strong fatherly interest in letting everyone see how *totally beautiful* you are. Cut your bangs!"

When the need was overwhelming, I would continue the assault. Fool that I was, I cried, "But, Daddy, if I promise to keep it tightly curled, can I keep it?" At least if I had to look weird onstage, I could let that curl hang down on dates that I was sure to get, thanks to my fascinating hairdo.

"All right. But I'm warning you, if I see that stupid thing in your eyes again, I'll cut it myself!"

I was okay for two days. I curled that hunk of hair with my clippies and bobbypins, and it was approved by Dad. On the third day, the temptation was just too much, and I let it hang down, just perfectly. I thought I looked *boss*! But in the morning I found out who really was boss! There on the floor was my curl, just where Dad had cut it off during the night.

Peggy:

One afternoon, as we prepared to leave a large department store where we had been signing autographs, we became separated from Daddy. We weren't concerned, because we had guards with us, and anyway Daddy loved to wander among people to hear their reactions to us. There were two little old ladies talking and admiring us. Dad stood right behind them.

"Look at them. Aren't they cute?" one said.

"They're not so cute," our dad interrupted.

Completely ignoring him, the other lady turned to her friend. "My, aren't they sweet?" she said.

"They're not so sweet, either," Dad retorted.

Now the ladies were irritated, but they did not turn to him.

Still composed, the first one whispered to the other. "Aren't they just darling?"

"They're not that darling, or sweet, or cute, believe me. I know!" repeated Daddy.

This was just too much, and the first lady turned around to Daddy and yelled. "Get off my back, mister!"

Just at that moment, Janet found Dad. "Come on, Daddy," she said. "We're going to be late."

Those ladies were dumbfounded when Daddy grabbed Janet's hand and whisked her into an elevator. He waved a facetious farewell to them, as the doors closed.

Dianne:

If things got dull while we were on the road, Dad did his best to spice them up. I remember the time we were being interviewed in Cleveland, Ohio, atop an extremely tall building. The glass-enclosed dining room overlooked the entire city. There was a huge bowl of fresh fruit in the center of the table. Daddy got up to pay the check, while we finished the interview. But then he paused.

"You know," he said. "We can't leave that great big pineapple sitting there. What do you say, girls? Let's take it home for breakfast tomorrow."

Then he picked up his hat and overcoat, slung the pineapple under his arm, and said, "See you guys at the elevator."

When we finished the interview a few moments later and headed for the foyer, we noticed almost immediately a large crowd and commotion at the elevators. As we approached, we heard giggling and laughing and people saying "What is it?" "Can you see what it is?" "Can you tell what is going on?"

We strained our necks to see over people, but could not get near enough. "I can't believe it!" was all we could hear. "What's going on?" "What does it look like?" "Tell me anything."

"Look, there's The Lennon Sisters," one man said.

"Yeah, great, I know. But what's that?" another man re-sponded. "What is it? Do you see it?"

We looked around for Dad. Maybe he knew what was happening. Suddenly, we heard his voice. "Come on girls. The elevator is here." So we pushed through the gaping crowd and took a look into the elevator. There stood Daddy in the corner, one arm of his overcoat draped normally over his arm. His other arm was buttoned into the overcoat, holding the upside down pineapple through the neck opening. The green stalk looked like a necktie, and Dad's hat was firmly ensconced on the pineapple's head. Daddy was talking to the pineapple head: "Well, they should be here any minute now, and then we can go home."

Kathy:

Dad's job on the road was neither an easy one nor a pleasant one. He worried about the many things that could go wrong. For instance, microphones. "Why do they build a twenty-million-dollar arena and put in a ten-cent sound system?" He worried about the lights. "What? No spotlights?" He worried about the bands. "No piano? How can they get their key to sing?"

Until the first show was finished, he *knew* nothing would work. I guess we did perform under some strange circumstances. When we played Salt Lake City for the Utah State Fair, we were told they had a 21-piece band. The idea sounded terrific! Most of the time we only had six or seven musicians. It did seem strange, however, that when we arrived for rehearsal, there was no bandstand set up. Finally, after waiting around for about ten minutes, Dad went to find the man in charge. He didn't have far to go, because coming through the door toward him was the agent, followed closely by a 21-piece marching band—complete with drums, tubas, silver feathered hats, and a glockenspiel.

We were as flabbergasted as Dad. No piano, no guitars, no bass! Those were the instruments we had to have. So we sang to thousands and thousands of people without any accompaniment at all for the duration of the Fair. I guess no one minded that, though. I remember that after each performance, we would sit and sign autographs by the hour—and I mean by the hour. Daddy felt that was part of our job, too—to be there until the last person was given our signature, a handshake, and a smile.

We were frequently amazed when the people remained in their seats or grandstand bleachers during a rainstorm. And in the Midwest, in the summertime, it rained! Yet most State and county fairs were held with no covering at all for the stage show. We sang many nights in pouring rain, shivering in light summer dresses, terrified to touch the dripping microphones for fear of getting a shock. During those downpours, the band members played only until they could no longer read any of their music. Then they ran for cover. By that time, the ink on our orchestrations was running as fast as they were.

Janet:

We never acquired the knack of how to dry out our music sheets. Sometimes, we would lay out the sheets, piece by piece, all over the hotel room—and, when no one was looking, along the halls and corridors. The ones placed over lamps dried fastest, though they turned a little brown around the edges; the ones near a heater curled; the ones in the hallways got trampled. And trying to separate the really waterlogged pieces was like trying to pull two wet Kleenex tissues apart. Half of the trumpet solo was permanently married to the alto sax obligato. We tried using hair dryers, but they took too long, because for one sheet to dry in this way, we needed about fifteen minutes. Not only did we acquire charley-horse of the arm muscles, but multiply one piece of music by twelve instruments, times fifteen songs; well, you get the idea. At one point, we asked the manager of the motel where we stayed if we could use his clothes dryer. That was not bad, but the music came out minus some of the more important musical notes, which remained inside the lint screen.

Peggy:

Dad worried when we had to perform in the rain, although part of his philosophy was, "If the people will brave a storm to see you, then you owe it to them to give it your best." At those times he was very protective. He would run around getting himself soaked, trying to find some kind of shelter for us. Once he even stood behind us onstage holding a blanket over our heads. As we would come offstage, he was waiting with our coats and warm blankets. He would rush us off to bed, making us gargle with Listerine (his panacea for everything), and pray that we wouldn't catch pneumonia. We never did. But he came close to it.

We were engaged to play Freedomland, New York, a huge amusement complex in the Bronx, reminiscent of Disneyland, *sans* Mickey and Donald. It was in Freedomland that Kathy and I did something awful to Janet. She was sick, sicker than we knew at the time, and we sympathized with her—but only up to a point. She had a sore throat and a chest cold, and it was not a quiet one. She would sniff and snort and sneeze and wheeze and cough and sputter and hack and blow, until we were just crazy. It was not so bad during the day, but all night long it went on. After three nights, Kathy and I could stand it no longer. We took the sheets and blankets from one of the beds and made a very comfortable bed for Janet in the bathtub. It was soft! Honest! It's just that, with the bathroom door closed, we could get some sleep.

But then we were quite remorseful when we arrived home and Jan was found to have strep throat and mononeucleosis. She stayed in bed for over six weeks.

Then again, I remember when we played Buck Lake Ranch, an amusement park forty miles from Fort Wayne, Indiana. We just drove and drove out into the countryside, for what seemed like forever, and never saw a building or a house. But three miles or so from the park, we had to stop. The two-lane road we were traveling was jammed with traffic.

Dad was concerned, because we had a rehearsal and an afternoon show to make. So he got out of the car to find a policeman; there were quite a few up ahead. "Officer," he said, "I'm trying to get to Buck Lake Ranch."

"Well, so is everybody else, mister."

"You mean for the next three or four miles all these cars are going to Buck Lake Ranch?"

"That's right," the policeman said. "Don't you know The

Lennon Sisters are singing there today and tonight? Better get back in your car and take your turn like everybody else."

"But, officer, we *are* The Lennon Sisters!"

With that the officer laughed and told Dad to bring his car around on the grass and follow him. We drove for three miles on grass, daisies, and rocks. But we made it. Nestled between two vast grassy knolls was an old barn made from handhewn logs slapped together. It was an outdoor shell theater and very picturesque. The crowds could watch the show by sitting on the hillsides with their picnic baskets. It was simple and pleasant. This was not going to be half bad. But the other half was.

There was no orchestra, only an organist. She was a sweet little old lady who played in church, and she assured us she could play anything. So we handed her the music to our opening song, "Sugartime." She tried to play it, stopped, started, stopped. "Let me see now. I know I've played in this key before...." Then her hands just froze. She was scared to death. We let her rehearse that two-minute number for at least half an hour, knowing she was never going to make it, but we didn't want to hurt her feelings. Since the time for the first show was racing towards us, we finally had to tell her we would sing *a cappella*. While we were fixing our hair and dressing, we could hear her out on the stage, desperately trying to get through the first eight bars of "Sugartime." She just wouldn't give up. We imagined her being forcibly removed from the stage, still pumping out notes that didn't work.

It's hard to describe the crowds that came to hear us. The only thing we might compare it to are the pictures of Woodstock in the 1960s. There were over thirty-thousand people sitting upon the hillsides at Buck Lake Ranch that day.

When we had finished our shows and were preparing to leave . . . ,

Janet:

. . . the owner of the place asked us to come to his house, situated on a rise behind the stage. He came out of the front door holding what looked like a moneybag. It *was* a moneybag! It was a small gunnysack with dollar signs printed on it, tied at the top with a piece of rope. "I always pay in cash," he growled.

In that bag was four-thousand dollars in cash. He had sent a sizeable deposit to our manager in Hollywood, and now he was paying the remainder to us in cash! Dad couldn't believe it. We drove back to Fort Wayne that night, along those dark Indiana backroads. Dad was terrified. "Everyone around here must know that old man pays in cash, he's so outspoken about it. Lock the doors. I'm going to take off down that road and not stop until we reach safety. You guys watch for sneaky-looking cars or anyone trying to follow us. Let's get out of here!"

There he was, our great protector, shivering in his boots. And us? How do cars look sneaky anyhow?

We did reach Fort Wayne and our hotel in relative safety, except for Dad's frantic driving. He did some pretty frantic running, too. From the car up to the hotel room. He slammed the big double doors to the room and put chair backs under the doorknobs. We slid our rollaway beds up against the chairs and collapsed onto the beds. "Okay, kids. I think we're okay. It's Sunday night, and I can't get to a bank until tomorrow, so we'll have to keep this money here tonight."

There it was, sitting in the middle of the floor. Then Daddy became curious and as silly as we were. "Let's open the bag and take a look at all that money," he cried. It was more money than we had ever seen at one time, and all in dollar bills. I think Dad was so relieved at not having been conked on the head on that dark, lonely road that he became goofy. He grabbed handfuls of money and threw it into the air. We joined his reckless abandon, dancing around the room, jumping on the beds, and shouting, "Millions, millions; look at all that money. Millions!"

At Du Quoin, Illinois, in the summer of 1963, we appeared at the annual Music Festival. The racetrack where we performed was in the middle of a huge field of green grass six feet tall. As evening approached, the heat became oppressive. Lightning flashed on every horizon, and rising from the grasses like a plague came swarms and swarms of mosquitoes, locusts, grasshoppers, and gnats. As the main spotlight flashed on us, a cloud of insects attacked us, settling on our heads and arms and legs. I recall we were wearing blue chiffon dresses, and when we were hit by those bugs, our dresses glowed green. While we snapped our fingers to the songs, they became bloodied with the bodies of gnats and mosquitoes. They were in our mouths and down our clothes. It was so awful we needed nerves of steel to get through that show, but the worst song to endure was "Ave Maria." Fortunately, the song called for the spotlight to be dimmed, and I'm not sure whether there were fewer bugs because of it or we just couldn't see as many. I know we could feel them. About halfway through the song, I began my recitation. I was in agony, as a large green praying mantis crawled up my neck. The remainder of the performance was spent slapping and hitting at bugs; whenever we took a step, it sounded like a crackling fire, because there were so many insects covering the stage. When we undressed that night, we found little green bugs embedded in our skin from top to bottom.

At home, we showed Mom the Des Quoin morning papers that had headlined the story of the insect infestation. She needed no further proof than that which fell from our music sheets—a three-foot square, two inch pile of dried, pressed green bugs.

At Maryville, Tennessee—up in the Smoky Mountains, about thirty miles from Knoxville—we performed for the Hillbilly Homecoming, an annual event that brought all the backwoods people together. They displayed their handicrafts, home-baked goods, and moonshine whiskey.

The small booths set up in the meadow held snacks for the folks to buy, but they were not the usual fare. There was fried catfish and hushpuppies, and they tasted better than any hot dog. The people dressed in costumes and drove their horses and buggies or antique motorcars up the winding mountain ridges. We sang in a wooden glen surrounded by trees so green they were blue, and the hastily erected platform on which we stood had the pungent smell of freshly cut pine. There was a little old lady dressed in black, who had brought her rocking chair with her, and as she closed her eyes and rocked with the music, the smoke from her corncob pipe trailed off into the woods. All the children were dressed like Huck Finn, and I somehow got the feeling they were not in costume. And the men really did sell Mountain Dew, White Lightning, Kickapoo Joy Juice, or whatever else they happened to call it.

We were invited by the Alcoa Aluminum Company to stay at their executive lodge, a retreat hidden fifteen miles higher up the mountains. It was located on the far side of the river that tumbled down the mountain. In order to reach the estate, we had to use a private ferry. Our first crossing was at night. The river was wide and deep, and the little wooden raft that held our car seemed to bob and weave its way across. But once on the other side, we forgot the shaky journey. There in the moonlight, lying low against the trees, was a hunting lodge reminiscent of the ones in Victorian novels. We were assigned rooms in the long, porch-like wing of the house. The furniture was antique, and the floors were polished hardwood; the curtains and bedspreads were white eyelet, and the walls were painted an icy blue. We fell asleep that night snuggled under the luxurious satin-covered down quilts.

The next morning we awoke to a light tapping at the door. There, standing over six feet tall, was a servant dressed in butler's livery with sparkling white gloves. "Good morning, ladies," he said in a deep, bass voice. "I've brought your breakfast." There were bowls of fresh wild raspberries and hot buttered melba toast and ice-cold milk, served to us on silver trays.

We stepped outside into the golden sunlight reflecting off the river. The beauty of our surroundings was awesome in the daylight. There was an immense lawn extending from our doorstep down to the riverbank. Towering mountains shot up on the other side of the river, all of them thickly forested with pines. To the side of the building was a small golf course that would have been coveted by any country club in the world. Behind the lodge were more hills extending straight up into the air. And a very curious archway cut the lodge itself into two sections.

We commented to our host that the architecture of the building was unique, but he replied that it was more unique than we could imagine. "You see, when Alcoa Company decided to build this hideaway here, they were unaware of a singular fact of nature peculiar to this land. Each year the wild boar that live in the hills make a strange migration. They come roaring out of the mountains on the other side of the river and swim across. Then they stampede across the meadow and take an ancient path right through this spot and up into the hills in back. Now, there is no way to tell these animals that they can't use their old stomping grounds any more. So we just built around them." (Now, why couldn't they have thought of that in *Elephant Walk*?)

Kathy:

For a decade, we worked annually on the famous Steel Pier in Atlantic City, New Jersey. It had four areas of entertainment—the outdoor amphitheater for the water circus, with its famous diving horse, the ballroom for dancing at night, the small auditorium for Tony Grant's Talent Show, and the huge stage-show theater where we appeared. The weather was usually humid and hot, and the days were long and tiring. The general schedule of performances then was 12:30 p.m., 2:30, 4:30, 6:30 and 8:30. Depending on the crowds, there were at times six shows daily.

Our small dressing room, which was backstage, had two tiny windows. We could view the beach below us, and we became quite adept at predicting the admission count for the day and—consequently—the number of shows. We prayed the sun would continue to shine, because, if it rained, the bathers would scurry to the pier and fill up the theater seats, and we would have to do added shows. After our performances, we would change out of our costumes and proceed to the backstage door. There were long lines of people, and as we opened the doors, we were bombarded with flashing bulbs. Half blinded, we found it difficult to sign our names when all we could see was a big black spot in the autograph books.

Once we had a brilliant idea to autograph all the pictures before the pending tour. We each wrote our names on thousands of photographs while at home and on the airplanes, thinking we could just pass them out after the shows. We were taken aback when, after handing them out to the crowds, the line continued to form with the same people walking up with picture in hand, saying, "We love your autographed picture, but we want to *watch* you sign it!"

The first time we appeared in Atlantic City was the summer of 1957. We can remember driving onto the pier, which was no different from driving onto our own Santa Monica Pier, but as we looked up over our heads, we were shocked to see our names in a lighted marquee 25 by 50 feet, alongside the theater. Then, as we looked out over the ocean, we were surprised to see a small airplane over the coastline, flying a long banner of cutout letters fluttering the words, "Lennon Sisters in Person." That was the first time I felt like A Star!

Dianne:

Although we think of Bill Lennon as the ideal father, one side of Dad that did not often show on the surface was his vulnerability. To the family, however, he often had a haunted look about him, and it would manifest itself in hypochondria. As a father of eleven children, he was enveloped by many pressures, some of these inflated beyond reason by his own fears. That heavy, worrisome side would show itself in a quiet, preoccupied facade, and at other times he clothed this part of himself overtly with humor and teasing. He found escape and therapy by thrusting himself into sports activities with the neighborhood kids. Frequently he just went to bed to bury his head in his pillow, occasionally asking one of us to rub his back to ease his tension. As we matured, we sensed his inner turmoil and were quietly supportive of him. We could not, however, alleviate his stress.

In July of 1960, we began the last tour of personal appearances as a quartet. In a few months, I would leave the group to marry.

Caught up in the eager anticipation of my wedding, we were unaware that Dad had begun to move at a slower pace. We were performing at the Maumee Fair in Toledo, Ohio, glad that it was the end of a two-week tour. As was Dad's custom, he joined us in our finale, and it was quickly apparent to all for of us that something was wrong. His face had a pained expression, instead of the look of fulfillment we usually saw when he sang with us. It seemed an eternity until we could get offstage. By that time Dad was pale and weak. "It's probably just the strain of this tour," he explained. "It will be good to go home tomorrow and rest."

But that tomorrow was not a restful day at all. Dad woke me very early in the morning, saying that he had called a doctor about chest pains he was experiencing. "Don't wake the girls unless I call you, Dee Dee," he said. "I'm going to see a doctor right now, and hopefully I'll be back before they wake up. It should still give us plenty of time to catch our plane home."

With a strong embrace and trembling lips, Dad said, "Say some prayers for your old Dad. He'll need them." Then he took a taxi out to the city.

It was about an hour later that the doctor called and told me that he was putting Dad into the hospital. He had found some irregularities in his heartbeat, and it was best to be safe. I didn't know where to turn—in a strange city, hundreds of miles from home, and no Mom to fall back upon. Then I thought of Father Marty. That's who I would call. Father Martin Matulik was a close family friend, working in a parish in Canton, Ohio. He would know what to do.

I woke the other girls, explaining as much as I knew, not really sure of the seriousness of Dad's problem. Together we telephoned Father Marty. The sound of his voice at the other end of the line brought instant tears of relief. "Please come, Father. We don't know what to do next. We need you."

Father Marty was on his way. It's a good thing he was a huge man, because as soon as we unlocked our motel room door, he was smothered with hugs of gratitude. We threw our suitcases into the trunk of Father's car and headed for the hospital. Father and I went up to Dad's room. Dad looked pathetic and lost until he saw Father Marty's gigantic frame come through the door. "Father, I'm so glad they thought to call you."

"Bill, they couldn't get rid of me now, even if they wanted to!"

The doctor suspected a mild heart attack was responsible for Dad's pain and explained that he must remain in the hospital for at least three weeks.

I telephoned Mom. She was so far away and had seven small children at home, including five-month-old Kippy. She knew her place was with Daddy. Father Marty made airline reservations for Mom to fly to Toledo immediately. Of course, the only way she could be with Dad was for us to go home to look after the little ones, so we had to catch the first plane back to Los Angeles.

We gave a quick, tearful farewell to Dad that afternoon. It was hard to leave him all alone. "Say 'hi' and kiss the little kids for me," he said. "Tell them Daddy will be home as soon as he gets well."

Dad did come home three weeks after entering the hospital. And what a homecoming that was!

With Dad, surprise birthday guests at President Dwight D. Eisenhower's party, October 12, 1959. *(The Lennon Sisters Collection)*

Our surprise meeting with Senator John F. Kennedy, during his presidential campaign trip, Detroit, Michigan, summer 1960. *(The Lennon Sisters Collection)*

10

People Who Need People

Peggy:

Washington, D.C. October 12, 1959. The Correspondents Association Press Club honors President Dwight D. Eisenhower. The occasion: The President's Birthday. The place: Sheraton Park Hotel.

We received the formal request from the Press Club asking us, The Lennon Sisters, to surprise the President. "You are favorites of his and would add greatly to his evening's entertainment," the invitation said. Hal Holbrook, John Gary, and Mahalia Jackson were also to perform at this huge stag dinner. We felt honored by the request.

There was an incredible amount of red tape, including a security clearance, before we could attend such a gathering. We were informed that we might not be able to go because our Gramma Lennon was from Germany and her brother Max had served in the German Armed Forces in World War I. However, the clearances finally arrived, and we headed for Washington on an overnight flight. A chauffeured limousine whisked us from Dulles Airport to the Sheraton Park Hotel, where we had brunch with some of the Press Club dignitaries. At noon, still caught up in a whirlwind of excitement, we received an unexpected phone call from

Mr. John Malone. He was a gentleman we had met in California, a friend of Lawrence Welk's. He worked with the Federal Bureau of Investigation and directly with J. Edgar Hoover.

"Girls, I'd like to visit with you. I know you are only here for one day, but perhaps you might like to take a tour of the FBI building." He asked if he might pick us up and be our guide.

Just after a rehearsal in the early afternoon, another black limousine awaited us. This time it took us to the big, gray fort-like FBI Building. In addition to the personal tour of the Bureau, Mr. Malone invited us to meet J. Edgar Hoover. "When Mr. Hoover heard you were coming to visit, he asked me to bring you up to his office. He's a real fan of yours. Would you be kind enough to have your picture taken with him?"

Mr. Hoover's photographer was a busy one. Hoover, it seems, made it a point to have his picture taken with thousands of the famous and the infamous.

When we returned to the hotel, we had to endure three or four hours of nervous anticipation. We ordered room service, but it was difficult to enjoy a calm, leisurely dinner when we knew that we would soon be performing for the President of the United States. Dee Dee's fiance. Dick Gass, stationed at Fort Bragg, North Carolina, had been granted a three-day pass so he could come to Washington to be with her. Two of his paratrooper buddies came with him. "The guys back at the barracks won't believe this. It's a good thing we took those pictures with J. Edgar Hoover."

"Yeah, but they'll never believe we went to President Eisenhower's birthday party."

Just as we were finishing our dessert, Dad emerged from the bedroom in a black tuxedo. Some of us were able to stifle our laughter long enough to swallow. Janet and Kathy sprayed the table with chocolate cake and milk. "I sat in front of the mirror and practiced looking sophisticated," Dad laughed. "But it's no use. I still look like a beetle with its wings folded back."

We were escorted down to the ballroom. Two Secret Service agents accompanied Dad and the three soldiers to a table out on the dance floor. The whole atmosphere backstage fit in perfectly with our state of mind, our shaky knees, and knotted stomachs. The stage manager, a tiny, nervous man, fairly flitted from place to place, shushing the orchestra, which was "tuning up much too loudly," and telling each performer again and again where to stand and where to exit.

The man's complete loss of control had us laughing, even through the M.C.'s announcement: "Mr. President, we have a special surprise for you tonight. I give you . . . The Lennon Sisters!"

And there we were, singing and smiling to the notes of "Honeycomb." I strained my eyes to find the President in the crowd, and to see if he was enjoying himself. The several songs we had chosen to sing went by quickly, and suddenly it was over. Once again we were backstage with the raving little tyrant stage manager. "Stand aside, girls. You've done your twelve minutes. Wait over there!"

We retired to our designated corner, and while still collecting our thoughts we noticed a young man enter the side stage-door and approach our distraught stage manager. After a few moments, we heard, "But sir, they can't. It would ruin my whole schedule. We are already three minutes over. Please!"

Some more whispers. "Very well. There's only one solution." With that the stage director hurried to our sides. "Girls, this is *not* on my agenda, but the President has sent a courier asking that you sing another song. The only thing I will allow is that you four can go out again to lead the Happy Birthday song." The little man, completely falling apart, shoved us through the curtains onto the stage. (The President never realized the great commotion he caused, but he had won a mighty battle against a little general.)

We were informed that we would be able to meet the President and many of the dignitaries, including the President of Mexico, Juan Mateos. We did not have to wait long before we found ourselves face to face with President Eisenhower. Kathy remarked later how surprised she was at his ruddy appearance of health and vigor, and that he was so much taller than she had expected. "Hello, girls," he said as he shook our hands. "I'm thrilled that you came and sang for my party. I've watched you for so many years, I feel I know you." We looked at Dad's face then, and each of us saw in it all that our hearts were feeling.

"Mr. Lennon, I have to ask you something," the President said. "Mamie wants to know if you have ten or eleven children. I say ten and she says eleven."

"She's right, Mr. President," Daddy replied.

"Girls, I think Mamie knows more about you than you do about yourselves." Then he laughed at his own humor.

We watched a great display of diplomacy as he greeted and talked with each person in the reception line. He seemed a very gracious man. When the President's entourage departed, we walked out to the alcove at the main entrance to the hotel. Mr. Eisenhower and President Mateos were in the first car, their nations' flags blowing in the breeze. The car paused as it passed us. The President leaned across Mr. Mateos and rolled down the window. "See you on Saturday night, girls," he shouted. "We'll be watching!"

And the procession of limousines drove off into the night.

Janet:

There were other cars and other Presidents during 1960. In February that year, our friend, Father Ed Ramacher, asked us to perform in St. Cloud, Minnesota, for a $100-a-plate dinner benefit. When friends or strangers called Dad for favors, it was very difficult for him to turn them down. So we trekked off to the Midwest to sing a few songs.

Father Ramacher expressed his gratitude when he picked us up at the airport, and again when he drove us from our hotel to the auditorium. "By the way," he said. "Some of the merchants in town bought each of you—you too, Bill—a raffle ticket for a new car."

In front of the auditorium stood the shiny new black Lincoln Imperial. "Well, you guys," Kathy said, "I received my learner's permit last week. There's my car to go with it."

After we had performed our part of the entertainment, Father Ed asked me to remain on the stage, while the other girls took seats next to Dad. I could see Kathy was fidgety as I walked to the microphone. "Do us a favor, Janet," Father said. "Draw the winning ticket."

Father blindfolded me and swirled the metal-screened barrel, loaded with ticket stubs. We knew there were only about one-hundred tickets sold, and we held five of them in our hands. Our chances were one out of twenty. I reached into the drum and carefully selected the winning ticket. I absolutely knew whose name was on that ticket. Father Ed asked me to remove my blindfold and read the lucky name.

"Oh, no! It's my sister Kathy!" I screamed.

Kathy:

I *screamed* right along with Janet. I almost fell right off my chair. Father Ramacher came over to me, picked me up, and led me to the microphone. I couldn't breathe.

"Oh honey," Dad kept saying. "You really have to give it back. This is embarrassing."

Probably for the first time, I ignored Dad and his unselfish feelings, grand as they were. It was definitely my own car, and no one was going to take it away from me. Father Ramacher came to the rescue. "Ladies and gentlemen. Isn't this wonderful?" he said. "But Bill Lennon keeps telling her to give it back. He does not realize that all of you have one or two cars just like it sitting in your garages. That's why you bought these kids those tickets. Right?"

The crowd stood up and applauded, while I held *my* keys to *my* car firmly in *my* hand. The following day the front page of the local newspaper held my picture, captioned:

DODGE DARLING WINS LINCOLN *

And the following month I used my brand new Lincoln to bring home our brand new brother, Christopher Joel Robert ("Kippy"), born March 12, 1960.

Peggy:

That summer, because of Dad's illness, we were left without tour chaperones. We had to prepare for another scheduled tour, this time to Milwaukee. Uncle Ted Lennon and

---

* *For clarification, the Lawrence Welk Show, on ABC-TV was sponsored by the Chrysler Corporation, makers of Dodge automobiles. Ford Motor Company's Lincoln-Mercury Division produces Lincoln automobiles.*

Aunt Peg volunteered to accompany us. They had eleven children at home, and the trip was a decided change of pace from changing diapers.

They also quickly grasped the importance of a sense of humor on the road. One afternoon between performances, an official from the Wisconsin Fair asked us to come over to his house for a while. "We'll bring you back in our car. My wife will fix you a little snack, and you can just kick off your shoes and relax."

As we pulled into their driveway, we were greeted by excited groups of kids on bikes and skates, their autograph books and cameras in hand. Twenty minutes later, we were able to "meet the wife," and when we sat down on the sofa in their family room, a cold drink in our hands, we could turn and wave at all the people staring through the big picture window at us. "While you relax we thought you might enjoy some soft organ music by our little ten-year old Debbie. Her teacher says she's really good for her age. So just sit back, kick off your shoes, and relax."

This situation has happened to us countless times, and was exactly as we had described it beforehand to our Aunt and Uncle. It was only after we had returned to the solitude of our dressing room that we could finally "just kick off our shoes and relax."

We had a week of rest at home, and then it was off again, this time a tour with Pat Boone, to the Indiana and Michigan state fairs. Uncle Bob and Aunt Jeanette Lennon came with us this time.

The Indiana State Fair at Indianapolis was one of the biggest in the United States. We could feel the excitement and grandiosity as soon as the huge grandstand and fairgrounds came into view. The fair was like none other. Pat Boone was *the* Number One teenage idol at that time, and the crowds were tremendous.

One afternoon Pat, his road manager Don Henley, and the four of us were sitting in our dressing-room trailers, bemoaning the fact that we never got to go to see any of the fairgrounds. Pat's bright idea was to disguise ourselves and move out onto the midway. "It's the only way we will ever get to go on the rides and see the sideshows."

When we managed to scrounge up scarves, wigs, old hats, and jackets from people backstage, off we went. Janet and Pat ran for the Ferris Wheel and jumped onto the last empty seat. As the rest of us stood in line below, we could hear them laughing down at us. In a few minutes Don decided to get even. "Hey," he said in a loud voice. "That looks like Pat Boone on the Ferris Wheel. And that girl with him looks just like Janet Lennon."

A crowd started to gather, gawking and pointing. Before anyone could recognize the three of us, we made a mad dash for the dressing room, leaving the high-perched Pat and Janet to the mercy of the crowd.

From Indiana the whole show traveled all night to Detroit by bus. What a trip! There were thirty of us packed in like sardines. We had not traveled this way before, so we experienced what it must have been like during the "Big Band" era. The musicians tried to catch some winks, but Pat climbed onto the overhead luggage rack and threw things at them, while singing at the top of his lungs. About 3:00 a.m., Pat decided we were all hungry and needed breakfast. He instructed the driver to stop at the nearest depot, and we dragged our travel-weary bodies into the station. His boundless energy carried him from one vending machine to another buying all of us a breakfast: peanut butter 'n' cheese crackers and coffee and Hershey bars. Was this really the big time?

We arrived at our hotel in Detroit early the next morning. There seemed more activity than normal for such an early hour. "Senator John Kennedy is to stay at our hotel," the manager told us. "He campaigns here tomorrow."

We longed to catch a glimpse of the handsome John Kennedy. We were in our room when his motorcade pulled up in front of the hotel the next day. Hearing our screams, Uncle Bob ran into our room to see only derrieres and legs sprawled across the window ledge, which was ten stories up. "Girls," he said, "get away from that window before you really fall for him!"

We composed ourselves somehow and chattered away as only girls can about his gorgeous hair and good looks. And we got to see him in person—from only ten stories up.

The next morning Father Marty telephoned from Ohio. "How would you like to meet Senator Kennedy?" he asked. "I know Kenny O'Donnell, his aide, and he'll arrange it. Wait for his call. Don't leave your room." Soon, Secret Service men came and escorted all six of us to meet the next President of the United States.

Standing next to Senator John F. Kennedy was a much better way of viewing him than seeing him from a ten-story window ledge. He walked right up to us when we entered his room, and he took our hands in his. "I believe you girls go to school in the parish where my sister Pat is a member," Senator Kennedy said.* *He* knew something about *us*!

He asked us if we would take a picture with him. "I don't know what this will do for your careers, but I'm sure it will help mine," he said. As a postscript, John Kennedy was quoted as "having met The Lennon Sisters in Detroit," in the Theodore White book, *The Making of the President, 1960.*

Janet:

Our final appearance prior to Dee Dee's marriage was in September of 1960, at the famous Corn Palace in South Dakota. It was a bit difficult to believe that, after all the years, this was to be our last performance as the *four* Lennon Sisters. Accompanying us as road manager was Bob Lido, member of the Welk band and our baby Kippy's godfather.

We gave two performances each day at the Corn Palace, one in the early afternoon and one in the evening. Between shows there was a five-hour nothing-to-do period. At that time, 25 years ago, Mitchell, South Dakota, was not exactly a booming metropolis. After we walked from one end of the town to the other, we still had four and a half hours to kill. There was one theater, so our first afternoon was spent eating popcorn and watching a movie. We had received several offers during our Mitchell stay to "spend a few hours at our house and just kick off your shoes and relax." But we declined in favor of sprawling on our beds at the Hotel Lawler, watching television, and calling

---

* *The Senator was referring to Patricia Kennedy Lawford, who at the time lived in Santa Monica, California.*

room service for one of their famous homemade pies.

On our final day in Mitchell, Senator John Kennedy, still very much on the campaign trail, was scheduled to speak at the Corn Palace between our two shows. We were so excited we could barely concentrate during our first performance. We ran offstage, hoping to see him waiting in the wings to give his speech. Instead we saw the same performers we had seen each day—Zippy the Chimp, The Barrington Balancing Troupe, and Jo Ann Castle. We could tell by the look on Jo Ann's face that Kennedy had not arrived. We changed out of our costumes quickly, all the while retelling Jo Ann for the umpteenth time that we really had met him, and that he was gracious and handsome and charming, and that he really did know us.

"When he gets here," I told Jo Ann, "you go out into the hallway. We'll wait in here in our dressing room because we've already met him. That will leave more room backstage for people who haven't had a chance to look at him." A knock at the door silenced us.

I opened the door to a tall, stately, sandy-haired woman. Although we had never seen her before, she had that unmistakable Kennedy look. "I'm the Senator's sister, Eunice."

"Come in, Mrs. Shriver, please," I said.

She explained that the Senator had heard we were appearing there, and he wanted her to make sure we would wait until he arrived so he could see us again. "His plane is a little late," she said, "but he should arrive shortly. Now, before I go out and check the stage for him, do you think I could get some autographs for my children?"

When Mrs. Shriver left the room, the five of us stood gasping. "I don't believe all this," Jo Ann Castle finally said. "He really does know you. Let me get my camera, and you girls can take a picture of me with him. Do you think he'll do it for me? Oh, I'm so excited! I'd better comb my hair. Is my makeup all right? Where do you think we should stand?"

As she ran down the hall for her camera, we began to laugh, for as amusing as she appeared, we all knew how she felt. She rejoined us in a few moments, and this time we left the door ajar so we wouldn't miss him as he passed through to the stage. It was not too long before we heard a great deal of commotion down the corridor, and suddenly he was in our doorway. "Hello, girls," he said. "How have you been? Did you bring your Aunt and Uncle with you this time?"

Again he overwhelmed us. Jo Ann instantly went into action, throwing her camera to me, and in one quick lunge was at his shoulder. "Quick, Jan. Snap it now. Maybe you could take several. Is my hair messed up? Maybe I should get on the other side of him . . . ." We had to bite our lips to keep from laughing when she quickly jumped onto a bench directly behind Senator Kennedy and put her head close to his. Someone, I think it was Dee Dee, managed to introduce Jo Ann, and though he tried three times to shake her hand, she was too busy posing. She could only think of getting a picture with him to prove to anyone that she was next to John Kennedy.

That trip, the last we made as a quartet, was the end of an era for us, and in essence, the end of our youth. In some ways, we were glad that Dad had not accompanied us; he would have made these final days miserable for himself and for us, because he hadn't yet dealt with the fact that Dee Dee was really quitting. Without having to cope with Dad's emotions, we were free to cope with our own.

On our plane trip home that autumn, Bob Lido ordered a bottle of champagne. With glistening eyes, he lifted his glass and said what each of us was feeling. "Dee Dee, this is the end of one life and the beginning of another. May you have all the happiness in the world. Here's to you and Dick."

Now it would be the *three* Lennon Sisters.

Kathy:

The three Lennon Sisters—how strange that sounded. But the truth of it had to be acknowledged. Peg and I were challenged by the myriad problems confronting Janet. This shy young girl who used her sweet, soft voice to sing lullabies, or an occasional solo on the show, now had to tackle the lead singer's spot in our nationally famous musical group. She had very little confidence in herself, so it was up to Peg and me to convince her she was more than capable of handling the job. It took a while for her to gain the assurance she needed, but we did a few small concerts in northern California that fall, and they helped strengthen her voice and her feelings about herself. Daddy helped matters; reluctant though he was, he allowed her to grow up. No more braids and bobbysocks. She was an equal partner now!

In October of 1962, the three of us had a weekend engagement in Kansas City. Since we would be gone such a short time, Jan, Peg, and I thought it would be fun to take our Girl Friday, Betty Sanford, with us. At rehearsal in Kansas, I began to feel a familiar gnawing ache in my right side. During my adolescence, I had been troubled periodically by this dull, persistent pain. When I complained, people would say, "Oh, that's just Kathy going through her routine. She just doesn't want to do the show." It did seem worse when we had shows to do, so I thought perhaps it was caused by nerves. The accusations were hurtful, and I wondered if I had a psychological problem. The symptoms, resembling appendicitis, had me at doctors' doors for years. But no cause could be found for my discomfort.

We returned to our hotel after the first show, and the pain in my side became excruciating. I was rushed to Menorah Hospital. Doctors examined and tested and found nothing. The appendicitis symptoms were once again dismissed. Peg and Jan did two more shows alone and then had to fly home to tape the Welk show. Betty Sanford stayed with me; I mean, she really stayed with me. Betty was the next best thing to having Mom present. She refused to take a hotel room and insisted she would sleep in the hospital. My doctor, David Waxman, gave her special permission. Further tests were negative, and the pain eventually subsided.

Six days later, Betty and I flew home; it had been a disastrous trip. The travel and hotel expenses were compounded by hospital bills (although to this day, I never received Dr. Waxman's bill). To add insult to injury, the promoter of the boat show, instead of paying us, took the money and ran off to Europe.

Over the years, we have taped about two dozen television shows in New York City. The show schedules—for Perry Como's show, Gary Moore's show, Ed Sullivan's, *etc.*—were such that on some days we would have only a one-hour rehearsal. That left time for doing nothing—or something, depending upon our whims. The best time was evening, because we didn't have to dress to do a show; we didn't have to eat a fast dinner, and we didn't have to rush anywhere. We found the nightlife of New York glamorous and stimulating. In the glow of Times Square we mingled with the teeming crowd: socialites dressed in furs rushing to theaters, hobos warming their hands over open fires in trash cans, and vendors selling hot roasted chestnuts on streetcorners.

We were able to obtain tickets for some of the "sold out" Broadway shows, taking advantage of our connections in the entertainment business. We were captivated by Robert Preston as *The Music Man*, and enchanted by Mary Martin in *The Sound Of Music*. It was an honor to be asked by these legendary performers to come backstage so that *they* could meet *us*.

One of the more pleasant aspects of our travels was the fact that we made some lasting friendships along the way. There were people in almost every city who *became* that city to us. Father Bill Green from St. John's Prep School in Brooklyn *was* New York. Every time we had to tear ourselves away from home and go to New York, we alternately groaned with displeasure and laughed at the thought of spending a few days with Father. It was he who forced us to be tourists, in spite of our trepidation. He introduced us to the Statue of Liberty, the Empire State Building, Rockefeller Center, *etc*. And he also introduced us to the Joseph Lang family in Flatbush. It was their old green station wagon that Father borrowed to show us around the city, and at the end of each day, it took us through the Brooklyn-Battery tunnel under the East River to the Lang home, which was our main anticipation when going to New York. There, Joe and Margaret and their ten children became our family for awhile; we helped with dishes, shared their meals, played with each new baby, and slept two and three to a bed. That was our New York!

In Dubuque, Iowa, we stayed with the Ang Kerper family. We had been introduced to them by Lawrence Welk, in Cedar Rapids. We latched onto them, and they *became* Iowa to us. They took us water-skiing on the Mississippi River. Ang was the manager of the huge Dubuque Meat Packing Company. He gave us a private tour through his plant, where somewhere along the way we lost our taste for sausage.

Perry Como introduced us to Cuzzie and Elaine Mingolla, whose door was always open if we were anywhere near Boston. Their home was a large comfortable estate in the country. Elaine pampered us by showing each of us to our own bedroom suite. Across each bed she had carefully laid out one of her own silk peignoirs for us to wear. Although Cuzzie Mingolla was a prominent, successful businessman, all he wanted to do when we were around was be our chauffeur. Sometimes he drove us as far as three or four-hundred miles to reach our destination. They were New England!

The year 1962 brought about a change from the routine county and state fair circuit—our first nightclub engagement. Our performing at Blinstrub's in Boston allowed the three of us to put together an hour show that was more diversified. After years of working, our repertoire of songs was more than adequate. The difficult part was not the selection of songs, but the proper pacing for the show. On the Lawrence Welk Show, our songs were seldom longer than two or three minutes. To do an hour show meant that we had to sing at least 25 songs. So our solution was to break our act up into four sections and also to bring with us a special guest star. Our brother Danny was twelve years old then, and he had been singing with us at a few benefits in the Los Angeles area. We were proud of his talents, and we felt our audience would enjoy him

After nearly a quarter-century, Dan recalls that he was nervous during that first show, but it went fairly well, from his point of view. Dad came into the dressing room and told him there were two young female fans outside. He flushed with embarrassment and instructed Dad to tell the girls he was sick and couldn't come out to see them. Instead, Dad told the young ladies Dan would come to their table. Trapped again!

"On the way to their table," Dan told us, "something occurred that to this day I cannot explain. Suddenly I felt like a Star, deigning graciously to pay a visit to a few worshipping admirers. In a haze of illusion, I introduced myself and proceeded to weave a tale of my glamorous life in Hollywood—how Annette, Cubby, Karen, Johnny Crawford, and I would stay out until the wee hours at teenage nightclubs dancing, dining, and kibitzing; how long, gleaming cars would pull up and wheel us to our poolside homes.

"What was wrong with me? I wondered. On and on I rambled, as I shrank smaller and my fantasy began to fill the room with grandeur and opulence." He finally excused himself to prepare for our second show saying, "You will stay, won't you? I'd so love it."

"Floating back to the dressing room," he said, "I felt giddy and finally nauseous. I had succumbed to the demon of the stage, even if only for a few minutes. But soon I returned to my life of Monopoly, football, and First Fridays with no champagne breakfasts."

These hour-long shows were tiring because of the many quick costume changes and the high-energy level we had to sustain throughout each night. And the close proximity of the audience to us was a startling new experience. We knew they could see every Clearasil-covered blemish.

But I think with this engagement we finally proved to Daddy and to ourselves that we could go on successfully as a trio.

We were away from home so much of the time during our teenage years we hardly had time to think about—or even care about—the balancing and budgeting of money. There was little to budget, because we did not have an allowance, and only if we really needed or wanted a particular kind of clothing or some beauty supplies did we ask Mom if we could "borrow some money." I can honestly say it was of no concern to any of us, nor did it occur to us, to feel the money we were earning was for personal profit. It just went out to pay the bills.

The first time it crossed my mind that perhaps I might want to be responsible for some of the money I earned was when I considered buying another car. When I spoke to Mom and Dad about acquiring one, they told me we would all have to discuss it with Beverly.

Our secretary at this time was Beverly Benenati. During our busiest years, she was employed at our home five days weekly. Our familes were close, and because of that very friendship I could talk to Bev about anything. It wasn't until this financial discussion, based in part on curiosity and my need, that I came to learn that there was a difference between a checking account and a savings account. Bev told me I should be interested in my own finances. She felt it was essential for my future to become aware of money matters. "Your mom and dad want you to care about your funds. I think it's time to help you."

Beverly sat me down and showed me what I was earning and where it was going. I asked if it was possible to start a personal checking account. I did know it was a State law to deduct a certain amount of our weekly salaries and hold it in savings bonds under the State child labor laws. This had been taking place since 1957. But that fund was not mine until I reached age 21. Beverly, Mom, and I agreed to withhold a certain portion of my weekly check. This gave me the chance to handle and budget my own income. So, at twenty years of age, after eight years of working, I had my first checking account, eventually my own savings account, and then I graduated very quickly to—credit cards.

In the summer of 1963, Peg, Jan, and I agreed to limit our touring to those trips we would take with the Lawrence Welk organization. We fully realized that our Dad would be disappointed, because he viewed us almost as good will ambassadors to the people of our country. This decision to pull back from touring was among the first that we made for ourselves in order to enjoy other aspects of life. It was for us a business decision. Dad was hurt for awhile, but in the end, he—who had also programmed us to think and act for our own good—supported this change in our professional life. When we began our travels, we were just four little girls whose only knowledge of America was through books. Seeing it for ourselves, however, was a much more exciting and educational experience. Some places were quite lovely and serene; some were chaotic and anything but beautiful. Strange, different, but every bit a part of America.

How surprised we were to meet communities of Amish and Mennonite peoples, their simple way of life preserved through their communal farms and unmechanized, unhurried existence. Along the highways of central Pennsylvania or upon a backroad in Kansas, we would come suddenly upon a horse and carriage with its occupants all in black and gray, ladies in bonnets, and men with long beards. Occasionally we would meet families in stores in small towns and watch their little children stand and stare in silent amazement at the shelves of brightly colored toys. All this seemed to bring to life Jessamyn West's family in *Friendly Persuasion*. How charming. How strange. Time stood still for them. And these people, without television sets or even radios, who did not have an inkling who or what The Lennon Sisters were, gave us a fresh perspective. We could look upon them without being looked at ourselves.

We were taken aback, too, when we learned that in southern states a culture had formed that was different from the one in which we lived. We were amazed to find segregation in many forms, with "white only" and "colored only" signs on drinking fountains, bathrooms, and separate seating sections of our audiences! For us, it had been a word rather than a fact. We were unaware of the problems facing Southern people, black or white, who were attempting to recover from centuries-old social problems.

We found the American Indians colorful and inspiring; they, too, struggling for their existence and self-esteem. From the Black Hills of the Dakotas to the pueblos of New Mexico and Arizona, they nestle on lands from the mountains to the plains, holding tenaciously to the cultures of their individual tribes. Most fascinating to us were the Blackfeet Indians in Montana. We came to know their chief, Earl Old-Person, and to our great honor and pleasure we were made members of his tribe. Our adopted names are Princess Arrow Woman (Peggy), Princess Flying Woman (Dee Dee), Princess Shining Star (Janet), and Princess Morning Star (me). We have lovely beaded necklaces and headdresses, and we will always cherish our adoption papers from the Blackfeet Nation.

Living in Southern California we had little knowledge of the strange things that cold weather could do. Imagine our surprise when, after leaving Los Angeles at over eighty degrees one day in January, we arrived in Winnipeg, Canada, that evening to face minus-forty degree weather. We had made the mistake of wearing naugahyde coats, and our first venture out into that weather was a disaster. We had to walk about fifty feet from the airplane to the terminal building, and in just that distance, walking at a normal arm-swinging gait, our coats actually froze and cracked at the elbows. It was in Winnepeg that we first observed cars being plugged in for the night, and we were given an electrical cable to attach to our automobile battery. We plugged onto a warming device at the curb, so that the battery fluid would not freeze.

In Minneapolis, we were introduced to the marvels of ice fishing, something we had thought existed only within the pages of a

Jack London story or a *National Geographic* magazine. With icy-cold fear, we drove onto a huge frozen lake. All the way across, the ice was splitting under the pressure of the car's weight. "This lake is frozen so deep it's impossible to fall through," our driver told us, but it did nothing to relieve my gut feelings that death was imminent—particularly when the sound of the cracking ice echoed like distant thunder, as each new split traveled the entire length of the lake, vibrating the water beneath it. Looking out the window of the car, we saw other cars, and near them little shacks measuring four-by-five feet. These huts, with no floors, sheltered fishermen from the winter winds. Inside, just like Eskimos in cartoons, men in parkas fished through holes cut in the ice. Each shack had a small stool, kerosene stove, blanket, and smelly fish bait. An exciting winter palace for four girls from California!

Dianne:

> *There is a destiny which makes us brothers.*
> *None goes his way alone;*
> *All that we send into the lives of others,*
> *Comes back into our own.*

> —Edwin Markham

Our Dad believed this, and he had the patience of Job when it came to going through every letter from friends and fans and attending to the volume of materials that came to us. As our manager, he felt his individual attention was required on each letter that accompanied the sheets of music, the tapes, and records sent to us by professionals and amateurs. His idea was not to involve us in these matters, although occasionally he called us in to listen to what he called his "little beauties." We kept a list of ones most remembered and requested by our family.

> *Fi-Fi my little toy poodle*
> *You make my heart go doodle doodle!*

And Number One on our sisters' and brothers' Hit Parade:

There once was a monkey who
Wasn't happy in a zoo.
So he cried the morning, afternoon, and night,
And the tears ran from his eyes,
Down his shoulders to his thighs.
You could swim in them or paddle a canoe,
Boo-hoo-hoo, Boo-hoo-hoo,
Boo-hoo-oo-oo-oo-oo-oo-oo.

One of our all-time greats:

Lickety-Lennon Sickety Sisters—
For Lickety-Lawrence Wickety-Welk—
And his Chickety-Champagne Mickety-Music—
On Tickety-TV for Dickety-Dodge . . .

Swamped by mail and besieged in person by hopeful composers and aspiring performers, Dad rarely asked us to interrupt our schooling, at-home-rehearsals, or household chores, just to listen to a personal audition. But there was an exception one afternoon.

"Daddy, a man is at the door," one of the little kids said that day. "And there is a big camper filled with kids out front."

As Dad came to the door he was greeted with: "How do you do, Mr. Lennon. My name is George Osmond."

He told Dad he had driven his family out from Utah in the hope someone would listen to his sons sing. "I feel my boys are talented, and we would appreciate your opinion. We came here because our family is much like yours, and we thought you might be able to help us find the right way to get our boys started."

We girls were not at home at the time, but Dad waved in the Osmond family and then met Allan, Wayne, Merrill, and Jay. Mr. Osmond reported the two older boys were back home in Utah, and Olive—Mrs. Osmond—was out in the camper with their two babies, Donny and Marie.

After hearing the boys sing, Mom and Dad were so impressed that they arranged for the Osmonds to return in the early evening.

When Jan and I came home from school, Mom met us at the door, telling us that we were to eat early. "Dad has some friends coming over at six o'clock, and he wants you to meet them," she said.

After dinner, Dee Dee and her husband Dick came over. Dad ushered all of us out to the den. He had, true to form, arranged everything perfectly—chairs set up, the phone unplugged, the curtains drawn. There, standing against the wall, were four darling boys in red blazers and straw hats. "Hello, hello, hello, we are the Osmonds . . . ," they sang.

We were enchanted by their harmonious blend and the vocal power coming from this young group. They were adorable and radiated a strong personality. We were captivated by their barbershop quartet, thrilled as much as Dad had been.

We were hesitant to bring them to Mr. Welk, because his reaction to new talent could be very unpredictable. He was forever asking the members of his organization to find fresh songs and new faces for the show, but at the same time he made it known that he alone was the final judge.

With mixed feelings we asked the Osmonds to meet us at the Aragon Ballroom the following Thursday. Since they had no place to stay, Dad gave them the keys to our small guest house in Malibu for a few days. Their performance that Thursday afternoon had the band members standing and applauding with great admiration. The Osmond boys charmed everyone—almost. "Bill," Mr. Welk told Dad, "I'm not looking for amateur talent, and we have to continue with our show's rehearsal."

We were disappointed. Yet, sure of their talent, we told them to enjoy the beach house, and we would call them soon. His next approach was to call his brother Jim. Uncle Jimmy Lennon was still announcer for Friday-night boxing on a local television station. He used some of his clout, and the next night the boys appeared in a time slot between the preliminary bout and the main event.

The following week the Osmond family left for their home in Utah. But they did not pass into oblivion. Dad's persistence proved the key that led to a phone call we received.

"Hello, who am I speaking to? Is this one of the girls?"

"Yes, this is Janet."

"Janet, this is Jay Williams, Andy Williams' dad. And I need to know who those darling little boys were with your Uncle Jim at the fights the other night. I saw them again on a Disney Show. They remind me so much of my own boys, you know—Andy and his brothers. Andy must have them on his show. How can we get in touch with them?"

"Mom?" Janet yelled. "Do we have the Osmonds' phone number and address?"

Mom told Jan we had their address but no phone number, so she passed on the information to Mr. Williams, and the rest is history.

Contrary to most jobs, a performer needs an audience, and his career cannot survive without fans. From the very beginning of our singing career on television, we looked forward to sitting on the Aragon ballroom floor with our boxes of fan mail and packages. We have received thousands of handkerchiefs, hundreds of pieces of baby clothes for our children, hand-knitted afghans and shawls; one lady crocheted gowns for storybook dolls, which were copies of our bridal party gowns.

It is human nature to favor the youngest of a family, or in this case, a group; consequently, Janet was absolutely deluged with gifts, from hair-ribbons to dolls—especially dolls. They would arrive from all over the world—handmade Indian squaws, antique china-head figures, cuddly floppy rag-dolls, and many, many more. In their bedroom, Jan and Kathy had a doll display-case that they constantly rearranged to make room for a newly-arrived treasure. Most of them are now a part of Kathy's antique doll collection.

From the end of the 1950s to the mid 1970s, one man sent Kathy, Jan, and me Waterford crystal every birthday, anniversary, and Christmas. We would receive a big silver package with a sticker from Donavan and Seaman, bearing a tag: "From your loyal fan." He remained anonymous for eleven years. When we finally met this generous man, we asked him why Peggy never received anything from him. His explanation was logical, and left us all laughing. "My wife," he said, "is an Aries, and Peggy is an Aries, too. I never got along with my wife, and I don't think I would get along with Peggy, either."

Throughout these past thirty years or so, some names have changed, but the content of our fan mail has not:

Dear Girls,

How you remind us of our granddaughters. We love having you in our home, especially little Janet. She's our favorite . . . .

Dear Lennons,

I do want you to know we have grown up together. My grandparents made me watch you every Saturday night, and now I watch you because I want to . . . .

Mom and Dad received many letters from parents of children who were ill and bedridden: "Could your girls sing my child's favorite song? Is it possible to have your girls call my son or daughter any time that's convenient for you?"

Many times we visited those children who could not come out to the fairgrounds, and their homes and hospital rooms were a regular stop on every tour.

Of course, there were the weirdos. Dad usually sheltered us from them, but as we grew older, he made us aware of their existence. It took us many years before we realized how sheltered we had been. Dad had such an innate trust in human nature that he gave everyone the benefit of the doubt and believed no one would do us harm if we were kind to them. This trust only added to the delusion of our "odd" fans that they could become part of our family.

There was an 82-year-old man who admitted to communicating with me every Saturday night over television and said I had asked him to fly out to California to take me back east with him. He showed up at the ABC studios three years in a row, with the same contents in his shaking hands—a purple satin Seagrams pouch filled with old broken jewelry and a one-way airplane ticket for me to return with him to Boston.

One outstanding character introduced himself to Dad. It was unforgettable. Around his neck hung an eight-by-ten glossy picture of Kathy's face, and with self-assurance he announced, "Mr. Lennon, you are a lucky duck. I'll be so proud when I'm your son-in-law. I wouldn't mind driving Kathy's brand-new Lincoln at all."

And we're still keeping an eye out for the man from St. Louis who wrote that he was going to roller-skate all the way out to California to marry Peggy.

Peggy:

And that reminds me of a summer, years ago. We picked up notes tied onto rocks that had been thrown onto our front porch—all with the same messsage: "Janet, please come across the street to talk to me. I am going to be your husband—Tom."

We would peek across the street, but never could see the stone-tosser. After two or three days, a couple of teenage boys walked up the front steps. One stood at the end of the porch. The other—resembling a dapper, pipe-smoking Sherlock Holmes—knocked at the front door. Dad opened the door and was greeted with, "Mr. Lennon, I presume. I must speak with Janet." Dad told the boy that Janet was upstairs and asked him what he wanted. "Well, sir, if I must talk to you, will you relay my message to Janet?" He continued, "My name, sir, is Lyle and I am a friend of Tom Flanagan's. You know him as Janet's fiance. Well, I am to be his best man, and I must give Janet her rings."

By then he had opened a box and was holding a wedding band set in his hand. "Tom, sir, is an extremely fine gentleman, and I am proud to be here as part of the wedding family. Come here, Tom."

Then Dad said, "Janet is not engaged to anyone, and there will be no wedding."

"I must talk to Janet myself," Lyle replied. "Because I know she knows of the wedding plans. Come here, Tom!"

As Tom stood shaking at the end of the porch, Lyle then said, "I flew all the way out here from New England, and I'm going to be Janet and Tom's best man. He's my best friend."

By this time, the persistence of Lyle pressured Dad to say, "All right. I'll get Janet to come to the door herself to tell you she does not know your friend Tom and that there will be no wedding."

As Jan, Mom, Dee Dee, and I listened to this conversation, Dee Dee's husband Dick went out the front door to see what was going on. Dick came running in to us, laughing. "This is too much. This guy thinks his silent friend is going to marry Janet. This is unbelievable!"

Once again, Dad went to the door to tell Lyle that we had never heard of Tom Flanagan and he was sorry that both boys had a misconception of the situation. "Janet is in no way, shape, or form ready for marriage," Dad said. "And you boys will just have to fly back home."

"But Mr. Lennon, please let me hear it from Janet's lips. I know she must love Tom, and Tom wants her for his wife. Right, Tom?"

Janet finally came to the door to tell Lyle she really did not know Tom, nor was she in love with him. "You'll just have to go home now. I'm sorry."

This must have convinced Lyle, because he turned slowly away, put his arm around Tom's shoulder, and dejectedly lumbered down our walk, saying, "Don't worry, Tom. We know Janet loves you, and you love Janet, and you'll be together someday . . . ." As Lyle and Tom reached the corner of the street, Lyle suddenly left Tom standing, ran back up the walk to the house, and knocked once again. Dad and Dick opened the door this time. Lyle jauntily removed his pipe from his mouth. "Uh, excuse me, Mr. Lennon," he said. "If it is true that Janet does not love Tom, do you think I have a chance?"

In any event, we did answer our fan letters, Daddy setting aside small stacks for each of us to write some response. He, however, answered the bulk of the correspondence himself. We established many friendships through the mails. In each new city we were curious to meet the faces of some of the letter-writers.

Eventually the fan mail became too much to handle alone. It was then that our friend, Madolin Wilson, who at that time was also our bookkeeper, offered to organize a fan club. Her solution was to send out a newsletter every three or four months, with pictures and facts about us and our family. Madolin's husband Bob, who was at that time redecorating and restoring the interior of our home, was also a part-time photographer. So his talents were put to good use, and he became our fan club photographer.

Betty Sanford was again called upon to render her services in the fan letter department. She has remarked that Dad felt our fan mail was very important and that it should be handled with as much care as any personal letter. The mail would arrive by the box loads; one box could hold 3,000 letters. Ninety-nine percent of them were great. The sick ones were just that—really sick.

We knew some of the fans' letters by sight. Some wrote every week. Whenever Betty or Daddy came across an unusual one, they would share it with us to see how we wanted it answered. When we had the time, we pitched in and helped.

"One time an older man sent Janet a check for ten dollars," Betty recalled, "so she could take her family out for a soda."

Early in our career, during 1957, we had been receiving letters from a family in Portland, Oregon. The father, Dan Cason, had written Dad and told him how he and his wife Shirley, had their own personal Lennon Sisters. Actually, their three daughters, Shirleen, Kathleen, and Madeline, "loved to dress up and imitate your girls." Dan went on to tell Dad, "Bill, I feel I know you and I'm wondering if there is any chance you and the girls could send my three girls autographed pictures." In his letter he sent a photograph of his daughters standing in front of their two-story home, posed as if they were singing. We sent them a picture and continued to correspond for a few months.

One night, as we were packing to go to Spokane, Washington, Dad decided to call Dan Cason. "Hello, Dan Cason? This is Bill Lennon. The girls and I are going to be stopping in Portland at 3:00 a.m., en route to Spokane. Could you possibly bring the girls out to meet us?"

Dan laughed. "Are you kidding?" he said. "They think it's a big deal to know the principal of their school. Of course we'll bring them."

Dad gave the flight number to Dan, and then told us we were going to have a chance to meet the little Cason girls. On the plane that night, we could hardly sleep. We were so anxious to meet our pen pals. The plane landed in Portland, and as we entered the airport terminal, the Cason girls screamed and ran towards us. What could we do but scream and run toward them!

We asked Dan Cason to write us and tell us his impression of that first meeting.

"To be expected," he said, "the Lennon girls were tired, sleepy, and not really given to gush out with a showbiz performance. But the image was not tarnished in our girls' eyes by the rollers in the hair, the wispy strands escaping from Janet's pigtails... My three little girls were awestruck. Never before in their lives had they beheld such a glorious ensemble. From that hour-layover on a chilly windswept March morning, friendships began and resulted in an everlasting bond.

"Striding with his daughters and looking like a combination coach and fashion plate was Bill Lennon. Bill Lennon—the very name is as indelible as any performer's or athlete's we have had the pleasure to know. He walked with an athletic stride; a big, sincere smile was all across a tanned face; and, as though he was welcoming an adversary at a tennis match, he raised his arm and said laughingly, 'Hi, Dan. How are you?'

"I had never met the man, but I knew I had known him for a lifetime. Easy-mannered, in a crisp collar and well-tailored suit, he told me—without saying it—we would always be friends, and we were. The girls were giggling now in their newfound acquaintance, and Bill and I simply talked about the things two fathers talk about with seven little girls in their care."

The Cason family came to visit us many times. Not just for an evening or two, and at our encouragement they stayed in our home. During these visits, we developed strong emotional ties. It took very little persuasion to convince them to move from Portland to Venice. They rented a small house two blocks away, but until they could move into it, they lived with us. All nineteen of us shared beds, dishes, curlers, one bathroom, and the ability to find humor in almost everything.

Dan Cason's favorite story of this time concerns the day he and Dad went out into the country. "Here we are," Dad told Dan.

Dan recalls that he looked around and said, "Where are we?"

In the middle of practically nowhere, "stood a little fellow, probably a millionaire, in front of a replica of what had once been a vegetable stand," Dan said. "Although it hadn't collapsed, it seemed like a good idea to walk up to it sideways. Once we got within range of the contents, however, one didn't have to be a farmer to see that it was the real thing. The Horn of Plenty should have seen it. All Bill wanted was corn, three bushel baskets of corn.

"We returned to the home patio, and Bill prepared a fire in the patio pit. After the fire was going, it was time to round up all the burlap bags we could find. Everybody had a job to do, and as I remember, nobody did it. But burlap bags we got. Now, at around 4:00 p.m. it was time for the corn. Everybody stood and watched as Bill dumped the cobs into washtubs of brine. Around 6:30, the kids were beginning to complain, and the laughter and clowning were diminishing, and the corn was receiving a few glances.

"Nana spoke for everyone by asking when that 'darned stuff' would be ready. None of this fazed Bill, as he was in charge, and he would say when it was ready. The hour of 7:30 came and went, with Nana declaring something about 'that nut' not knowing what he was doing. Then 8:30 came and went. The adults stood looking at each other, and Nana stated that 'these poor kids are going to starve.'

" 'Okay, we're ready,' Bill called out. And to everyone's delight, he reached for the brine-soaked corn, spread the brine-soaked burlap on wire grates over the charcoal beds, and began stacking the corn on the burlap, then more burlap, then more corn, exulting all the time that an epicurean delight awaited us. Around 9:30, with everyone finding fault with everyone over absolutely nothing, Bill assured each and all that it would be well worth waiting for. Nana said, 'Baloney! I'm going to my room. If that nut ever gets ready, you can bring it to me.'

"Around 10:30, Bill told the remaining adults that the magic time had arrived. I never revealed my feeling to him, for though I was no cook, I could only reflect on my wife Shirley popping some cobs in boiling water for a short time, slapping some butter on the golden kernels, and it tasting every bit as good. But Bill had had his hour, not only in the sun, but the moon and stars as well."

11

Some Day My Prince Will Come

Dianne:

There are many advantages to being the oldest child in a large family. There are also disadvantages. And for me, the subject of dating qualifies under both categories. When I was in the seventh grade, Dad and Mom decided to help organize a teenage club in our parish. So my first real boy-girl relationships were at our church recreation hall.

We met every Friday night from 7:30 to about 10:00. The evening's activities included table shuffleboard, cards, darts, ping pong, crafts, and/or dancing to records. Usually it was "and." Though I had many childhood crushes on boys, my first real boyfriend was Mike Gass. The Gass family was one of the large families in our parish, with eight children. Except for their oldest son, they had a boy or girl in the same class with each one of my sisters and brothers. Mike and I enjoyed attending the Friday night meetings of the teenage club, but we also enjoyed taking the bus to Culver City Saturday afternoons to see a movie. Many times he just dropped by the house to help me babysit—and, of course, watch television. Dad loved that, because Michael always brought a box of butterscotch candies, which disappeared quickly. I liked visiting Mike's folks, who lived across the street from Grandma Lennon. His dad had a wonderful sense of humor, and his mother made me feel at home at any time, allowing me to help feed and dress her three youngest daughters.

Real dating began for me when I reached ninth grade at St. Monica High School. It was the usual sock-hops, football games, movies, Goody-Goody Drive-In for a milkshake, Tony's Pizza Parlor, and assorted school activities. At home I did not have what could be termed the usual father. He was not an Ozzie Nelson nor a Robert Young, nor even a Danny Thomas or Hugh Beaumont; our dad had prepared and studied his own courses on fatherhood.

When a guy came to pick me up for a date, he was greeted with, "How fast do you drive?" Dad inspected the car and gave him a quick, practiced lecture on the dangers of speeding, and then, to relieve the pressure a little, he would pipe, "Let me see if your socks match."

But the boy got the message!

After each date, I would sit on my folks' bed and tell them about my evening, knowing full well that Dad would question me about everything.

"Did you sit close to him?"

"Yes, Daddy."

"Did he hold your hand?"

"Sometimes . . . ."

"Did he, maybe . . . kiss you goodnight?"

"Daddy!"

"Well, if you kiss him, you gotta marry him."

During my first two years of high school, I was presented with a problem that none of my brothers or sisters had to go through. Dad and Mom slept on a hide-a-bed in the living room, *right next to the front door*. It is not easy to kiss a boyfriend goodnight, knowing that your dad is right on the other side of the door. Especially *my* dad!!!

The guys, however, liked Dad, because he always seemed to have time for them, whether it was a game of football in the street or a quick golf lesson on the front lawn. He loved kids, and every kid knew that. I don't believe they resented Dad's over-protectiveness of any of his daughters—on the contrary, they respected him for it.

During the high school years, I had many boyfriends. Tom was a great dancer and my best girlfriend's brother. I went with Pat for quite a while, until he borrowed and lost my dad's 9-iron golf club. Bob was a superb athlete and came from a big family like mine, but he loved to sing when we danced, and it always made me giggle. Everyone knows you can't be romantic and giggle at the same time. Now Freddie was the boy who taught me how to shift the gears of his 1954 Ford—a lesson most girls of the time learned, to enable their boyfriend's to put one arm around them while driving. (It is a shame that, for the last few decades, automobile manufacturers have deprived the youth of the steering wheel gear shift! And thrust them into bucket seats as well!)

During my memorable senior year, I had a crush on Pat Young, the all C.I.F. (California Interscholastic Federation) quarterback of our league-winning school football team. And he liked me. As if that were not exciting enough, I was elected Homecoming Queen of 1956-57. What more could a senior girl ask for?

But because of our busy work schedule as The Lennon Sisters, I was not able to join many clubs or groups during high school. There were very few days in my junior and senior years when I did not have rehearsals, dress fittings, pictures, or interviews after school hours. So my friendships with the other girls were limited. I think they even thought of me as a bit of a snob due to my natural shyness and lack of involvement in school activities.

The 1950s decade has enjoyed a great revival recently, and I'm glad I was a teenager then—poodle skirts, ruffled petticoats, jeweled angora collars, ponytails, the bop, and the hop.

It has been said that we were a naive generation, and I think we were. But I'm thankful that my dating years were free of many of the added pressures that kids nowadays have to face, along with the normal ups and downs of just being a teenager.

Dick Gass and I started dating in the fall of 1957. (Dick was the older brother of my first boyfriend, Mike.) I had graduated from high school that previous June and had spent a long summer on tour. It was on October 16, at Mimi's second birthday party, that I "arranged" our first date. Dick's mother had brought her two-year-old Debbie to the party. As Mimi was opening her gifts, I casually asked Mrs. Gass what Dick had been doing for the past few years. I had seen him walk to Mass every Sunday with his girlfriend, and I thought, frankly, he was really cute. I kept prodding her all afternoon, hoping that she might mention it to him. She did—and he called that night to ask for a date. I admit to this creative manipulation, and at his call could scarcely believe the scheme had worked.

However, my excitement was short-lived, for our first date was a real bomb!

Each thought the other wanted to go to the St. Monica alumni football game and dance. We had both recently broken up with long-time steadies, and we felt all eyes on us as a new couple. Besides that, he was a good dancer, and I couldn't dance anything but the Balboa, which Daddy had taught me. The whole evening was a disaster—I should have taken as a bad omen the fact that I stepped into a huge mud puddle before entering his car.

By the end of the evening, I was sure that he never wanted to see me again, and I could not blame him. Nevertheless, with that in mind, I acted against Dad's principle that girls-should-never-call-boys-on-the-telephone to invite Dick to go ice-skating with me and a group of friends. On that date I spilled a chocolate chip milkshake all over him in the car. From that time on, we never dated anyone else.

We really got along well, but we did meet with one obstacle—my little sister Mimi. She was my special girl, and vice-versa. I took Mimi everywhere with me. I loved to buy her frilly dresses and curl her hair; I even took her to the studio rehearsals at ABC. I was her Dee Dee, and she was not about to share me with this stranger. But—like it or not—Dick Gass became a big part of my life very quickly, and every time his car pulled into the driveway, she began screaming, "Don't go, Dee Dee, don't go."

Thus, Dick first bestowed the nickname "Screamy Mimi" on my baby sister, and it remained with her for several years. In order to get me out the front door without Mimi hanging onto my legs, Dick used to tell her that he was taking me to the dentist or the doctor.

Most of our dates were spent riding the trams along the beach, walking down by the ocean, or dancing.

Knowing he might be drafted into the Army, Dick enlisted, so that in two years he could fulfill his military obligations, and then we could marry. We did not tell anyone our plans, but I think almost everyone knew we were happy with each other. In June of 1958, he left for Fort Ord, California, and after basic training, he volunteered for the paratroopers and joined the 82nd Airborne Division at Fort Bragg, North Carolina. This was the only time during my singing career I was glad we did tours, because whenever we were anywhere near the east coast, Dick would somehow finagle a pass to come see me. We ice-skated in Rockefeller Center, New York, and walked along the boardwalk in Atlantic City.

Dick obtained a two-week leave in July of 1959, in order to come home and visit. One night, as we drove up the coast, he suddenly asked me if I would like an engagement ring. We had not planned to get engaged until he was out of the service, but I ecstatically accepted. The following day we slipped away and purchased my ring, but decided to wait one more day before announcing our engagement. The ring burned a hole in Dick's pocket. On the Fourth of July, we drove up Pacific Coast Highway to a favorite restaurant, The Sea Lion, to have abalone. He gave me my ring, and we drove straight back home to tell my folks. But no one was home! The family had gone to watch the fireworks on Ocean Park Pier, and had left early to find a good location in one of the parking lots along the beach. By this hour, we were so anxious to tell somebody that the twelve-house drive from my parents' to his parents' seemed like an eternity.

In great excitement we ran in and blurted out that we were going to be married. His mother, in the middle of changing sheets on her bed, hugged us both. But Dick's dad spoke nonchalantly. "I never doubted it for one moment," he said. They had been very special people to me, and I was proud that I would become their daughter-in-law.

We took to the road to track down my folks. One hour (and four parking lots) later, we found Dad's station wagon filled—Dad, Mom, nine brothers and sisters, and three neighbor children! Dick had prepared a little speech, but after hearing the noises of the fireworks and seeing the huge gang in the car, he simply said, "Sis and Bill, we're engaged."

The kids began yelling and hugging us. Mom, feeding baby Annie a bottle, said, "I'm so happy for you." Dad, on the other hand, could not speak. He opened the car door and got out, walked once around the car, got back in, and sat down. I'm sure he could not believe that one of his girls was really going to leave him. "Dee Dee, you couldn't have a nicer guy," he said after a long time. That was all. It was over, the news was out, and we had survived it. What an Independence Day! (Dad went to bed for a month.)

Still, we had to settle with Mimi. I went into her bedroom the following morning and held my little sister on my lap. The news that

Dick would be gone for a year and a half before he would whisk me off may have soothed her, or the fact that I would not move too far away after my marriage, allowed her troubled little mind to accept the inevitable. At least, as well as any three-year-old girl could accept the thought of losing her big sister to a man.

A few days later, Dick was again in North Carolina, and I was back at work, touring for the summer. It was not until the following April that he was home for good. He returned to cable-splicing for the telephone company, his job before entering the Army. I decided I would quit singing when we married, and I told my parents that all I wanted to do was stay home and raise a family. They both understood my feelings, but it was hard for Daddy to accept the fact that I would leave the quartet. What would the other girls do, since I was the lead singer? Would the public accept The Lennon Sisters as a trio? We had a whole summer of touring to talk and plan for the big change; Dad tried hard to change my mind. Even Mr. Welk invited Dick and me to his house one evening, to try to convince me to stay.

It was Kay Esser who gave me the last little shove to stick by my decision. She wrote me a letter that I still read on occasions. "Dee Dee," she wrote, "Everything you have ever done in your life, you have done because you felt it was right and good. You are making this decision with the same reasoning and deserve to be a wife and mother which you've waited for all your life . . . . Be happy in your decision. Your Dad loves you and will be happy for you and Dick . . . ."

It was what I needed to hear. Through it all, Mom supported me and told me to leave Dad in her hands.

It was settled! On October 16, 1960, three years from our first date, and on Mimi's fifth birthday, I became Mrs. Richard Gass— and no longer one of the singing Lennon Sisters.

What a wedding it was! Dick and I were the first in our big families to marry, so the guests were numerous—1,500 to be exact. Our little church could not hold more than half that number, so the overflow spilled into the streets. The wedding party was almost as many, it seemed. Seven bridesmaids, including my sisters, dressed in long, aqua-blue chiffon dresses. Peggy was my maid of honor, wearing a gown of pale yellow. All my attendants wore large tulle picture hats and resembled old-fashioned Southern belles. Dick's

brothers and several friends served as ushers, dressed in white dinner coats, black pants, and red boutonnieres. Nearly stealing the
spotlight from the bride were the two adorable five-year-old flower
girls, Mimi Lennon and Debbie Gass, followed by six-year-old ring-
bearer, Billy Lennon.

Daddy left the house for the first time since his heart attack to
give me away. I'm not sure whether he held me up or I supported
him, but I hung onto his arm for dear life. I remember looking down
that long aisle toward the altar, as Daddy and I shared a special
inside joke. Seeing Dick's smiling face at the other end of that tunnel
reassured me that our moment had finally arrived!

After we had recited our vows and the wedding party had left the
altar, the Mass was supposed to begin, leaving Dick and me kneeling in the center of the sanctuary. It was then, with our backs to the
congregation, that we recognized the sound of something taking
place behind us—the collection baskets were being passed. At our
wedding! Dick and I stared at each other in utter disbelief.
Although humiliated, we could do nothing about it—until the
ceremony was over. Later, we confronted our pastor, begging to
know why the collection had been taken. His answer was simple:
"It was a Sunday Mass, and many of those people were fulfilling
their Sunday obligation. Supporting their parish is part of their
duty. I realize now that many of those people were not Catholic,
and I probably should not have done it. It was not a good decision on my part."

(I really did not want to write about this incident, but my sisters told me I should, as it would give Dick and me an opportunity
to explain—nearly 25 years later— how embarrassed we were
about the situation. What could we say? It was over and done
with. But for years Dick's friends from the telephone company
and people from the Lawrence Welk organization asked us,
"What did you two do with all that money collected at your
wedding?")

Our wedding reception was held at the Aragon Ballroom. We
stood in the receiving line for nearly three hours and never did
get anything to eat—except for the taste of a small piece of cake and
the glasses of champagne that were used for the standard wedding pictures.

Later, when we had changed into our going-away clothes, we

Dee Dee and her date, Dick Gass, 1958. *(The Lennon Sisters Collection)*

When we were three—Dee Dee "retired" to married life. *(The Lennon Sisters Collection)*

When we were three—with Andy Williams on his TV Show, 1962. *(The Lennon Sisters Collection)*

Dee Dee returns to us, and we're four Lennons again (Janet, Kathy, Dianne, Peggy). *(The Lennon Sisters Collection)*

drove to my parents' home to pick up my trousseau. This quick stop proved to be a most fitting and well remembered beginning to my new life. As we ran up the stairs to snatch my suitcases, we passed Dad and Mom's bedroom; the door was open, and we could see Dad lying on the bed, taking his required afternoon nap, still recuperating from his recent illness. Unable to attend our reception, he had gone home after the ceremony. "I'm not asleep," he said. "Come in for a minute."

In the dimly lit room, Dick and I sat at the foot of Dad's bed. He took my hand in his. In those few quiet moments, the three of us shared few words together, but our emotions were deep, warm, and good.

Our honeymoon was spent driving through northern California, thanks to Kath's wedding gift—the use of her brand new Lincoln. Finally, Dick and I were alone for ten whole days—at least, we thought we were alone. The second day, we stopped at a grocery store to buy some popcorn. As we stood at the counter to pay, we noticed several people glancing our way and smiling. Dick looked around to see what was causing the commotion and saw our wedding pictures plastered across the front pages of all the newspapers, captioned, "DICK AND DEE DEE ON HONEYMOON."

Another incident still makes us laugh. On our wedding night, as I was changing into a beautiful negligee, Dick went into the bathroom to shower. A few minutes later, the door opened and there he was—dressed in a dark purple satin robe similar to a smoking jacket. I tried not to laugh, but he looked too debonair for the unsophisticated guy I had just married. As my laughter became tears, he began to laugh at himself.

"I *knew* this would happen," he said. "My mother forced me into packing Dad's robe. I've never even worn one in my whole life, but she insisted that I couldn't go on a honeymoon with Dee Dee without a robe."

Knowing Dick's wonderful old-fashioned mom made the situation funnier. We were going to enjoy our new life together, with in-laws like ours. We couldn't miss. And the relationships we had with each other's parents continued to grow through our married years, bringing us all closer—especially Dick and my dad. They became truly best friends, attending track meets, football games, boxing matches, or any and every sporting event together. Once in awhile, Mom and I were allowed the privilege of tagging along; knowing they shared a companionship that was unique, we enjoyed these events even more. I think it was the mutual respect of character, the love of sports, and the genuine appreciation of the humor in everyday life that brought those two men so close. I know that I have been blessed with the love of two men in my life—my dad and my husband. When Dad died, a special part of Dick's and my life ended, not a part we shared with each other, but a part we had each shared with Dad.

I retired from the entertainment world, and for more than three years I was a housewife. I loved every minute of it—it's what I do best.

In the autumn of 1963, the telephone company employees went on strike, and for five-and-a-half months Dick walked the picket line. The next January, we adopted our little Mary, and then I became pregnant. Dick was still not back at work.

On a Saturday morning in February, I was surprised by a telephone call from Mr. Welk. "How are you, Dianne?" he began. "I have heard that you have a new baby and that Dick has not been able to work for several months. Maybe I can help you out. Would you like to come and sing on my TV show for a while? I'd love to have you back with us." He said that I could leave whenever I wanted.

It was a very tempting offer for us. As new parents, and planning for the future of our fast-growing family, we decided to accept the proposal. I returned to the work I had thought was behind me. Children have a way of enriching and yet altering their parents' lives!

Living so near, our own parents proved to be a great asset to me when I returned to work with The Lennon Sisters and the Welk organization. Dick's mother and dad were directly across the street; having raised their eight children, they welcomed the chance to babysit for our little girls. With my parents just a few houses away, babysitters were plentiful. So, as I re-entered the world of entertainment, two-and-a-half days a week each grandmother took and spoiled a granddaughter and the grandpas teased and enchanted the children who were with them so frequently. This situation made it easier for me to return to work. I knew our baby girls were receiving all the love and attention they needed, and so too were their grandparents.

Peggy:

When I was an eighth-grader, a member of the first graduating class of St. Mark school, Venice, I tried out for the lead in the Stephen Foster musical that would be presented at the end of the school year. My self-confidence, singing voice, and natural brown locks were just the right thing for the part of "Jeannie With The Light Brown Hair." I was really good—I can't lie!

I didn't lie to my family either. They couldn't stand the new me. Lost in my loveliness, I would glide down the hall, singing, "Beautiful Dreamer."

"Prepare the way for the star," I would hear one of the family say. "Oh no, here she comes again," would be whispered, one to another. Of course, I didn't know what they meant. I mean, I could *not* learn my lines unless I practiced them over and over again, now could I? They no longer called me "The Madonna," but chose then to call me "Prima Donna." You can't win!

My personality of angel-actress was somewhat subdued by the time I was in high school. Or at least tempered by more mature thought. It was not easy to blend the two qualities of angel and actress and have them be compatible. Once, I remember arriving home with a date and having to fight the guy off after a goodnight kiss. "What's the matter with you?" he yelled. "How can you dance and laugh and have a terrific time the way you did tonight, and still be so holy, too?"

Of course, I never saw that boy again!

I dated my share of guys when in high school, although I was not extremely popular. Not by a long shot. I was friendly with most of the girls in my class, but I felt like an outsider. I doubt anyone knew that. Throughout my four years at St. Monica High, I dated the star football player. Len Kelly and his fellow lettermen were the popular clique in school. They dated the cutest, most popular group of girls, and I was included in their parties and fun. I don't think I would have been in that group if it weren't for the fact that I was Len's girl. I did not smoke or drink, not because I was a prude, but because I just didn't like the taste of the stuff. Also, I was not about to break the law buying those things and ruin my health at the same time; that was plain stupid. I guess it's safe to say I was not your basic wild party girl.

My sisters and I have been laughing about dates and miseries we went through as teenagers—everything was ruled by emotion. That was my tie to Len Kelly. He was fun, he was a letterman, his family was terrific, and there was that chemistry that drew us together. Nothing on the intellectual level, but he was fun to be with.

Once, on a tour, I had received a letter from him telling me that he would be at the airport to pick us up. As I walked down the ramp, I saw him standing there, six feet, two inches tall, broad shouldered, sheepish grin—and bald as a cue ball! I was furious. He wasn't the world's most handsome young man, but with his shaved head he looked like a human bullet. How could he humiliate me like that? I stormed right past him and didn't stop until I was in the car.

But Len did have a way about him. I even believed him when he told me that the coach made *all* the players shave their heads for spring practice. Yet, not one other guy at school was bald. See what I mean?

I enjoyed high school, and my grades were above average. I might have gone on to a university if I had not been a working girl. I still have hopes of going to college one day, but at the present rate I won't get there until I am eighty!

As I grew older, I found myself once again considering a religious vocation. Only this time I felt myself in a position to compare and decide. I had not found a man who cared to share my deep thoughts and philosophies, so perhaps this was God's way of showing me the path. Certainly, I had no inkling of what lay ahead for me.

In the spring of 1962, we toured the southern states with the Welk band. On one of the milk-run hops we so often flew, I took a seat next to a relatively new member of the band, trumpet player Dick Cathcart. He was a quiet person. I think he had been with the show three or four months and had made few acquaintances. Sitting with him, I mentioned this fact. "Well, Peg, I know I'm not the most outgoing person, but I've met and worked with a lot of people in my life, and it seems the ones to whom I give my friendship have hurt me. I guess you could say I'm gun-shy."

We talked, too, about music, commenting on his unique style of trumpet work, particularly his solo performances. He played all the great jazz trumpet solos for Jack Webb's *Pete Kelly's Blues*, both the film and the television series. I had some of those record albums and told him how much I loved his playing. But I really made a fool of myself a few minutes later. "You know," I said, turning back to Dick. "I think the greatest jazz or Dixie music I've ever heard is on an album you've probably never heard of. It's an original composition on the sights and sounds and essence of New Orleans, written by Paul Weston. You'd just love it. It's the most creative and best-played music I've ever heard. It's called 'Crescent City.' "

He nodded his head as I continued talking. "And Pete Fountain gave me a copy. He said it's the only album he plays when he's away from New Orleans. I've listened to the album so many times it's worn thin. I think if I were an orchestra I could play every note from memory. The musicianship of the performers is just extraordinary. I'll see if I can find you a copy. You really should hear it."

In the special way that is only his, Dick quietly unfastened the band of his wristwatch. He turned the watch over for me. On the back, engraved in gold, I read: *To Dick, thanks for Crescent City, Paul Weston*.

"So you know the whole album, huh?" remarked Dick. I just sat there in my embarrassment. I had never stopped to read the back of the album cover. Dick had played all the music; that great trumpet work I so admired was his. (Years later I was to recall that incident when lying in the labor room with our first child, timing my pains to that same watch.)

We became friends from that conversation and trip, and something stirred within me when he remarked that he knew I was a Catholic and that perhaps I might know answers to some questions that were puzzling him. He told me he was taking instruction in the Catholic faith, that he was searching for truth. It was a trying time in his life. He was in the process of divorce, and he sorely missed his three children.

In the months that followed, we grew closer. How could this be happening? All those feelings I knew existed, but not for me, began to well up in me until all I could think of was Dick. My good sense told me that this was a situation I had no right to encourage. Yet, at the same time, Dick realized we were in love. That was an agonizing time for us; we had no choice but to acknowledge our dilemma. We were trapped by our love and our circumstance. Here we were, Catholic in our beliefs, knowing that we could not marry without Church approval, and we wanted that desperately.

Then began two years of investigation by the Church Tribunal to see if circumstances surrounding Dick's first marriage would permit the blessing of ours. We did not date, but met occasionally at my home or at the studio for lunch. Mom and Dad were terribly upset by our relationship. I assume if my daughter had come to me involved in a similar situation I too would worry. Here was a man sixteen years older than I, divorced, and the father of three children. The law of averages said there was very little chance of success if we married. But for some reason, I knew this was my destiny. Dick and I wondered if God could have made a mistake, having us born out of time, so to speak. We prayed together, knowing that if this was God's plan for us, we would accept it.

My parents liked Dick well enough, but they had great concern regarding Church law and reactions from family and friends to this unusual relationship. Dee Dee had married the boy next door. With so many unattached men around, why *couldn't* I have chosen one of them? We had to live with hurt feelings and confused ideas.

Dick toured with us in the summer of 1963 and conducted our music. It was wonderful to be able to see him every day, but I lived with the thought that perhaps we would be faced with Church disapproval of our bid. We returned home from that trip, feeling lost at having to return to everyday life. Then Dick phoned. "How would you like to go to dinner tonight with a single man? I just received our papers from the Church. Everything is okay!"

And indeed, everything was okay. Mom and Dad gave their blessing. "How can we object? The church approves. You both know the problems involved. And we love you."

We married the following spring, on May 24, 1964, at St. Mark Church. The logistics were incredible, and at one point Mom suggested we save our money and run off to Las Vegas.

"No, no," Dad said. "I gave Dee Dee and Dick a big wedding, and I'm proud to give you one, too." So Church of St. Mark it was; and thousands of people lined the streets to glimpse my finery.

There were a few problems. Little brother Joey, who was then nine, was our ring bearer. Dressed in his tuxedo, he looked splendid—but just a little flushed. The closer it got to the time for the wedding, the redder he became. Then his face broke out in spots. Measles! He went to the church anyway. "I just can't miss Peg's wedding." I shudder to think how many others may have felt a little flushed two weeks later.

Ten-year-old Mimi was dressed in a pink gown with a little flower basket about her wrist. As she was about to lead the procession down the aisle, she turned around and started screaming. "I can't go down that aisle by myself. I just can't!" And she cried and wailed until we finally coaxed eleven-year-old Carrie, Dick's daughter, to proceed first. Carrie was crying, too, but Screamy Mimi was louder.

Father Joel was at the altar, and Monsignor Wade, our pastor, gave a beautiful homily. And then Father Marty married us. Or at least I think he did. I got confused and called Dick "Richard Charles" instead of "Charles Richard." Dick could not get the ring on my finger, and Father Marty growled in his booming voice, "Let her put it on herself, schnookie. You'll break her arm."

After the reception, held at the Miramar Hotel in Santa Monica, I realized that I had left my makeup case at home. (How could I let Dick see me without makeup?) So we returned to Harding Avenue. Makeup case in hand and about to leave again from the house, I answered the ringing telephone. It was our pastor—he couldn't find Father Marty, and the marriage certificate hadn't been signed. Dick grabbed my hand and shoved me out the door. "Honey," he said. "If after that two-hour ceremony and all those prayers and all the hullabaloo we still are not married, then we'll just have to live in sin."

We spent two days at the Madonna Inn in San Luis Obispo, California, about three hours drive from Venice. The beautiful hotel complex was named after a man named Madonna, not the Blessed Mother. But what more fitting name for the honeymoon hideaway of the former "St. Therese?"

Kathy:

Being in the public eye was like living in a fishbowl at times. This could have caused difficulties in my being accepted by my teenage peers. However, I was treated as one of the gang, and dated boys from my school. I fell in love many times, but my first real steady was Ken Del Conte, the boy who had everything. He was a great athlete, very handsome, and he was the first write-in candidate to be elected student body president at the University of Southern California in forty years. He was also crazy, fearless, and enchanting in his attentiveness. About once a month throughout all the period of our dating, Ken would stand beneath my second story window and serenade me with his guitar.

"Tell him I'm asleep," I'd whisper to Janet. "Tell him I'm not home. Tell him anything. He'll listen to you, but get rid of him. If he wakes Dad, I'm grounded. It's way after our curfew . . . ."

Dad was especially strict on the nights before we had to leave on tours. It was a must to be in our beds by midnight, so we could be up early, rested, and ready for the plane flight. But one night before I left on a tour, Kenny took me to see the movie *West Side Story*. We were home a little after midnight, so I quickly and quietly said goodnight to him and slowly crept on my hands and knees up the stairs, careful to bypass the squeaky fifth and ninth steps. Relieved to hear Dad snoring, I climbed safely into bed. After a time, though, I heard the melodic strains of the love song from *West Side Story*. It was Kenny under my window. "Maria . . . I just met a girl named Maria . . . ."

"Janet, tell him to go away!" I whispered. She went to the window and tried to get rid of him for me, but he would not be dissuaded. He started to climb up to the window, and nothing would stop him. "Oh, go away," I insisted. "Daddy will ground me if you wake him up."

"I can't get down," Kenny said. "I had a wineglass in my pocket. I was going to give it to you, but it broke when I was climbing up, and if I try to climb down I'll cut myself. You've got to let me in."

I was in a state of panic but decided the only thing to do was to let him in and hope he could slip out of the house without waking everyone. Janet and I laboriously removed twelve louvres from our window so that Kenny could crawl his way into our room. "Now you must leave, please," I begged. Kenny went out my door and tiptoed down the stairway, skipping steps nine and five. I heaved a great sigh of relief when I gently closed the front door and triumphantly returned to bed.

The next morning, I was still in fear that Daddy had heard the whole episode, but he didn't say a word about it. Janet and Peg and I made all the preparations to leave for the airport. We kissed Mom and Dad goodbye. But as I was going out the door, Dad's voice wafted after me. "Goodbye, Maria . . . ."

Two USC friends of Kenny's were Tom (Turbo) Trbovich and Terry McGee, whom we had known at St. Monica High School. Those three, with Peg, Jan, and me, became the six inseparables. As buddies, we went everywhere together. They would take us to the studio and then pick us up after the shows, drive us to the airport when we left for tours, and meet us after almost every trip. Like countless others, they became part of our family. And while we were on the road, their interest in the family did not stop. Those guys would take at least four or five of our little brothers and sisters to drive-in movies, slot-car races, or to the beach. It would be an understatement to say that we six had fun together. There were the USC Sigma Chi fraternity parties, beach parties, penny arcade ventures, miniature golfing escapades, and all the excitement that most girls have in their college days, but without the obligation of the book reports, theme papers, and exams.

I dated Ken for three years before we began to have problems. "If you argue before you are married," Mom and Dad always said, "you will argue after you marry. People don't change, basically." I realized that they were right and that this was not the man I wanted to live with for the rest of my life. So I decided we would go our separate ways.

In 1966, when I was 22 years old, my heart was captured by one of the musicians in the Lawrence Welk band. He was a well-respected performer, shy and kind, and handsome. In our developing relationship, although there was a twenty-year difference in our ages, we had a wonderful rapport and kinship. I told my parents of my feelings, and their concern for me was deep. I followed their advice and sought counseling. I was advised to wait. He was divorced, and perhaps the Church would not approve this marriage.

I had been taught to make my own decisions, to choose those things that I felt were the right things to do, to trust myself to find the key that was essential to my own well-being. And I begged my parents to trust me to find that key for myself. However, the laws of our Church were in conflict with my spirit.

During that era of closed-mindedness and strict tradition, Jews married Jews, Greeks married Greeks, Blacks married Blacks, Protestants married Protestants, and "good Catholic girls" wouldn't dare to date a non-Catholic or a divorced man. In today's society, with its deeper understanding of humanity, this experience seems alien. But this was my first real conflict with my parents and our beliefs.

For many months we agonized over whether we should marry. Often we ended these conversations in tears. At one point, he voiced a willingness to leave the Welk group so that we would no longer be subjected to each other. I asked him to attend a series of classes given by the Church, so that he might learn more about Catholicism and try to understand my family's pressures. But it was difficult for me to accept the tenets of the Church. I sought the advice of a Paulist priest who worked with problem marriage cases. The conclusion was that the Church had its rules, it was all black or white. In this case, there was no approval. "If you cannot obey the rules, then you must find your own peace with Christ," we were instructed. "Whatever you decide," the priest said, "be happy and live with it."

In June of 1967, I made my decision. I told my parents; I wished I could spare them grief, but I did not want to do anything behind their backs. We talked with Dad and tried to allay his fears and disappointment. "I want her to be able to make the choice for herself," was my dad's response. My mother asked one more time if we could wait. She pointed out that, if I married, I would "be throwing your life as a Catholic out the window."

"I still feel I am a Catholic," I said, remaining painfully firm, "even if I am not allowed the sacraments of the Church." Mom and I talked and cried together. I was able to understand that it was not within my parents training or their tradition to even contemplate, let alone accept, their daughter marrying someone outside of the Church.

We made our plans, deciding to take advantage of the annual Lawrence Welk engagement at Lake Tahoe to have our ceremony there a few days prior to our opening show. The evening before we left for Lake Tahoe, we dined with Dee Dee and Dick. Jan had given birth to baby Billy two weeks earlier, and Peggy was due to deliver her baby any day. Actually, I was not sure if my sisters could compromise their religious beliefs and go with us, and I was afraid to ask, for fear of putting them in a very awkward position.

I still had some misgivings. When we applied for our marriage license, I was recognized. As a prominent Catholic in the public eye, I had a sudden vision of newspaper reporters and movie magazine photographers up in the trees trying to get the story. At that point, I was even concerned about ruining The Lennon Sisters' reputation.

Although I had cherished dreams of a wedding gown, a veil, and all my family and friends attending, our marriage was just the two of us exchanging vows in a small chapel in an old Victorian house. Our gala wedding breakfast was at a coffee shop in Carson City, after which we drove up beautiful Highway 50 to Lake Tahoe. At my request, we stopped at small St. Theresa's Catholic Church, and in that sanctuary we knelt and recited a prayer. I took the gardenia I had been given that morning and placed it at the feet of the statue of the Blessed Mother. I remembered my sisters had presented their bridal bouquets in the same way.

After the Lake Tahoe engagement, we returned home. I had called my parents several times during our three-week stay there. On the last phone call, I told Mom our arrival time in Venice, and she said she would have a big pot of spaghetti on the stove.

When we drove up to the front of the house several hours later, my heart was pounding. Daddy came out to greet us. I'll never forget the look on his face. He smiled grimly and said, "Well, how was the trip?" That was all. The house was quiet, although most of the kids were around. I felt I would cry, so I ran upstairs, claiming I was going to get some things I needed. I rummaged around in a bottom dresser drawer, trying to keep myself occupied when my baby brother Kippy appeared at the door. "Did you really get married?" he asked.

"Yes, I got married, Kippy," I replied and put my arms around his six-year-old hips.

"Did you have anybody else for your ring bearer?"

"No, Kippy. You know I could not have had anyone else but you."

After he left the room, I cried. I was not afraid of the love I was feeling, but I was strangely afraid of—and for—the great love of my family.

My marriage lasted twelve years, nearly half of my adult life. We had moments of great beauty, and there were sad times. I have respected his request by not mentioning his name nor detailing the years of our marriage. Relationships are long or they are short, but I believe most are divinely inspired. We extend our commitment to a relationship beyond what may seem benevolent, but we care about ourselves and those we love, and at some point we have to be able to say aloud to the deepest corner of our soul: *I Did My Best*. And when a relationship has the two persons dividing, we want to say our loved one did his best.

Real love never goes away. It just takes its given place within the heart.

Janet:

"See that guy over there? I just know I'm going to marry him someday!" Kathy and I were standing on the ABC Sound Stage, preparing to rehearse. The side stage door had just opened, and a very handsome guy stuck his head in and looked around. In those days, about mid-1964, I was just out of high school and still on the lookout for cute guys. But this time an overwhelming feeling crept over me . . . .

I was twelve years old when I experienced my first real crush. A highly emotional age I admit, and to me Stan was "the end." He was an eighth-grade classmate. He was not only a nice boy, but he looked just like Ricky Nelson without his braces. That's as close to perfection as anyone could get. We attended our first mixed parties together, and we loved dancing to rock and roll. Dad teased me, saying we looked like we were plowing the north forty.

Stan and I shared a common interest in sports. He was heavy into Little League at the time. I don't think he ever kissed me, because we were both too shy. However, to this day, the smell of L. B. Butch Wax drives me wild.

When I entered high school in 1960, I was a very young fourteen years old. I had a public image to uphold, and I desperately wanted a calm private life, like other girls. Frightened of the responsibility involved in growing up, I chose instead to cling to childhood, which to me represented security. So I played with my dolls and dressed in identical outfits with my girlfriend, Joni Esser. On the first day of high school, we called each other and decided to wear our Tyrolean-print dresses with the peekaboo sleeves. Hers was blue, mine was pink. We were so excited that morning, looking like a couple of Bavarian Twinkies as we walked down the alley and into the main yard of St. Monica's High. You tend to grow up really fast when a whole schoolyard of your peers points at you and laughs.

High-school dating was rather sporadic, since we were at the peak of our traveling years. I was not at home all that much; Kathy and I did our studies on the road more than in classrooms. But I did have a special boyfriend throughout those four years. I consider the tall, dark, handsome, witty Santa Monica surfbum Nicky to be my "first love." I centered my whole life around him, and he in turn centered his entire life around his surfboard. Oh, I did date a lot of other boys during those years, but my heart belonged to Nicky. It didn't matter how many times he stood me up; I made excuses for him. Mostly the kind that had to do with the rising and falling of the surf. When he did show, I would be dressed up and ready; he would be just off the beach, half-dressed, and in bare feet. But personality? Absolutely. Even Dad and Mom were charmed by him; all he had to do was smile with those big dimples, and everything was all right.

I did not sit at home alone, though. I'll never forgive Kathy for the time she fixed me up with a blind date so she wouldn't have to attend a big dance with her blind date alone.

The guys arrived to pick us up, and I knew from the way he handed me my extra-long wrist corsage (which went halfway up my arm) and—of all things—clicked his heels and said, "Good evening, madam," this guy was a real winner! Within five minutes I learned from him that he spoke five languages fluently and he had acquired his fine dancing skills at cotillions. When he dragged me across the floor during the polka and made a complete spectacle during the Mexican Hat Dance, I glared daggers at Kathy. She laughed. I didn't!

It was an exhausting evening of the two-step, the waltz and turkey trot, a samba or two, and when we arrived at my front door, he kissed my hand gallantly and said, "Au revoir, mademoiselle."

To which I replied, "Sayonara, fella."

So much for blind dates.

I had a seasonal romance with a boy from northern California, whom I saw each summer at Lake Tahoe when we would appear at Harrah's Club. I was fifteen, and he was seventeen when we first met at the lake. He washed dishes at the club to earn money for college. We liked each other right away, and soon we were dating between the early show and the late show every evening. He taught me to water-ski and he took me to local parties with other kids who were working at the lake for the summer, and to the beach. Every year until I was eighteen, we enjoyed those three weeks together at the lake, knowing we might never see one another again. Although we would write back and forth for a while after the summer, we never did see each other again after that last summer passed. But such are the memories of summer love—intense, short, out of mind when autumn breezes commence.

When I graduated from high school in June 1964, I began to panic. Dianne was married, Peggy was married, two of my girlfriends married by fall, and I was on the pathway to spinsterhood. Where was that true love I had heard about? Naturally there was always Nicky, but even if he had ever asked me to marry him, I could not count on his showing up at the church on time, or even in shoes; especially if the surf was up.

One morning I walked into work at the Studio with the usual Saturday morning blahs, and there he was—my match. That cute guy I had prophetically told Kathy I was going to marry was a page at ABC and was answering telephones in the audience section of Studio E. I could feel my heart leap, and with all the confidence I could muster—in those days it took a great deal of mustering to get up my confidence—I walked over to him and introduced myself.

"Hi!" he responded. "My name is Lee Bernhardi . . . ." And we talked all through the morning, as if we were old friends.

Lee seemed to possess all of the qualities I had been searching for. An ex-college-football player, he loved sports, he loved children, and he had a great sense of humor.

The next week his parents came down to Los Angeles from their desert home to see the Lawrence Welk Show. Lee asked me if I would like to go on a double-date with them to a football game. I was thrilled! My head was so high in the clouds that evening at the game that I tripped and spilled our hot dogs and Cokes all over both of us. Lee could not have been too disillusioned, though, because he asked me to marry him less than a month later. Nothing appealed to me more, but I knew my parents would caution me that I was too young to think of marriage. Although Dee Dee and Peggy had paved the way for the rest of us by this time, we waited; but only for a few months. When the clock struck midnight on my nineteenth birthday, Lee slipped the ring—a beautiful heirloom passed down through the family—on my finger. We were engaged! And I was happy.

Although Mom and Dad were not quite as excited, they did give us their blessing. Mr. Welk, on the other hand, tried to dissuade us. "Janet," he said. "I think you're too young." We waited a year before finally marrying. Our wedding ceremony took place in May of 1966, at St. Mark Church, the same church where Peg and Dee Dee had taken their vows.

Also expectedly, there were TV cameras and movie magazine photographers everywhere. But I felt like the perfect bride, and I knew I would be the perfect wife. I had designed my wedding dress and all the bridesmaids' outfits. All the people that Lee and I loved were with us at the church, and it was our day.

When Daddy walked me down the aisle I could see Lee ahead, shaking in his shoes—not from cold feet, but from a bad case of the flu! He had a fever of 103, and he was miserable throughout the ceremony. Later we stood in line for almost four hours, greeting people at our wedding reception. By the end of that time, Lee was fading fast, and—as always—I was starving. So we drove off into the sunset, to starve a fever and feed a wife.

12

Sunrise, Sunset

The Lennon Sisters:

We loved Lawrence Welk, and we will be forever grateful for the many invaluable opportunities he afforded us. For his encouragement, for the rewards of fame, and for assuming the initial control of our professional development. But he was and always will be, for us, two very distinct and different persons.

He was charming and warm, and his sense of humor bordered on the ridiculous. Practical jokes and mischievous pranks were a part of his character. Our fondest memories are of the times we sat in the audience seats at the ABC studios and listened as Mr. Welk told us of his life on the farm and his old band and touring days. He loved to make us laugh, and we had a warm rapport with him.

Mr. and Mrs. Welk and their son Larry, Jr., were often at our home for dinner. We would play "Lennons' baseball" together in the backyard, using a whiffle ball and bat, and he would hold our little sisters and brothers on his lap and ask them to sing for him. Then he would clap and laugh with them and bounce them on his knee. In turn, we spent lovely evenings together in the Welk home, and occasionally we were invited to his country club. Our families were close.

Mr. Welk loved the way we sang, and he complimented Daddy time and time again for his ability to bring out the best in our young voices. In fact, when Mr. Welk was putting together a glee club, he asked Dad if he would coach them and see if he could instill in the group an awareness of the same feelings and phrasing that he so admired in us. But Dad, realizing his limitations, said that he didn't read or write music, and perhaps Mr. Welk could find someone better qualified to handle the task. But Mr. Welk truly wanted Dad's opinion and advice. When he was searching for new talent for his Top Tunes and New Talent Show, he once again came to Daddy and asked if he could travel the country to find fresh faces and voices for the show. But working with us and traveling took up too much of Dad's time already. Dad recommended his brother Ted, saying that Ted knew more about music than he did, and he had a sharp mind that would enable him to work in any other capacity in which the organization might need him. This arrangement worked out well for everyone. Uncle Ted has since become Executive Vice-President of the Welk Corporation, Teleklew.

Sometime during the second year of our work on the Lawrence Welk Show, Dad and Mom were asked by executive producer Don Fedderson if he could speak to them about a series that he was casting. He wanted the series to be called "My Four Daughters," and it would star Fred MacMurray and the four of us. Of course Dad was flattered, but he had several reservations, all of which he presented to us later. "It's really up to you girls to decide if you want to do this series. But I think you need a more normal home life than this would afford. Even though Mr. Welk agreed that you could take the new series and still sing weekly on his show, I feel that you could not do justice to both." He pointed out that we would certainly have to attend school on the set of the series. "It would mean," he added, "working seven days a week."

We agreed with Dad; it was inconceivable to do both shows and maintain any semblance of a normal life. Our first loyalty—and young as we were then, we knew this—was to Lawrence Welk. It was with some feelings of regret that we declined the offer. (That series became the very popular "My Three Sons.")

During the first years of our association with Mr. Welk, we had no glimpse of any negative side of his multifaceted personality. We were young and eager and attentive to his wishes; we idolized him and were more than happy to do what he requested of us. However, we could not live in a dream world forever. Inevitably, that bubble had to burst.

Perhaps it was because we were so very young that we were not fully aware or attuned to another side of Lawrence Welk. But that side was there, and as we grew older we came to see that oftentimes his conduct seemed erratic. So, for protection, we learned to avoid any situation or make any comment that might bring about a confrontation with him. Our personal contacts with him were fewer and fewer. We found ourselves frequently trying to second-guess him and, in a sense, manipulate our behavior to please him. We would find that the very same song he loved one day would be rejected the next day. Slowly, we were losing confidence in the talent for which he had so often praised us. Finally, it came to a point where we were forced to feel we were auditioning each week for the spot on the show that had already been ours for many years.

And. to put it bluntly, we felt we were in a rut. We were now women. There were new songs and sounds that we wanted to sing, some of the music of The Beatles, The Fifth Dimension, and The Association. No one, especially the young people of the '60s, could close their ears to the new musical changes. But we were not allowed to perform them. In order to expand our audience and our image, we felt we needed to grow musically. However, we were constantly being stifled by negative reactions.

There were many incidents that took place that finally led to our break with the Lawrence Welk organization. After much discussion, we chose not to relate certain matters. Several are personal, and revealing them would only serve to reopen wounds better left healed, as they have by now. But we were collectively disappointed and deeply hurt by untrue accounts that were widely publicized at the time we left Mr. Welk. So we will detail here only the final meeting that caused our eventual termination with the Welk organization.

In the spring of 1967, we were restless and very disturbed by the growing deterioration in our relationship with Lawrence Welk. Janet was soon to give birth to her first child, and with our families growing rapidly, we decided to approach Mr. Welk to ask him for a raise. We explained that now we were young women, and that our responsibilities to our families weighed heavily. At the time we were each drawing $210 weekly, which was scale for a solo artist under the AFTRA code. (During the first seven or eight years of our Welk association we drew group scale, *i.e.*, approximately $120 per week each. But with our growing popularity, it soon got to the point at which we appeared in at least six numbers per show each week. After a good many meetings, Dad's persistent and forceful discussions finally persuaded Mr. Welk to pay us solo scale wages.)

Now, years had passed since that initial raise. Our popularity on the Welk show was at its peak, and we felt some justification in requesting further consideration. However, Mr. Welk seemed shocked at our request, and he asked if he could take some time to think about "this conceivably dangerous situation." We agreed and left it at that.

Most performers can depend on their personal managers to help alleviate any undesirable condition that may exist. Sam Lutz, Mr. Welk's personal manager, also represented us. Understandably, Lawrence Welk came first with him; we had no one we could turn to. It was at this time that Lee Bernhardi, Janet's husband, helped solve our dilemma, introducing us to Bob Eubanks, the well-known host of the popular television show, "The Newlywed Game." Lee was stage manager for the show, and he and Bob had become golfing buddies.

"Lee knew I was just new in the field of personal management," Bob has said. "He asked me if I would be interested in representing the girls. I was surprised, since I knew they were still with Lawrence Welk." Lee told Eubanks that we had no contracts with anyone and that we were not satisfied with our manager. Lee asked Bob to at least talk with us.

Bob introduced us to his associate, Steve Wolf. They presented a plan that seemed to us ideal, and realistically attainable. It was explained that we could be spending less time working and making more money just by doing three or four highly lucrative appearances each year than by working the weekly routine of the Lawrence Welk Show. And we were reminded that we would have an opportunity to develop a more varied musical style. They acknowledged our financial responsibility, but realized that our main concern was spending a maximum amount of time with our families. They seemed aware of the fact that a weekly television show was a secure job—no doubt this was probably why we had stayed with it so long and at such a low salary. Their presentation was an accurate one, and we were impressed with Bob's and Steve's business acumen and their sincerity. Despite the risk, we made the decision we felt to be in our best interests, and we signed management agreements with Webco: Bob Eubanks and Steve Wolf became our new managers.

During our annual three-week engagement at Harrah's Club at Lake Tahoe, there was a definite underlying tension between the four of us and Mr. Welk. It was sad, really; non-verbal admiration and love for one another, which we desperately wanted to retain, mixed with the strength of both sides truly believing in its own convictions. These ambivalent feelings continued throughout the summer months.

In early autumn, Steve and Bob called us into a meeting to tell us of the many offers they had obtained for us. They put it all down on paper, showing us that, in order for The Lennon Sisters to earn the amount of money equivalent to what we were being offered, Mr. Welk would have to pay us three times as much as he was paying at the time. (We were impressed at the money that was offered us for short term engagements, or even one-shot appearances.) Bob and Steve encouraged us to consider leaving the Welk show.

We hated to make the decision; the old loyalty to Mr. Welk was still strong. We did not know what to do. We had heard nothing from him about our request for a raise. Feeling we needed more advice, we called our uncle Ted Lennon, who was Executive Vice-president of Mr. Welk's Teleklew Productions. As our uncle, he was in an awkward position. He attempted to have us see the disadvantages of leaving Mr. Welk. He did not think we could sustain our popularity if we threw away our weekly showcase on television. Certainly, we could agree with his reasoning, but at that moment our popularity was not our main concern. We were confident that we were capable of earning more money while still being able to spend a greater amount of time at home.

Faced with our seemingly immovable opinions, Uncle Ted said the decision was solely ours to make. He advised that we would have to "work it out with Lawrence."

Much as we disliked doing so, we made arrangements to meet with Mr. Welk at his new home in the Santa Monica hills. At Mr. Welk's request, Uncle Teddy picked us up and drove us to the secluded residence. When the door opened to us, there was an unforgettable pregnant silence. We knew Mr. Welk dreaded this meeting as much as we dreaded it. He deferred a confrontation as

The Lawrence Welk band—and girls looking like paper dolls. The Lawrence Welk Show, ABC Studios. *(Courtesy of Teleklew Productions and Lawrence Welk, Jr./The Lennon Sisters Collection)*

With the very lovely and pregnant Rosemary Clooney, and her two oldest children, Bell Telephone Hour, 1959. *(The Lennon Sisters Collection)*

1967. Singing "Greensleeves," one of our last appearances on The Lawrence Welk TV Show. *(The Lennon Sisters Collection)*

With the very handsome and talented Pat Boone, on tour, summer 1960. *(The Lennon Sisters Collection)*

long as possible by showing us through the beautiful, tastefully furnished rooms. How very different this experience was compared to the first house tour we had been given twelve years before in November of 1955.

The fateful moment arrived. Since we had expected a private meeting with just the five of us, we were quite surprised when Mr. Welk asked Uncle Ted to remain with us to be an intermediary. This only added to everyone's discomfort. Mr. Welk had hoped that Uncle Ted could still persuade us to his point of view, to have things remain as they were. Uncle Ted must have been torn between his fondness and loyalty to Mr. Welk and his love for his nieces. We were sorry that he had to be there at all. We had well-established goals in mind and a belief in the reasonable fairness of our request. As the tension mounted and a general uneasiness filled the room, Peggy began.

"Mr. Welk, we all know why we are here," she said. "We've come to the point where we are needed more at home, and yet we still have financial obligations that have to be met. As you know, we have growing families, and we have been shown ways to make enough money and still be able to spend more time with them. We would have to leave your show, because we couldn't do justice to you or anyone by dividing what little time we do have, trying to satisfy all sides."

She paused; there was no response. "We'd be foolish," she continued, "to ignore this opportunity, and yet we don't want to leave you if at all possible. That's why we have come to you, to see if there is any way we can work something out."

We sat in silence for a moment. "We believe," Peggy went on, "we've contributed a great deal to your show and in some ways have been partly responsible for its continuing success. After twelve years, we feel we are not being unreasonable in asking for double scale."

Mr. Welk was noticeably shaken, but then, so were we. "Do you realize what you are asking?" he said in a trembling voice.

"Yes, we do," Janet answered.

"Girls, you are so far off base," he said. He told us someone might be steering us in the wrong direction. "How could you ask for more money?" He reminded us that we were members of the

American Federation of Television and Radio Artists. "Well, the union sets the scale, and my policy has always been," he added, "to comply with union rules."

He stood up and began to pace up and down the room. He asked how we thought he could have a show at all if "everyone came to me and asked for a raise?" And then he asked us to suppose what his sponsor would say "if I asked him to double *my* salary?"

Of course, we had no answer for that. We were talking about hundreds of dollars, and he was comparing that with thousands. We began to realize that we would never make him understand our point of view. After a moment's silence, Kathy spoke up. "Mr. Welk, if we can't discuss this sensibly, then maybe we should leave, but we truly feel there is an alternative. If you don't agree, which is your prerogative, then we will just quit."

"Wait a minute," he said. "Why do you have to quit?"

"We have given you our main reasons, and we are getting more offers to do other shows," Peg said. "If we can't make what we need and want on your show, then we'll have to get it elsewhere."

Mr. Welk shook his head incredulously. He told us he didn't believe this could happen, that we were up in the clouds, and that no one who had ever left his show had ever done anything professionally afterwards.

"Well," answered Dee Dee, "if we have to, we'll sure give it a try."

The conversation took strange twists and turns after that, and it was difficult to make much sense out of anything. We were in tears, but we knew what we were asking was reasonable and right for us. He still held us in his Svengali-like grasp. We wanted desperately to soothe his anger.

"What are we going to do, girls?" Mr. Welk asked finally.

Before this meeting, we had accepted in our minds and hearts what we had to do. It was a calm and logical decision. Either get the raise or quit the show! We were ready for Mr. Welk to exercise his right, as boss, to refuse us. What we did not count on was our emotional exhaustion. We were drained, and when we faced the actual decision, we backed down. We could see the inevitable outcome; there would be no raise. Mr. Welk told us we could work on our own if we wanted to accept other offers, but if we desired to work his show, we should inform him of our schedule, and he would try to work us in. We took the compromise and agreed to try it for awhile.

Emotionally, we could not make that final break.

"Steve and I then went to ABC," Bob Eubanks has reported. "We told them we were unhappy with the Welk situation and that, unless the money could be improved, The Lennon Sisters would leave the Welk show."

The American Broadcasting people were concerned, suggesting that, Bob Eubanks said, "ABC guarantee The Lennon Sisters one-hundred-thousand dollars a year with four-thousand dollars to be applied to each Lawrence Welk show on which they appeared, the remainder to be worked off doing variety shows on ABC and other networks." We learned that, when ABC executives informed Mr. Welk of this, he turned down the offer immediately, indicating that no one on his show would make a thousand dollars a week!

Bob Eubanks recalls that the ABC executives indicated an interest in developing a Lennon Sisters Show. "As I remember, we completed a thirteen-week cycle with Welk," he said, "appearing only every two or three weeks, because the Lennons felt they had to live up to a commitment they had made with Welk."

We appeared every second week on the Welk show, but we felt an uneasy pressure that increased with each appearance. Then in March of 1968, we played the Carousel Theater in Los Angeles. Just before we were to go onstage, Dee Dee phoned the ABC studios.

Jim Hobson, our director, answered.

"Jim, this is Dee Dee," she said. "I'm just calling to find out what songs we are going to sing this week and what time is rehearsal for the Welk show."

"Didn't anyone call you?" Jim asked. "Didn't Sam Lutz talk to you?"

"No," Dee Dee responded.

"Well, just a minute."

Dee Dee waited for several minutes, and time was drawing short for our entrance onto the Carousel stage. Finally, Sam came to the telephone. "You are not going to be on the show." He told her that we could not be fit in. "You girls have too busy a schedule, and we think you'd better not come in."

Sam may have thought Dee Dee would ask for an explanation, but she didn't. "Okay," was her reply. "That's fine with us."

And so it was over . . . .

The dozen years had come to a close, not with a hand-wringing dramatic scene, but with a simple phone call. It was hard to believe, but looking back on that last Welk show, we realize that everyone seemed to know about this termination except us. Each member of the crew at one time or another had come to us and put his arm around our shoulders. "You know we love you guys," many had said. Woody, our stage manager, had been especially attentive. He gave us some photographs of the four of us with him, taken at the previous show. He had signed each copy with an appropriate phrase that had special meaning to each of us. We loved them, yet we did not make the connection that something strange was going on.

The thing that has hurt us the most was that, after so many years of such close association with the members of the show, we were not given the chance to tell all of them, person to person, "Thank you" and "Goodbye."

Our good friend, Perry Como, during our television series
season, 1969-70. *(The Lennon Sisters Collection)*

Kathy as "Tondaleo Lamour," with her co-star, the great Bob
Hope, in a scene from one of our television series shows, 1970.
(The Lennon Sisters Collection)

13

When You Walk Through A Storm

Kathy:

Our new freedom gave us the opportunity to branch out musically. As we began making more guest appearances on other variety television programs, we were surprised and delighted by the matter-of-fact willingness of the production staffs to arrange songs and choreography for us. It opened a whole new way of appreciating music. Our sound remained the same; we would never change that. We still phrased lyrics personally, just the way Dad had taught us. But now we were able to sing modern harmonies and current songs.

Our new managers kept us busy during that spring season of 1968.

In early summer, executives of American Broadcasting Company approached us about doing a television special that would serve as a pilot for a weekly variety series. This seemed too good to be true; the income from our own weekly show could advance us more quickly toward our goal of retirement. Best of all, no more touring. We would be working on home territory, Los Angeles.

We signed a contract to perform a fall television special, to be taped in September with Jimmy Durante, Bobby Goldsboro, and Hines, Hines & Dad as our guest stars. It took a bit of doing to get used to the idea of "our show." We put in long, hard weeks rehearsing, both singing and dancing. We had limitations as to what we could do, because Janet was seven months pregnant with her second baby. But we were certainly proud of the show and eagerly awaited the coming of spring, when it would be aired over the network; the only ratings we needed were those that validated the fruits of our labor. (Janet's labor produced John Frederick on October 31, 1968.)

Regardless of whether or not this special would give us our own television series, something wonderful happened to us during those weeks of preparation and taping—Jimmy Durante! Few words can describe that unique individual and personality. He stole his way into our hearts like some magical leprechaun. He has left his indelible mark on our lives. We were his "goils." I doubt that he ever really knew us individually by name—no, that's not right. He did know Janet, calling her "da little one," although she was far from little at that time. "Da little one is gonna have a little one," he loved to say.

It was hard to say goodbye to Jimmy at the conclusion of our taping, and we hoped we would be able to work with him again, and soon. Jimmy had class, something that he admired in others. His professionalism and manner brought out the best in people, onstage and off.

During the next months we busied ourselves with guest appearances on television shows, and in May we were booked into the Frontier Hotel in Las Vegas. It would be our first encounter with the Las Vegas showroom crowds. How would they accept us? What kind of act would we put together? It frightened us. But a very strong-willed, optimistic gentleman entered our lives at this point, and played a big part in helping The Lennon Sisters grow in ability and confidence. Jack Regas was a choreographer, and we had previously worked with him on a television guest appearance. Because we had felt at ease with him, we engaged him to choreograph our Las Vegas act.

Jack turned out to be exactly what we needed. Instead of renting a rehearsal hall in a cold, barnlike studio, he took us to his home. There, in his basement, we spent many hours learning basic dance moves and steps. He never lost his patience or his sense of humor, and we appreciated that. This tall, handsome, silver-haired man had the dark eyes and brows of paintings we had seen of Satan—hence, we told him that he looked like the Devil.

We were to lean heavily on Jack, and he supported us both mentally and physically. In a few short weeks, his creative talents and our own hard work culminated in our first Vegas act. We were by no means dancers, but with our growing confidence, we could move around the floor with greater ease. It was also a big help to us to know that the headliner of our Vegas show would be Jimmy Durante.

For instance, while we were dressing for the opening-night performance, Jimmy barged through our door. "Don't worry goils, I'm havin' it changed," he called out.

"Having what changed?" we chorused as if coming in on cue.

"Dat marquee out front of dis hotel. Our names are gonna be da same size. It's equal billing or nuttin'."

It happened that the letters of our names were only three-quarter size of the letters of his name. "Don't be silly, Jimmy," I said. "That's how it should be."

A star is a star is a star—he wouldn't listen. "It's gonna change," he insisted. And it did!

While appearing at the Frontier, our special was aired on ABC television network. When the ratings were announced, our show had drawn the biggest audience for any special so far that season, and not just in the Midwest, where one could expect our followers to be, but in New York and Los Angeles as well. It was a thrill for us, and Jimmy was exuberant. He walked around with clippings about the high ratings, showing them to everyone. Soon ABC announced our show as a weekly series beginning in September, and Jimmy Durante's appearance as our weekly guest was part of the deal. Their suggestion of title was: JIMMY DURANTE PRESENTS THE LENNON SISTERS HOUR.

With such a title it was hard to tell whose show it really was— and it caused a great deal of confusion. But it drew viewers from our audiences and also from those who followed the Great-Nose-And-Voice Man, a combination ABC believed would be difficult to surpass. The name stayed. Our managers, Steve Wolf and Jim Rismiller (due to professional commitments, Bob Eubanks had relinquished his half of the partnership) sat in on the coordination of the show. It was through mutual agreement and talks between ABC and Wolf and Rismiller that our television staff was pulled together. And our own corporation, Maryco, went into full production.

We returned to our old, familiar studio, back with all the crew with whom we had grown up. Our staff helped us feel a lot easier about this huge undertaking. Each week Jack Regas choreographed a big opening production number for us. If we were tired or could not get a step, he would say, "There is no such word as 'can't.' Now, we'll start from the top again."

And we did. He and his assistant, Marie Roe, made us look like true dancers. We had eight professional dancers (four men and four women) allotted to our show, and Jack and Marie took full advantage of their talents. So did we!

"Buddy, show me that funny little step one more time . . . . I can't get it—er, I mean, I find it very hard to do." After weeks of these strenuous dance routines, and at the height of her frustration, Dee Dee yelled out to Jack: "I brought a written excuse from my mommy today. She says I don't have to do this number."

On taping day, awaiting the "five-four-three-two-one" from our stage manager, our assistant choreographer Marie Roe, standing next to the cameras, whispered loudly, "EeTeeCee, Chickees." (She had told us from the beginning of our association with her that, if you smile with your eyes and mouth and stick out your chest, the rest would all fall into place. E.T.C., Eyes-Teeth-Chest—a lesson we've never forgotten!)

As we finished our production number, four pairs of eyes looked in the direction of the "Devil," craving his approval. With that evil smile, it was hard to tell whether Jack liked it or was gloating over the fact that we would have to do it again. Once this extravaganza was on tape, the rest of the show was a breeze.

To follow the opening production number, we welcomed our television audience to the show, and then proudly announced our guest stars for the week. When I say proudly, I mean it. The guest list for those 21 shows read like a *Who's Who* in Entertainment! Jack Benny, George Burns, Sammy Davis Jr., Don Ho, Glen Campbell, Ed Ames, Robert Goulet, Raymond Burr, Danny Thomas, Martha Raye, Louis Nye, Rosie Grier, Kate Smith, Jerry Lewis, Jack Jones, Walter Brennan, Dinah Shore, Monty Hall, Perry Como, Mike Douglas, Jimmie Rodgers, Jimmy Dean . . . .

And then there was Bobby Goldsboro, Milton Berle, Norm Crosby, Ferrante and Teicher, The Lettermen, Mel Torme, Joey Bishop, Desi Arnaz, Hines, Hines & Dad, Fess Parker, Sonny James, John Hartford, Vic Damone, Jo Ann Castle, Colonel Sanders (minus chickens), Rich Little, Corbett Monica, Merle Haggard, Roy Rogers and Dale Evans, and . . .

Not to leave out, of course, John Gary, O. C. Smith, Noel Harrison, John Stewart, John Byner, Wayne Newton, Tony Randall, Arte Johnson, Leslie Uggams, Kaye Ballard, Charlie Callas, David Frye, The Watts Community Choir, Senor Wences, Al Martino, Buddy Ebsen, Lorne Greene. On just one show we had Bob Hope, Andy Williams, and The Osmond Brothers. Awed by this? You bet!

The true essence of Jimmy Durante emerged during the third segment of our show. Jimmy's solo—and what a gem it was. The stage was completely bare except for a wooden chair, which he straddled, hat cocked on his little bald head. And he sang his heart out . . .

> *You mus' remember dis,*
> *Ah kiss is still ah kiss,*
> *Ah sigh is justa sigh;*
> *Da fundamental tings apply*
> *As time goes by . . . .*

All eyes and ears in the studio focused on Jimmy: you could have heard a pin drop. His way of touching your heart was supreme. Occasionally we sang a duet with Jimmy, following his solo. We loved it. It was like singing with Jiminy Cricket, and his raspy voice was unlike any other, as was his special pronunciation.

> *Inch woim, Inch woim, Measurin' da mar-golts.*
> *You and yur a-rit-matick you'll prob-ly go far . . . .*

We consider ourselves fortunate that some of his finest final performances were captured on tape for our TV show.

Many of the vignettes with our special guests are unforgettable. Peg dressed as a Roaring Twenties flapper, singing, "Hey, Big Spender" to Jack Benny; the facial takes from this notorious penny-pincher were some of his best, with Peggy sitting in his lap lighting his cigar, vainly tempting him to "spend a little time with me." Janet dressed as Charlie Chaplin in an imita-

Appearing on the Jerry Lewis Television Show; our first wigs and mini-skirts. *(Photo by Curt Gunther/The Lennon Sisters Collection)*

Onstage at the Cocoanut Grove. Now, which two are pregnant? *(Photo by Las Vegas News Bureau/The Lennon Sisters Collection)*

With the incomparable pal of us all, Jimmy Durante, on our
ABC Television Show. *(The Lennon Sisters Collection)*

1970. A wide-mouthed Milton Berle, appearing with us on one
of our television series shows. *(The Lennon Sisters
Collection)*

Peggy with Jack Benny
("Hey, big spender . . .").
*(The Lennon Sisters
Collection)*

Various guises and disguises:

Kathy—a stripper? *(The Lennon Sisters Collection)*

Janet, as Charlie Chaplin.
(The Lennon Sisters Collection)

Dee Dee, serenading a doubtful Jimmy Durante ("Raindrops keep falling . . ."). *(The Lennon Sisters Collection)*

tion of the famous tramp character, while Andy Williams, with turtleneck and cap, dropped to his knickered knees to portray Jackie Coogan as "The Kid."

Perhaps our favorite portion of the show was spent on the "family room" production set. Bill Morris, our set designer, patterned it after Mom's den at home, with used-brick fireplace and clusters of family portraits hanging on the walls. The family room segment gave us a chance to talk about our families and our career. These informal moments helped us show our individual personalities; we were not just four peas in a pod. The songs we chose for this segment were usually sentimental in nature, and it was a very relaxing part of the show for us.

The work that went into preparing for each program was voluminous. Our writer-producers, Bernie Kukoff and Jeff Harris ("Bernie and da uddah guy," as Jimmy called them), presented their ideas to the staff—three writers, the director, set designer, the choreographer, musical director, the costume designer, and the four of us. The feasibility, both economically and timewise, was thoroughly explored, over and over . . . and over. When it was resolved, everyone went their own ways to develop their particular facets.

The gentleman who perhaps had the most patience was George Wyle, our musical director. Every note we sang was written by this man, and sometimes there were as many as twelve or fifteen songs in one week. He yelled and complained that he needed more time, but nobody listened to him. And then he had to meet with the approval of not one, but four critics. Maybe George himself said it best in a little poem he concocted later in that season:

> *I've got a tale that I'll tell you in sections,*
> *And while I recite, please make no interjections.*
> *It's of a season, of music and jokes,*
> *And about some of my favorite folks.*
>
> *One week would start with a ten-thirty meeting;*
> *Coffee and doughnuts if you felt like eating.*
> *Then we got down to the business in hand,*
> *'Cuz in TV everything must be planned.*

Now comes the moment of truth, we've been waiting,
Time to learn music, and it's so frustrating.
I think that I've earned my purple heart stripes,
'Cuz here's a few of my favorite gripes.

Peggy is late, but that's to be expected;
Dee Dee asks why was this new *song selected.*
Janet says, "Pick up the tempo a bit";
Kathy then says the exact opposite.

George had his problems, but he loved every minute of them. This man, whom we called "old man with big nose and white beard," more than filled his niche.

Our costume designer Bill Belew was presented with a few obstacles during the season. For one thing, Janet was expecting her third child in January, and for the first four months of our show, Bill had to work *around* her—and he did wonders, never seeming to become upset. "Well, Janet, I'll bet this will be the first time our audience has ever seen a pregnant hobo." He never caused Janet to feel different, although I'm very sure he could not wait for January to pass. After all, a perfect 34-34-34 figure was not exactly a perfect figure.

His designs for us were more extravagant than we had ever had before. This was the first time in our lives we could wear any kind of clothes we desired. Bill would come to us at the Monday morning production meeting and ask, "Which of you has the solo this week? I will design your dream dress, any color, any material, any style you want." He would beam with pride as we floated out in his finished masterpiece, and then exclaim to all who could hear: "Once again, I have made you a star!"

Oftentimes the guest stars would create great moments for themselves (and us) out of the clever ideas from our writers. I remember especially the skit with Arte Johnson and Jimmy Durante. Arte, outfitted as his famous "dirty old man" character, held Jimmy, similarly dressed, on his lap. With his arms around Jimmy, Arte commenced singing, "Climb Upon My Knee, Sonny Boy." Jimmy was a little heavier than Arte, and slowly began slipping off his perch. Arte, quick to judge a comedic situation, never changed expression, and in slow motion, the two tightly locked senile gentlemen lowered themselves to the floor. All the while, the words continued, "When I'm old and gray, dear, Promise you won't stray, dear, for I love you so, Sonny Boy."

I had an embarrassing moment during a skit I was doing with Bob Hope. In the scene, I played the part of Dorothy Lamour—Tondaleo—from one of Hope's well-known "Road" movies. During rehearsals, Bob gave me directions. "Honey, when you catch sight of me tied to the tree, run towards me, throw your arms around my neck, and kiss me. I mean, really lay one on me. Okay? Now, let's try it."

Wanting to please my erstwhile esteemed director, I threw myself into the part and my arms around Bob Hope. But as I came face-to-face with the man, whom I hardly knew, my enthusiasm suddenly diminished. How could I give a real kiss to a stranger, let alone this world-renowned superstar? Halfheartedly, I planted a peck on his cheek. I was humiliated when he pulled back and rendered one of his well-timed punchlines: "What are you? A member of the Girl Scouts?"

That particular show could have been classified as a Special, for, along with Bob Hope, we also had guest appearances from Andy Williams and The Osmond Brothers. Working with the Osmonds gave us a feeling of deep personal satisfaction, for the little, unknown boys we had met and helped years earlier were now famous the world over. The nine of us stood before the microphones to sing our song together, and all our eyes turned to our fathers, seated side by side. Their faces told us of their joy and their pride. Now, looking back at that time, it seems appropriate that Allen, Wayne, Merrill, Jay, and Donnie were on the final television show Daddy would ever see.

We completed five tapings of "Jimmy Durante Presents The Lennon Sisters Hour" on a Friday night. Everyone was delighted with the way our show was developing. We were happy then to have four weeks off to restore our energies and prepare for taping the remainder of the season. On Monday evening, August 11, we celebrated by having the whole production staff over for a barbecue at our parents' house. Everyone was in a festive mood—especially Dad, who was more than pleased that all the years of rough times on the road had culminated in a topnotch network variety show starring his four daughters.

During that evening, Dad took our executive producer, Harold Cohen, aside. And he voiced to Harold some of his concerns for us, and for our futures. Harold has told us that he has wondered why that night: "Was I the only candidate to act as an ear for his thought? Was it premonition on his part, a projection? Or was it a preparation for the future of The Lennon Sisters and the Lennon family?"

"Harold," Dad said, "now that my four girls have their own homes and lives, their only rehearsal time is necessarily spent at the studio. My teaching schedule at the golf range doesn't permit me the free time I'd like to have to be with them." Harold had known that we continued to ask Dad's advice and to take in all his suggestions.

"I can't always be there to give them advice," Dad told Harold. "Nobody could care about them the way I do."

"Bill," Harold responded, "no one can ever do for those girls what you have done. The way they sing and the kind of people they are is all because of you. And don't worry so much about them. I promise I'll always keep a special watch over them for you."

It was one of those rare times that Dad was unable to pass off some humorous reply. Harold reported to us later that Dad stood up and walked to the window with tears in his eyes.

Dianne:

The next morning, Dad was elated, highly unusual for him, because most of the time he dragged himself downstairs, popped a handful of vitamin pills into his mouth, and groaned to Mom, *a la* Ralph Cramden, "Sis, I'll never make it though the day." We had grown up hearing that same line every morning.

Most days I took my children over to have breakfast with their grandpa, and this day was no exception. He went through his routine of making puffed wheat disappear from his hand and reappear in little Tom's ear; his young audience loved it.

One of Dad's great interests was his job teaching golf at a nearby driving range. Unlike most golf pros, Dad enjoyed teaching groups of lady golfers. He loved to hear their laughter when he yelled, "Don't be noodle swingers! Grab that club and swing hard!" Also, he enjoyed their unending flow of questions about the progress of his grandchildren and what was next for his singing daughters. Though Dad never spent his time or his money clothes-shopping, he took great care coordinating his golf shoes and clothes each day before work. His only luxuries were many sweaters and six pairs of golf shoes—all in bright assorted colors. "Do you think the ladies will be crazy about me?" he'd say as he strutted around the house.

It was a hot August morning. Dad kissed Mom goodbye and went to his car. As he backed out of the driveway, he hollered, "Sis, I don't have my green golf shoes."

"They're in the car Dee Dee's driving," Mom answered.

I ran out and grabbed his shoes from my car, and, chasing Dad's still-moving heap into the street, I teased, "You big baby. We all have to wait on you."

Dad flashed his I-know-it-and-I-love-it grin, and drove off.

Peggy had planned to leave two of her four children at Mom's that day, because the Cathcarts were moving to another house. On her way she had to take her mother-in-law to the airport, so she would pass the driving range. She considered stopping so that her kids could visit with their grandpa for a few minutes. No, she thought, he'll see plenty of them over the next few days. After depositing the two littlest boys with Mom, and then Julie and Chris at my house, Peggy drove home to continue the moving chores.

With the heat of the day advancing, I allowed my three children and Peg's to play in our little portable swimming pool. My nineteen-year-old brother Dan worked at the driving range with Dad and rarely left to come home for lunch. So it was a surprise to see him drive up. "Hey, kids," I shouted to the splashing children, "your uncle Dan has come to have hot dogs with you!"

When I opened the front door to Dan, he stood before me, white-faced and trembling. "Dee Dee, just hang onto me real tight," he said.

"Is it Dad?" I asked, my arms around him.

"Yes," Dan answered grimly. "I just left the golf range, and he's dead. You've got to help me tell Mom."

"Are you sure, Dan?"

"I'm sure."

"Let me stand here a minute," I said, too shocked to move. We stood in the doorway, holding onto each other.

Then the kids burst in from the outside, dripping wet and shouting, "Uncle Dan's here! Uncle Dan's here!"

At once I ordered the children to get their towels and robes and get into Dan's car. "We're going to Grandma's," I said. I then phoned my husband Dick. He was not in his office, so I ran across the street, hoping that my mother-in-law or Dick's father would be at home. Luckily, Mr. Gass was home for lunch. Embracing him, I blurted out the sad news, asking him to notify Dick and have him come to my mother's. After a sorrowful kiss, I ran back to join Dan and the kids in his car.

As we drove toward Mom's, Dan looked over at me. "He was shot," he said. At that moment, I presumed that Dad must have been struck by a stray bullet, fired by someone in the fields surrounding the golf driving range. I turned to the kids and blurted, "Now, all of you say some Hail Marys for your grandpa, because he's up in heaven now."

Danny and I were in a state of shock. We couldn't cry, and could scarcely think. There was so much to do.

"Mom," I called, when I had seated the grandchildren on the living room couch of the Harding Avenue house. "Will you come in here, please? We have something to tell you."

Mom knew when she entered from the kitchen that something had happened to Dad. "Your dad's had a heart attack," she said.

I held her tightly. "He's dead," I said.

Mom sank into a nearby chair, her moan one of utter despair. "My God, what will I do without him? Can I go to him?"

"There's nothing you can do for him."

"Are you sure?" she said, looking up at Dan.

"I'm sure," Dan said. "I saw him. It was an accident, Mom. He was shot."

She sat in the chair for a few more moments, crying and heaving great sighs. Then she asked us to bring all the little kids inside. Outside I found my nine-year-old brother Kippy, riding his bicycle. I put my arms around him, and then told him, Mom needed him with her because Daddy had died.

"Dee Dee, don't tease me about something like that," Kipp said. "It's not funny."

"I'm not teasing, honey," I replied gently. "Daddy really is dead." Kippy went inside, joining Joey and Annie, who were crying softly at Mom's side.

Billy, Mimi, and Pat were not at home, and Dan went across the street to a friend's house to find Pat and tell him first. He called Pat from the friend's backyard and put both arms around him. He told him then what had happened and asked for his help in finding Bill and Mimi, who were somewhere on the beach.

Once they were inside his car and heading for the beach, Danny poured his heart out to Pat. "This is such an injustice. How can this happen to such a great guy, when there are so many jerks who don't give anything to this world?" It was then that Dan finally told Pat the whole story: "A man shot Dad, and I saw him running with a gun in his hand and watched him drive away."

Once Dan and Pat had located him on the beach, our brother Bill knew immediately from the look on Pat's face that something was wrong. "Get Mimi," Pat said, and a few moments later he led them to the car. They all climbed into the back seat and huddled together.

"What's happened?" Billy asked.

"Daddy's dead," Pat simply said.

Mimi buried her head in Bill's shoulder and wept disconsolately. The sad group headed home.

Nana had just been informed, and she became hysterical. Mom shook her. "Now stop it! We've got little kids in the house," Mom said. "They don't know what's going on, and we've got to be strong for them. Please calm down."

Nana understood and began to help with the confused and tearful children.

I was now faced with the task of calling Peg, Janet, and Kathy.

"Kath, is Mahlon there?" I asked when I had dialed her home.

"Yes," she answered. "But he's in the shower. Can he call you back?"

"It's important," I said. "I'd like to talk to him right now."

Mahlon came to the phone. I told him about Dad. "Are you sure?" he asked.

"Yes."

"We'll be right over."

When he hung up the telephone, Kathy asked him, "Is it Kippy?"

"No."

"Mom?"

"No. It's your Dad."

"Is he okay?"

"No, he's dead."

"Was it a heart attack?"

"No, he was shot. It was a stray bullet."

It was not until they were driving down Venice Boulevard that the impact of what had happened hit Kathy, and she began to sob.

When they walked through the door, Mom threw her arms around Mahlon and said, "Oh, Bill loved you so much."

Janet, who was pregnant, was taking a nap when I called her. Fortunately, her husband Lee had been released from work early that particular day. It was one of the rare times he was home in the daytime. He, too, was napping, and the telephone awakened them.

"Are you sure?" Lee responded to me when I told him of Dad's death. Then he turned over on the bed and put his arms around Jan. "Honey, your dad is dead."

With her mind in a state of half-sleep she said, "Don't kid me." Then realizing what he had said, she too asked, "Are you sure?" Lee helped Janet rouse and dress their two boys, and they headed for Mom's house.

When I called Peggy's home, she was emptying the drawers in the childrens' bedroom and thinking how fortunate she was that the kids were not underfoot. "May I talk to Dick?" I asked.

"He's in the shower," Peggy said. "Can I have him call you back?"

"No. I'd like to talk to him right now."

Dick Cathcart came to the telephone, and Peg watched him as

he responded with, "Yeah ... sure ... okay." As he spoke, Peggy noticed that he began to shake.

He hung up and said to her, "Now, honey, somebody shot your dad."

Peggy looked at him unbelievingly. "Is he alive?" she asked.

"No," he answered.

Peggy leaned against the wall and slid slowly to her knees. "Are you all right, honey?" Dick asked.

"Yes," she said numbly. She started to cry, and Dick said, "The first thing we have to do is go over to Venice and pick up our kids. Your mother doesn't need any extra burden now." Peg decided to send Dick and his son John after the children so that she could stay and make arrangements for their care when they returned. This would enable her and Dick to go back together to Mom's by themselves.

During all this time that I was notifying everyone in the family, I hadn't broken down. I was still too stunned, too busy with details to feel the impact of what had happened. But finally, when my husband Dick walked through the front door at Mom's, the emotion of the whole thing came over me, and I lost control. Now Mom was crying, too. The release was necessary and good for both of us.

Then the doorbell rang. I opened the door to two men who identified themselves as members of the Los Angeles Police Department, Homicide Division. This was our first indication that we didn't know the circumstances of Dad's death. Mom and I seated them in the living room.

"We're sorry to bother you, Mrs. Lennon, but we'd like to ask you a few questions."

"It wasn't a stray bullet, was it? Why doesn't somebody tell me what really happened?" Mom demanded.

Then the lieutenant explained that Dad had been shot intentionally. Someone had run up to him with a rifle and fired at him. All of us were dumbfounded. We were still trying to absorb the news of Daddy's death; now came this unbelievable shock. Who would possibly want to kill Daddy? He didn't have an enemy in the world—everyone loved him.

The lieutenant apologized for asking questions at this terrible time. "But can you think of anyone who would have reason to kill your husband?" he asked.

"No, of course not," Mom said.

"Anyone at all . . . perhaps a jealous husband. Mr. Lennon taught lady golfers, didn't he?"

"Yes," Mom answered, "but that couldn't possibly be it."

These questions caused my thoughts to race. "Mom," I said, "there's only one person I can think of, and that's Chet Young."

"Oh no," Mom said doubtfully. "He couldn't have . . . ."

I reflected for a few seconds, then felt certainty. "He's the only person I can think of, Mom," I said with assurance. And then, for the first time in my life, I became angry enough to swear. "That damned . . . !". I named a woman who had written an article in a movie magazine about "the madman with the gun—with possibly murder in his heart."

Still, Mom wouldn't believe it. "You don't know for sure, Dee Dee."

"Mom," I replied, "I *do* know."

The police officers asked how I could be so positive. And who was Chet Young?

It was then that we all started to recall the problems we had had with this man. Slowly the story unfolded.

The first time we had been aware of Chet Young was on the back lot of ABC in late 1968. Originally, we thought he was a strange but harmless person who had become a very devoted fan. After each of our TV performances, he would be at the rear entrance of the studio, just staring—not like the other fans, who wanted autographs or simply wanted to say hello. We were unaware that he was dangerous until the U. S. Secret Service sent two men to our dressing room one night showing us mug shots of him.

We learned he had been sending threatening letters to President Johnson, stating that if the President did not let him see his "wife," Peggy Lennon, he was going to kill him. Chet Young had recently been released from a mental hospital and was now considered possibly dangerous, on the strength of these letters. We told the agents that Peg had been receiving letters for some time from Chet Young, but had never connected the name with the face at the stage door. We took the mug shots home and showed them to the whole family so that they might all be aware of this very sick man—not knowing where he might show up. The Secret Service men stationed themselves on the ABC studio premises for the next two weeks, but for some unknown reason, Chet Young never came back.

Then one night we were all at our family home for Sunday dinner when Kippy came running in. "I saw him! I saw him!" Kipp yelled.

"Saw who?" Daddy asked.

"Chet Young, around the corner at the MacDonald's stand. I'm sure it was him."

Dad was skeptical at first, but upon looking out the window he saw a man walking towards the house with his hand in his pocket. Indeed, it was Chet Young. "Girls, take all the children upstairs," Dad instructed the four of us.

Quickly, we gathered up the little kids and took them up to Mom and Dad's room. Dad went to his closet and took down the gun that he had kept hidden there for years.

Chet Young pounded on the door. Daddy had his gun ready, but he wasn't about to open the door. "Call the police, somebody," Dad yelled.

Uncle Tom Lennon got on the telephone and told the Venice police what was happening. "What has he done?" the officer asked.

"Nothing, yet," Uncle Tom replied, "but the Secret Service warned us about him. They also told us that you have been informed and that we should call you immediately if he showed up. He's made threats against the President, and he's considered a dangerous man. Please hurry, because he's banging on the front door, and we don't know what he'll do next."

"Sorry," Uncle Tom heard in his ear. He was told by the police that if Young had not done anything yet, there was nothing they could do. "I've heard nothing about this man."

About the time Uncle Tommy put down the phone, Young ran away. Dad tried to follow him, hoping to locate his car and license number, but he lost him in the darkness.

Two days later, our uncle Bob was driving to work and recognized Chet Young walking a few blocks away from Harding Avenue. He, too, had seen the mug shots and was positive of the identification. He quickly turned around and drove to our family home. Mom called the Venice police, who had by then been thoroughly informed of the situation, and they were at the house in minutes. Several squad cars scoured the area, but Young had again disappeared.

The same morning, our brother Pat was serving at the 8:00 a.m. Mass at St. Mark Church. From the altar he spotted a face in the congregation that struck him with fear. He managed to whisper to the priest to prolong the Mass until he could run home and tell Mom what he had seen. Hearing Pat's story, Mom called the police again, and they quickly had the church surrounded. When Chet Young left Mass, the police arrested him. He offered no resistance. Later that same morning, his car was found parked two doors from my home. Perhaps it was only a coincidence, but it scared us. We were glad he was caught. We were told that he would be confined to a mental hospital for good.

However, a few months later, he escaped and walked many, many miles to get back to Venice. He pounded on Mom's door and completely surprised her when she opened it. He was disheveled, covered with mud, and he asked for Peggy. As calmly as she could, Mom told him that Peggy was at work, and he headed for our church, a block away. After phoning the police, Mom called our pastor, who confronted the escapee and nonchalantly invited him into the rectory. There he offered him coffee and chatted with him until the police arrived. Again, Young was hospitalized.

Then the letters started coming again—weird, disjointed letters full of Biblical quotations, some of them xeroxed and sent to other members of the family. His letters to Peggy were all the same, loaded with endearments and signed, "Your loving husbin [sic] Chet." Soon they began to take on an angrier tone. He was obviously reading the fan magazines and believing the outrageous lies they printed. (The magazines, in an effort to shock and tantalize readers for the sake of sales, pounced on every shred of news or gossip, distorting our lives into their soap opera concepts.) Chet Young must have been drawn to the cover lines, which—for reasonable persons—were beyond belief. One of the themes that the magazines continually replayed was the myth that Daddy was trying to rule our lives. They proclaimed such bogus headlines as "Lennon Sisters Want to Quit, Dad Won't Let Them." He was pictured as interfering in our personal as well as our professional lives.

Chet Young apparently absorbed this poison, and injected it into his notes to Peggy and other members of the family. The tone of his messages became more and more threatening. They were full of photographs of President Nixon and pictures of Daddy and us from fan magazines. In several letters, he had circled photos of Dad and written, "This man is keeping me from my true wife."

One Sunday afternoon in March of 1969, the four of us attended a baby shower for Jo Ann Castle, given by Norma Zimmer. Many of the band members' wives were also invited. Since we had not seen many of these people for quite a while, there was a lot of catch-up conversation and gossip. As we were all seated for luncheon, questions were asked across the table about weird letters they had all been receiving. Since the writings were about Peg, they naturally assumed the four of us were aware of this man and could explain their meaning. As the truth was related, everyone was very intrigued and listened intently. One listener was more than just interested. She was the west coast editor of several fan magazines, and she locked in her mind all these extraordinary facts. Several months later, one of her magazines carried the title, "The Secret The Lennons Hid For Five Years . . . Peggy's Other Husband . . . The Whole Sensational Story." The article contained the information that the editor had heard at the shower, but with much embellishment. She wrote of the time that Chet Young had come to St. Mark. The article pictured The Lennon Sisters kneeling in prayer, and . . .

> Beside them [was] a madman, with possibly a gun in his possession. With probably murder in his heart.

And the story continued:

> The man named Chet believed he was married to Peggy Lennon. By all sane standards of behavior, this should mean that he would want to protect her, safeguard her. But the man wasn't sane. He was an escaped lunatic. Who could predict his behavior? Who knew if he had a gun hidden on his person—and if that gun might not be aimed at Peggy Lennon in some distorted sense of rage?"

The writer concluded with:

Is a madman stalking the Lennons again? At this point, with fear and trepidation, they can only sit and pray to God the man named Chet will leave them in peace.

We were enraged by the article and could not believe she would write such a thing. Surely Chet Young had read the magazine—he read all the fan magazines, so his letters indicated. He had no doubt seen his name in the story, had read that he was a "madman" who might own a gun, who might have "murder in his heart."

This article had been released just two weeks before Daddy's death.

When the two police investigators had digested this information about our confrontations with Chet Young, they seemed to feel that this was the logical lead to pursue. (Prior to this, they had thought that perhaps Dad's murder had some connection with the Sharon Tate and the La Bianca murders—later termed the "Manson" murders—that had been committed a few days earlier.) They asked if Young had sent any letters since the magazine had released the article. We rummaged through some of the unopened fan mail that Mom had received at her address and discovered a recently scrawled envelope. It contained a picture that had been cut from one of the fan magazines showing Daddy's head. Another cutout of a gun was aimed at him. Young had scribbled the words, "High Noon."

This corresponded with the account the officers gave us of Dad's death. Witnesses at the driving range had seen a man walking along the nearby railroad tracks, carrying a sack with something in it. Close to noon, Dad apparently recognized Young and realized he was in danger. He put his golf clubs into the car, presumably to come home and warn the family. (He usually returned home for lunch, but on Tuesdays he had a 12:00 noon lesson and did not arrive until 3:00.)

At exactly noon, this man took a rifle out of the bag and approached Daddy. There was a brief argument, and bystanders heard Daddy shout. "What ... No, don't! ... Somebody help me!" The gunman calmly took aim and fired. Daddy died instantly. The murderer placed the gun back into the sack, crossed Lincoln Boulevard to his car, and drove off in the direction of Marina Del Rey.

All the pieces fell together. There was overwhelming evidence that Chet Young had indeed been the man who had killed our dad.

Relatives and friends had begun to arrive at the house, and were all shocked and saddened. I had called Uncle Teddy at the Lawrence Welk office, and he rushed to the house. "How could this happen?" He immediately took upon himself the sad task of notifying Uncle Jack in Paris. Uncle Jim arrived and took care of the growing number of reporters and photographers gathered outside the house. Uncle Bob had taken his family fishing in the mountains, and did not hear the news until late that afternoon. He also came to Mom as quickly as he could.

Police protection was ordered for all of us, but rather than having guards at each home, Janet, Kathy, and I moved our families in with Mom. Twenty people all under one roof. It was not only safer for all of us to be together, but the constant camaraderie helped each of us to bear the sorrowful strain.

Kathy and her husband needed to go to their home and get some clothes and pillows. Police officers drove them to West Los Angeles and searched all their rooms and closets before letting them enter. When they returned to Mom's house, some of the fan magazine photographers rushed up and started popping flashbulbs in their faces.

"Can't you ever leave us alone," Kathy said, "at least today?"

"How long are you going to stay here?" they asked eagerly. "How does your mom feel?" They pushed their way through the reporters and the barrage of questions.

That afternoon, police officers arrived at Peggy's house in the San Fernando Valley. It was decided that she would be safer if she stayed away from Venice. "You and your family will have to stay indoors and keep the blinds pulled," she was told. "The man who shot your father may have more plans. We will be with you 24 hours a day for your protection." Every eight hours new plainclothesmen arrived to relieve those on duty inside the house. Five unmarked police cars were staked out in the area. Two officers were even stationed in a neighbor's house across the street that first day and night. Peggy's children had to remain in the basement playroom because the police didn't want them near any windows. The officers became instant babysitters, playing baseball with plastic bats and balls and enjoying the little ones as much as the kids enjoyed the policemen. This left Peg free to complete the packing of the remainder of their household; in spite of all events, they had to be out of that house in three days.

Meanwhile back at Mom's, the rest of us attempted to cheer one another, recalling what a character our dad was. We couldn't help but laugh at some of the crazy things he used to do. After the laughter came the tears, but then something new would come to mind, and we would be laughing again.

The following night the Rosary service was held at our little church. It was the first time any of us had seen Peg since Dad's death. We four gathered in the den and shared our sorrow. The Rosary was hard on all of us, but I think it was especially hard on our brother Billy. He was fifteen and as yet hadn't released his emotions. He told me, "You know, Daddy's father died when Dad was the same age as I am, and he went to work to help his family. Do you think I should leave school and go to work?" I assured him it would not be necessary. At the Rosary, Billy's sorrow finally overtook him, and he began weeping uncontrollably.

During the Rosary, we drew our strength from Mom. She sat straight and brave, a picture of composure. I could hear the words she had spoken to me the previous evening: "If I didn't have my Faith and Belief that I will see your Dad again, I could not accept all of this."

The funeral was held the next morning. The outpouring of love for Daddy was unbelievable. People came from all over the country—people Dad had befriended as only he could. There were hundreds of mourners: old high-school buddies, fellow workers from Douglas Aircraft and Edgemar Farms, all the Lawrence Welk band members, the production crews from ABC, golf students, boys and girls Daddy had coached on football and baseball teams. Daddy strongly believed in athletics for youngsters. so the family requested that, in lieu of flowers, donations be made to one of his favorite causes—Save Our Sports. Hundreds of dollars were contributed to help support athletic programs that were being eliminated from Los Angeles schools for lack of funds.

Dad had frequently stated that he didn't want a somber funeral, and it was not. There was much weeping, some by big burly men who loved him and would miss him. But there was also much joy and affirmation of life, recalling the funny, loving human being Daddy had been. Monsignor Edward Wade captured exactly the right spirit of Dad's humanity in his eulogy.

"Can't you just picture Bill up there organizing a baseball team and complaining to St. Peter about the umpiring?" Monsignor had everyone laughing through tears at the beloved man for whom they were gathered.

Mom once again was a pillar of strength. Seated close by her were the two bodyguards assigned from Robbery-Homicide Division of the L. A. Police Department. With Chet Young still at large, she and the rest of us were considered to be in danger.

The one element that disturbed the dignity of the funeral was the photographers from the fan magazines. They were everywhere, dressed in blue jeans and tee-shirts; they didn't even have the courtesy to dress properly! They shoved their cameras inside the limousine windows and exploded flashbulbs in our faces. Guards had to be placed at the doors to keep the photographers outside the church. It was worse at the cemetery. They climbed trees for camera angles and walked right up to Mom to photograph her at close range. (Because Dad had disliked the color black so intensely, Mom had chosen to wear a navy blue and white dress. Later, as might be expected, one of the fan magazines criticized her for not wearing black. We couldn't believe that people could be so disrespectful and insensitive at such a time.)

After the interment, literally hundreds of people came to the house on Harding Avenue—neighbors with arms filled with food, former boyfriends of ours who had remained fans of Dad's, our brothers' girlfriends who adored him (Mr. Groovy, they teasingly called him). Mr. Welk, who loved our family and admired Dad, despite their occasional battles, spoke to us with tears in his eyes. "If there's anything I can do . . . anything . . . , please let me know," he said. His wife Fern brought a big dish of chicken to the house, and so did Larry, Jr., and his wife Tanya.

Jimmy Durante came up from his vacation at Del Mar to see us. "I just can't believe it," he said tearfully. "How could a thing like this happen? Can I do anything? Maybe Marge could take the kids for a while. How about that?" We thanked him and the many others who offered to watch after the children, but we all agreed that we would feel better staying together as a family.

Andy Williams offered us the use of his beach house in Malibu. Bob Hope and Perry Como sent flowers with notes of sincere sorrow and offers of "help in any way."

The outpouring of love and sympathy from people from all walks of life was, for us, staggering. Mom especially was deeply touched, but never wept openly, until a special gift was presented to her from all the teenage boys in the neighborhood. They had all chipped in and had had a copper plaque made in Dad's honor. On it was simply inscribed:

In memory of William Lennon—
To The Man Who Never Struck Out—
The Harding Boys.

After the funeral, Peg and Dick returned to their house to continue with the moving. Police officers were with them at all times, and they pitched in and helped take down curtains and pack boxes. As with any large family moving from one home to another, there were endless boxes of junk that were stacked in the driveway for the trash pickup. On moving day, four extra plainclothesmen were assigned from the Metro Squad. When the trash truck arrived, the sight of all those boxes filled with who-knows-what proved too much for the drivers, and they understandably jumped at the chance to be scavengers. Just as they were knee-deep in discarded miscellany, two of the plainclothes officers came out the front door with more boxes. As the cartons fell from their arms, their shoulder holsters came into clear view. Fearing they had unearthed a gangster's den, or worse, the two drivers fell over each other trying to escape to the sanctuary of the truck, while stammering that they hadn't taken a thing and meant no harm.

Throughout the three weeks they provided protection, the policemen were extremely thoughtful and concerned. They brought toys for Peg's kids, who were finding it very difficult being cooped up in the house day after day. One policeman brought a large angel food cake. "My wife is having labor pains," he said, "but she insisted she wasn't going to the hospital until she baked you this cake." A few hours later, he had to leave his shift early to await the birth of his baby. Peg was happy to be awakened at three in the morning by a very proud father, telephoning to announce the arrival of his healthy son.

The police at the Venice home were equally conscientious. It could have been a great problem living with so many people in one house, but they seemed to enjoy the noise and confusion. Their patience and tolerance of the little kids went far beyond the line of duty. The children never left the house, except to play in the backyard. For the first few days, a squad car was parked in the backyard. So the officers who were assigned to that car also had yard duty. How exciting it was for the young children to wear handcuffs and pretend-drive their own police car. On one particularly hot day, one of the policemen asked Mom's permission to take all the kids up to Malibu. "I'll pick a deserted beach where they can play, and I'll watch them carefully." As the squad car filled with eager beachgoers, it was gratifying to finally see some happiness come back into those little faces.

Within the confines of the house, there was much for the adults to do. Just planning three meals a day for all those people took hours, and the volume of laundry was staggering. We had to keep busy. Consequently, Mom's big home was given a complete rejuvenation. We even found the mates to socks that hadn't been seen for years. Each morning, all the sleeping bags had to be rolled up so the hallways could become hallways again. Although our lives had been upset, the everyday chores had to be done. And it was good therapy for us.

Then the mail started coming. Every day the post office made a special delivery to our house, of bags and bags of letters and cards. Many were from acquaintances, but most came from total strangers, offering their sympathy. It seemed all of America had reached out to us. Eventually we were able to acknowledge every condolence.

We were instructed to open every letter as soon as possible, as the police thought Chet Young might send another letter that could give a hint as to his whereabouts. So after each mail delivery, we would gather to sort out the correspondence. No new letter ever came, nor could the police find any trace of him.

With Chet Young still at large, any of us could be his next target. But we could not stay in hiding forever. After two weeks, Janet and Kathy and their families returned to their homes, being assured by the police that by now the murderer had most likely left the city. However, our houses were kept under surveillance. Dick and I decided to stay, because there was evidence that Chet Young knew where we lived.

Soon we were faced with going back to our TV show. At our first pre-recording session, we sang "Heather on the Hill." It is a beautiful, lilting song filled with haunting harmonies. As I think now of the lyrics, I marvel at the strength we summoned to complete that song.

> *And when the mist is in the gloamin'*
> *And all the clouds are holding still,*
> *If you're not there, I won't go roamin'*
> *Through the heather on the hill.*

For the first time in all our professional years, there was no Daddy to look to after we had finished singing; no one to give us that extra touch that would take a song out of the ordinary and make it something special; no one to say, "That was beautiful, but . . . ." Always the "but," always the perfectionist.

We finished the recording, and—as if with one mind and one heart—we separated from one another and sought out secluded corners of the soundstage.

Out of sight, we wept alone.

"Oh Mein Papa." A television appearance with Dad. *(The Lennon Sisters Collection)*

On tour, appearing again with Dad, 1960. *(Photo by Jackson Studio/The Lennon Sisters Collection)*

14

From This Moment On

Dianne:

Time lessens the pain of the loss of a loved one, and thankfully, it enhances and renews all the fondest memories. Each little thing I had done with or for Dad, and that which he had done with or for me, slowly emerged from my deepest thoughts where they had been stored for years. It was the little things that I remembered: the tight grasp of his hand around mine as we walked along the fairways in the early morning when I was young; the clicking sounds of his golf shoes on the asphalt and the rattle of the clubs in his golf bag; the "wahoo" he hollered each time I sank a putt, which he had so carefully helped me align; stopping to share a milkshake at Chestnut's Drug Store (with two straws); many late evening visits by Grandpa after I was married, that made instant "Look-what-I-can-do-Grandpa" hams out of our three previously sleepy kids.

I recall today, in vivid pictures, the daily after-breakfast walks to Grandpa and Grandma's house, where the kids would hide so "Grandpa can't find us." How they giggled from their hiding places as he stomped loudly through the house. "Where are those bums?" he would bellow. "They'd better come out and kiss me, or I'll never let them come over here again." And the times that Dad took my three little ones fishing on the Venice canals with his own handmade poles and water-soaked, hand-rolled little balls of bread for bait; the red sweater he bought for me one day not too long before he died.

He had said to me, "It looked like you, and I had to buy it." And I remember the way he and Dick enjoyed each other, whether it was sports, music, lying on the beach, playing practical jokes, or just being together.

I feel that very few daughters have been blessed with so many close and special times with their fathers. I treasure mine.

Peggy:

> My memories are scattered—
> So many things mattered
> In your life—
> Daddy, I miss you.
>
> Your Strength in the Lord
> Was a blessing poured
> On my life—
> Daddy, I pray for you.
>
> Your tender, warm feelings
> That flowed through all dealings
> With life—
> Daddy, I admire you.
>
> Your wit and pranks
> That made me give thanks
> For your life—
> Daddy, I laugh with you.
>
> My sorrow increased
> By the goodness that ceased
> With your life—
> Daddy, I cry for you.
>
> Your faith from the start
> That gave me heart
> To face life—
> Daddy, I thank you.
>
> You, I remember!
> Your soul, a living member
> Of my life—
> Daddy, I love you.

Kathy:

As I look back over the years, I realize Daddy did not give out the hugs and kisses that often exemplifies a loving child-parent relationship. At the time, I was never aware of this, because his own way of giving love was, to me, so gratifying.

When he smiled at me, the warmth of his eyes said, "I love you." When he called me his "little bari-girl" (baritone), he was saying, "I love you."

As he rubbed the back of my neck when it wasn't even sore, his touch meant "I love you." When I was sick in bed, I always knew Dad was going to scratch my back and sing his corny songs, which all meant "I love you."

Often I stepped down from Mom's kitchen into the family room and heard my recorded rendition of "Malaguena Salerosa," and there would be Daddy, sitting on the floor with his eyes closed, lip-synching every word silently with a smile of fatherly pride that vibrated "I love you."

And oh, so many, many little things that maybe only he and I will know. I do become selfish, wanting to save them so they'll last through the years.

Janet:

Daddy, just the mention of your name can evoke more emotion in me than any other word. Your spirit is alive in me, as it is in all your children. To know any one of us is to know a part of you. And yet, I never really knew the whole you. I alternately loved and feared you, as one usually does when they respect someone so highly. I know you weren't perfect, and yet you were so unique I could never categorize you.

You made me laugh every time you did somersaults down our staircase, even though Nana admonished me "not to encourage the nut." You frustrated me each time you made me wear *Rubyred* lipstick when *Apricot Frost* was the thing. You gave me chills every time you sang your favorite, "Danny Boy," the tears of emotion welling in your eyes and mine. You made me blush every time you interrogated one of my boyfriends, because I never knew whether you did it to embarrass me or to protect me. You made me cry every time I watched you coach a group of little children, always able to convince the most uncoordinated of them that he was "The Six Million Dollar Man." You made me feel like the most important child in the world when you told me that I massaged your back and pounded your legs better than any of the other kids. I felt like your best pal on those Saturday afternoons at the studio when you would grab my hand and say, "Let's go out to lunch, just the two of us." I can just picture the Old Vienna, that little cafe where our whole lunch consisted of extra-thick chocolate milkshakes and mocha nutcake. Then our walk, hand in hand, to the miniature golf course next door where we would play a quick game before returning to the studio. You never did like it when I beat you. You made me feel so proud when, many years later, you held my firstborn, Billy, in your arms, calling him your "Golden Boy." I thank you for sharing with me your knowledge of sports; it's a little extra bonus I can share with my husband and children.

I can still see your smiling eyes and feel the warmth of your hand rubbing the back of my neck. We all came to know this gesture as your way of saying, "I love you; I'm proud."

I have to say these things to you now, these many years having passed, because I was too shy to say them to you in your lifetime.

Daddy, I love you.
Daddy, I miss you.
Daddy, I'm okay.

Dianne:

We still had to endure another ending. There was no break in the case of Dad's death for seven weeks. Once, our hopes were raised when an abandoned car was found near San Francisco, and proved to be Chet Young's getaway car. But there was not a trace of him.

We had resumed taping our television series in September, forced now to perform on a closed set. For security reasons we were not allowed to have a studio audience, and we still had assigned guards. In mid-October, two months to the day after Daddy's murder, my husband Dick came to the studio and asked us to join him down in our dressing room. "I've got something to tell you," he said.

We seated ourselves in the room. "While I was at your mom's tonight, Detectives Moon and Benson called from northern California," he told us. "A car has been discovered in the woods, with a suicide victim in the trunk. They are going to drive to the scene and make a positive identification." Dick said the detectives believed the dead man was Chet Young.

The following morning, Sergeant Moon called to confirm Chet Young's death. His body had been found in heaps of fan magazines and newspaper articles containing pictures and stories of Dad's funeral. Among them they discovered letters he had written, confessing he had shot our dad. His rambling notes stated that he truly felt Peggy was his "wife" and he had to kill anyone who came between them. There was also a list of people whom he planned to assassinate, including other members of our family, prominent politicians and entertainers, his former psychologists and psychiatrists.

He had scribbled a letter to Peggy, dated October 5:

> My precious wife, I managed to slip into town and buy four magazines which I have been reading . . . . thank you for not crying in the pictures. I know your little sisters and brothers are confused, but please explain to them that I had to do it for them . . . . my death is no waste . . . . I have died a man rather than a zombie in the hands of 200,000,000 capitalist pigs . . . . your devoted husbin [sic] . . . .

To end his life, he used the same rifle he had used to end Daddy's life. The long, drawn out months of terror were over. Our relief was indescribable.

How did we feel about Chet Young? We never hated him. We simply recognized him for what he was, a desperately sick man. It was our ten-year-old sister Mimi who best expressed our feelings. We had gathered to have a Mass at Mom's home, shortly after Dad's death, and when the priest asked for any special intentions,

Mimi spoke simply. "Let's offer this Mass for Chet Young. May they find him and give help to this poor, sick man."

It was difficult for us to return to the normal lives we had led only a few short months earlier, and to the routine of our weekly television rehearsals and show. Understandably our audiences were supportive, but they were also curious as to how we might react at any given moment. We kept our mourning inside ourselves, and naturally we were somewhat subdued. Again, at the studio, it was our friend Kay Esser who helped keep things going. When Bill Belew, our costumer, had mentioned at the onset of our show that he would need a good seamstress, we eagerly suggested Kay. The job was hers!

"Dee Dee, you know better than to walk barefooted on these cold cement floors," she'd reprimand. "You'll catch pneumonia." Or to Peggy: "I told you not to have that piece of cake at lunch. Now your skirt won't fasten. You'll never change."

To any and all of her mother-hen cluckings, we simply replied, "Nag! Nag! Nag!" as we ran out the door of her wardrobe room.

Kay's sewing machine never stopped humming. It's a wonder it did not completely explode when we had our Christmas show in preparation. That machine was used to sew most of the costumes for the four of us, and also clothes for our husbands, Mom, Nana, five brothers, two sisters, our ten little children, and even a big red bow for our dog, Mutt.

Our Christmas show mirrored the traditions of our family: lots of kids, Christmas stockings on the mantel, traditional Christmas carols, Santa Claus—and, of course, the Christmas story of the Christ Child. The setting was one huge living room bedecked with fireplace, staircase, and a ten-foot Christmas pine, all festively decorated. Santa had a big schnozz that year and handed out gifts to all the children; however, his eyes showed favoritism toward one little girl—eight-year-old Cece Durante. That show was merry and bright, although our hearts ached for the man who would not be home for Christmas.

The season of 1969-70 Mom busied herself admirably, her willingness (if not, indeed, her need) to babysit with my children created an ideal situation. My kids loved being at Grandma's house, and they soon became extensions of my brothers and sisters, using their same "cutie" verbal expressions and dressing in the same sleazy teenage manner that their aunts and uncles had newly acquired. I would drop them off at the Harding Avenue home each morning, the girls dressed in matching ribbons in neatly combed ponytails, and Tom with hair parted and combed to one side. Then, inevitably, I would return home to find them all in huge, baggy sweatshirts hanging to their ankles, and their hair hanging "au naturel." More little hippies from Venice!

I really lucked out with respect to dinners. Each night after rehearsal, Dick and I were treated to one of Mom's great meals. Not having to come home and spend time cooking dinner left me several hours in the evening to share with just my family. Dick and I know that some of our happiest memories were due to Mom's continuing refusal to let us help with the dishes. "Go on home and enjoy the kids," she'd say. "I've got Mimi here to help me." Moms know that bath times and before bedtimes are the best part of the day for young parents of little ones.

In order to take full advantage of those evening hours, I got up at five o'clock each morning to do the ironing, fold the laundry, and scrub the floors. About 6:30, I'd awaken Dick and we'd enjoy a few solitary moments together over breakfast. When the three kids made their early morning appearance, we were well into the cycle of our daily lives.

Kathy:

Can you believe Dee Dee?

In January, mid-season of our television series, Janet gave birth to her daughter, Kristin Leigh. Our newest niece made her television debut at only ten days of age. To everyone's amazement, Janet returned to work less than two weeks after delivery. To further our dismay, she did a song and dance with male dancers who whirled and tossed her through the air, as we all held our breath. Janet was the only person who took it nonchalantly—except Jack Regas, who just smiled his devilish smile and said, "I told her she could do it."

I think we were fortunate that most of the celebrities on our show were down-to-earth people. There's something to say for each one

Another guest of our 1969-70 television season was a 75-year-young George Burns, appearing here with Peggy. *(The Lennon Sisters Collection)*

NBC Follies, early 1970s, with the very gracious Sammy Davis, Jr. *(The Lennon Sisters Collection)*

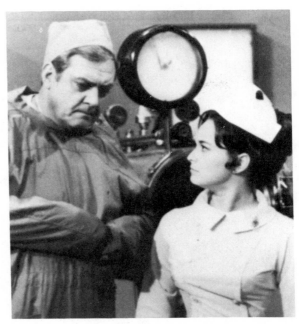

Raymond Burr as a Doctor with Nurse Peggy. *(The Lennon Sisters Collection)*

A young, dark-haired Merv Griffin, in song with the young(er) Lennon Sisters, 1971. *(The Lennon Sisters Collection)*

of them. But there was one instance when one "small" man proved how big he could really be.

One show was running several hours late, due to technical difficulties, and the audience had been sitting for quite a while. This time, one of the cameras had broken down, and we were informed there would be at least a thirty-minute delay before we could resume taping.

Sammy Davis, Jr., our guest, was in costume and waiting backstage to sing his medley when the camera failure was announced. Our stage manager informed him he could return to his dressing room and rest for a few minutes. But Sammy, sensing the audience restlessness over the delay, grabbed a microphone, walked up to the front of the stage, and proceeded to give an impromptu concert for the weary spectators. We learned again a lesson in professionalism.

Shortly after his appearance on our show, Sammy sent us a telegram asking us to join him on his opening night at his nightclub, the "Now Grove." Few stars can get the Lennon sisters out for an evening, but we are big fans of Sammy Davis, Jr., and so Dee Dee and I, and our husbands, went together to the old Cocoanut Grove. Just after dinner and before the curtain went up, Dee Dee and I sent Sammy a note. "Dear Sammy, we are here with our husbands and are eagerly awaiting your performance. Love, Dee Dee and Kathy Lennon."

Toward the end of the show, Sammy said to his audience: "I'm honored to have some very special friends in the audience." At this point, Dee Dee and I put our napkins on the table. "They are two of my favorite sisters in show business," he continued, "with whom I've had the pleasure of singing many, many times." Now Dee Dee and I pulled our chairs back and, blushing a bit, stroked the crumbs off our laps. "I love them dearly," Sammy went on. "And their husbands were kind enough to bring them to see me tonight." Making sure our hair was in place, Dee Dee and I got part way up out of our seats, when Sammy finished with, "Please give a big hand to two great singers, Dionne Warwick and Leslie Uggams!"

By the time we realized what he had said, we were halfway into our bows, so we just continued to bend forward and shrink down onto our chairs until our faces touched the hem of the tablecloth.

After Sammy's show, our husbands persuaded us to go back-stage and talk to Sammy. He immediately walked over to us. "Oh, kids . . . as I walked offstage, my manager handed me your note. I'm so sorry I didn't get to introduce you."

"Oh, don't worry about it," Dee Dee and I said with one voice, looking at each other. "We never expected you to."

Our series of television shows was creatively stimulating for the four of us. As for me, I welcomed the challenge to learn danc-ing and solfeggio (lessons in music sight-reading). But the hours spent on our feet, especially during dancing rehearsals, caused our legs to ache as each vigorous step pounded on the cement floor. I'm sure I spend more time than the other girls exercising my muscles. I'm pigeon-toed, and Jack Regas felt that by forcing my feet to point outward ("Think East and West!"), it would greatly improve my appearance and also my ability to dance. I remember looking forward each day to going home and luxuriat-ing in a tub of hot water, while studying my music.

Peggy:

While maintaining such a busy work-schedule, I could never really feel relaxed about leaving four children five days a week. I trusted the young French girl who was acting as our babysitter. Otherwise, I would not have left Sabine in charge of my little ones. Then, after the long day at the television studio, I would return home to find the house in a shambles. Dishes piled high in the sink, dirty clothes stacked in the laundry room, and beds still unmade. But the children were happy, and they loved Sabine. Actually, she was like them. I suppose it can be said that Sabine made a valiant effort at cooking for the children. But, as little Chris said, "Mommy, she cooks snails and things like flour and jelly pies. It's horrible."

So, in addition to cleaning the house after work, I myself made casseroles and soups for Sabine to feed the kids. Now that I look back on that time, I was the one who waited on Sabine hand and foot. But I suppose it was worth it. I can always say I once had a French maid.

Janet's three children had a wonderful English lady, Peggy Holladay. This Nanny fed, bathed, clothed, and disciplined Jan's kids, and sprinkled a bit of English culture on them so "Mummy and Daddy would be proud."

Janet:

All true.

Before long my youngsters were habitual 4:00 p.m. tea-drinkers, demanding lots of milk and sugar in their brew, just like English children. Peggy Holladay's talents seemed limitless. It was not unusual for me to come home after the long day's rehearsal to find my children attired in handknitted sweaters and caps. Many times, I found my young trio snuggled up to Peggy on the couch, while she read them her newly-composed poetry as their bedtime story. I was content that my children were well cared for, and I admit that I enjoyed those months of being Janet Lennon, entertainer. I can add, too, that I was glad to spend those days with my husband, who was our assistant director. An added compensation for the days away from home.

The show was doing well in its Friday night time-slot, but at mid-season ABC switched us to Saturday nights. It proved to be a grave mistake, for our ratings diminished. One day when we were rehearsing at the studio, our agent paid us a visit. "I have to talk to you," he said. But we knew by the look on his face and the tone of his voice: our show was cancelled.

Dear Jimmy Durante was in tears. "How can dey do dat to us?" he said. "We were da best ting on television. You can't get good, clean talent like dis anywhere else."

The news was a shock, of course. To everyone. We had to go back into choreography rehearsal for our last show, and on entering the rehearsal hall, one look at Jack Regas told us how everyone in that room felt. Dark glasses were the order of the day. Not only for the dancers, but the cameraman, lighting men, prop men, and the rest of the crew; for we had all been one big family. All Indians, no chiefs—a unit laboring to create the best possible show—and all of us were proud of our achievement.

We four had mixed emotions, hating to part from the fine people with whom we had worked those many months (and who had so warmly aided us through the loss of our Dad), and also looking forward to the end of the weekly grind. Before us lay the opportunity to rejoin our families and to lead normal lives.

We had learned that we were professionally capable of gathering up and expending the energies necessary for a weekly television show. At the time, we may not have been professionally mature enough to exercise whatever authority we had as the stars of the show. For so many years we had been conditioned to accept directions from others, to follow all the orders of those authorities who undoubtedly had our best interest in mind, who aided us to achieve whatever goals were placed before us.

It had always been difficult for each of us to express our own opinions, especially when we disagreed with any member of our staff, simply because we were afraid to hurt someone's feelings. Consequently, it was our own fault whenever we were unhappy with the finished product, whether the problem pertained to script, music, or wardrobe.

Since that time—perhaps because of it—we have learned the value of opening our minds—and our mouths—often.

The dancing Lennon sisters with the dancing Andy Williams, 1974. *(The Lennon Sisters Collection)*

15

Let's Go On With The Show!

Kathy:

When our television series was not renewed, the four of us had to sit down and re-evaluate our goals as a singing group. We had choices, many of them. Did we wish to begin nightclub and concert tours again? Or just do guest appearances on television? Or did we want to quit altogether?

Our first choice was to quit altogether. But our second thoughts were much wiser. At a new doorway to our professional life once more, and as married women, we had considerations of family life prodding us to carefully weigh our decision. If we could perform only in and around Los Angeles, we thought, and still contribute to our families' incomes, it would be silly to quit.

One decision affecting our careers had already been made. Steve Wolf and Jim Rissmiller decided to devote full time to their fast growing careers as rock-concert promoters. We needed a personal manager who would put up with our stringent conditions.

The answer came in the person of Harold Cohen. As executive producer of our television series, he had commanded—and then earned—our wholehearted respect. He was a kind, soft-spoken man, with varied experience as a former agent, attorney, and television and motion picture producer. He made us feel he truly cared about us as people.

"I promised your Dad that I would look after you, and I would consider it an honor to be your personal manager, come what may," he said. He—and we—felt we needed someone who could guide us without pushing, and he did not waste any time when we accepted his management offer. It took only a few weeks for Harold to come to us with an exciting proposal that we quickly approved. "Andy Williams would like you to appear on ten of his TV shows this season. I feel this could be a good move for you."

We did not know that those weeks with Andy Williams would grow into many years of deep, personal friendship, nor that the association would so enhance our professional life. We were immediately made to feel at ease, from the first day of rehearsals and our first performances on his show. There was no pressure, and the ideas that we offered and the suggestions for our part of the programs were considered. Many times they were discarded—but they were considered.

We were introduced to the new sounds of that time by Earl Brown, Andy Williams' vocal arranger. Earl's arrangements were challenging to us, in the harmonies he employed and in the feel he wished us to project. In order to learn these new vocals, we had to have him sing each individual harmony part on a tape cassette, which we would then take home to listen to and memorize. After several days, we came together to sing all the harmonies simultaneously. We were pushed by Earl to update our sound and arrangements, to take them out of the strict "quartet" harmonies we had been using since the beginning. And we loved it.

Choreographer Andre Tayir stepped into our lives (and soon into our hearts) during our Williams show appearances. He was, and is, a gentleman at all times—addressing us as "Ladies" and Andy as "Andrew." Andre's tall, thin frame is reminiscent of the fabled lanky schoolteacher, Ichabod Crane, with frizzled hair and deep-set eyes. He has a great way of making us do something we think impossible. "My dears," he says simply, "you can and you will!"

Although he is, to put it mildly, a taskmaster, he has a great capacity for fun. His subtle ways of showing displeasure are, in themselves, comedic. If we do not seem to be catching on to a certain dance routine, his dark glasses are put on to cover the huge black eyes that are upset by our clumsiness or disinterest. This brings an immediate reaction from us. "Andre's got his glasses on. We must be awful today," we tell one another. "Come on, you guys." And so we try harder and keep pushing ourselves until the dark glasses are flipped back onto the top of his head.

Every time we begin learning a new dance, Andre comes to work in tattered Levi's and scruffy unlaced tennis shoes. As our dancing improves, so does his appearance. Until one day he arrives in his crisp, blue denim trousers, home-sewn long-sleeved flowered shirt, and clean laced sneakers. Then we feel we have finally achieved his approval for hard work well done.

"One moment there is glee," he has said. "Another moment, a crinkled brow, but like a child changing, growing, and regressing, there are the proud moments of success when you know your guidance has made an impact.

"There are times when you have to put out tons of energy, mental and physical, and yes, spiritual, and you see it go down the drain. Working with four minds and four bodies is like a small army, especially when all four are creative. When they go in different directions, it's murder—but when things jell, it's like guerilla warfare, and the little army wins big."

Andre has always given us much encouragement and self-confidence by making us strive harder to achieve higher standards of performance. He has taught us to be open with each other and not hold everything inside. "Get it all out. It's good for the soul." We have come to depend a great deal on Andre's opinions and guidance.

Toward the end of that same television season, Andy Williams proposed to us the idea of working up an act with him, which he would take to Caesar's Palace in Las Vegas. It gave us great pride to think of accompanying *the* Andy Williams at *the* famous Ceasar's Palace. Certainly there was some panic about putting together a quality act, but Andy had us believing in ourselves because he believed in us. With complete reliance on Andre Tayir's directions, we accepted Andy's invitation.

"Okay," Andre said, the first day of rehearsal. We were in Andy Williams' office sorting out ideas. "I'd love to do something different with the four of you."

"Like what?" we chorused as one voice.

"Hold onto your hats, ladies," Andre replied. "I'd like to see you strip onstage."

Again, as one voice: "*ANDRE!*"

"I agree with Andre," Andy said. "And I get to watch all the rehearsals."

"*ANDY!*"

Andre explained that he pictured us in long, fitted sequinned dresses and stripping down to black satin corsets. Andy thought that sounded just great.

"Andrew! Let me finish," Andre said, his voice commanding. "You ladies will be completely covered, of course, but people will see that the Lennon Sisters have legs. In those outfits, I see you singing 'Cabaret,' and then you can quickly put on four Army jackets to end with "Boogie Woogie Bugle Boy!""

Staring into our deafening silence, he added, "Well, my dears, let me hear from you."

Dee Dee, the most conservative of us, was first to react. "Imagine, The Lennon Sisters doing a strip—it would shock everybody! What a great idea!"

With three "Why nots?" it was unanimous. Then Andre added, "What do you think, Andrew?"

Andy was silent for a moment. He looked around at each of us. "You girls sure don't act Catholic."

Janet:

We passed around and passed over and passed through many ideas, making lists of concepts and songs we might sing, and handed our choices to the vocal arranger and the costumer so they could begin their work. We began the sometimes tedious, ofttimes amusing task of learning words, music, and choreography. "Amusing" is the right word, because basically Andy and the four of us are singers. Getting all of us to dance in unison is a rather hilarious feat—especially since Dee Dee has found her terpsichorean equal in Andy Williams. Poor Andre now had two people with two left feet. His glasses were on and off his face several times a day. That gave us much-needed laughs in the midst of deep concentration.

The fittings for costumes were left until the last possible moment. ("I know I'll be at least ten pounds smaller by Vegas, so please don't take my measurements right away.") Andy had retained costume designer Ret Turner from his television staff. His designs for us were lavish. For the first time, we were glamorous women, draped in clinging beaded gowns. Ret gave us the extra sparkle we needed for that opening night.

Opening night—two frightening words. I don't think the anticipation and panic connected with that one phrase can be compared with any other. I really don't know how to describe it, except to say that if you could imagine those feelings at any other time, you would never put yourself through such torture again. After two days of rehearsal onstage to synchronize the sound, lights, and music, you realize that it is still all up to you.

Andy Williams told us that "When I walk out onstage and give my first smile, my top lip immediately sticks to my upper gum, due to the extreme dryness of my mouth, and I spend the whole first song frantically trying to bring down that lip. I feel like a grinning fool."

Working with Andy Williams gave us the chance to really see if The Lennon Sisters could take care of familes and work at the same time—and do justice to both. We were able to have our cake and partake of the frosting as well.

It's such a short, simple flight from Los Angeles to Las Vegas— or it can be a long, tedious drive. Unfortunately, we weren't given much of a choice. Packing for eight adults, fourteen children, and three babysitters for three weeks posed a problem we wouldn't impose on any airline. Not that they would have considered loading our styrofoam swim rings, vaporizers, footballs, hot plates, and pots and pans. On the other hand, it's amazing what you can stuff into the back of a station wagon. (Any automobile manufacturer could have used us for a commercial expounding on the delights of packing and traveling in such a conveyance.) Our children learned to tolerate sleeping on golf bags, and were experts at coloring and reading in the car without throwing up.

The bellboys hated to see us coming. We weren't exactly your run-of-the-mill weekend guests. Along with all of the above-mentioned, these poor guys had to unload four complete sets of costumes, including hats, canes, shoes, and props.

In Las Vegas, many people never see the sun. In a town where days and nights become confused and/or fused, we tried to keep our normal family routines.

Dee Dee and Dick and their three children—Mary, little Dee

Dee, and Tom—were usually up about nine o'clock. Dee Dee always cooked a big breakfast. (We could smell the bacon frying, all the way down the hall.) They were the first ones at the pool to stake claim on at least ten lounge chairs.

John and I rose early to play tennis. On the mornings we could talk Dee Dee and Dick into getting away from their kids, we would play doubles. Losers bought breakfast.

Juli, Chris, Joey, Mike, Jennie, and Betsy slept until noon, like their Mom and Dad. Peg and Dick kept their kids on their schedule of "stay up late, sleep late." The rest of us are glad they did, because their little voices were piercing, especially when you were rooming next door to them. Peg says the best source of discipline she used in the hotel was to threaten her children with a visit from the security guard. Silence or jail!

One of Peg's more memorable chaotic evenings caused a total change in little Dee Dee Gass' philosophy of life. As she and Dick and Dee Dee were going down to dinner, Peg's door suddenly flew open, and all the kids came pouring out, curious as to where the Gasses were going. Peg came running out after them, a plate of pancakes dripping syrup on the floor. She grabbed Jennie's nightgown, which caused Jen to fall on her bottom, and the syrup began dripping its way into her hair. All the time this was going on, Peg was screaming in a stage whisper for someone to retrieve Betsy, who had taken off naked down the hallway. Little Dee Dee, who had always said she would have at least twelve children, turned to her Mom and Dad and said, "I'm never going to have six."

Kathy was swimming instructor for all the children in the pool at Caesar's Palace. (What a shock it must have been for the gold-chained, hair-sprayed, lame-clad women lying on rafts in the pool to see twelve children, wearing their yellow plastic "floatees," attack the water like a swarm of frenzied honeybees.)

None of us had a pool at home, so swimming kept the kids amused and busy through the long, hot Las Vegas days. And it gave us a chance to spend time with them without having to worry about housework or phone calls.

We did have to take time out to sign autographs, though, and sometimes even our children were asked to write their names. That made them feel like real hotshots. But we quickly brought them back to reality by reminding them that their signatures were also required on the homework waiting for them upstairs.

When we'd had enough sun, most of us would head for our rooms to nap. Some days, though, we had groceries to buy and laundry to do. The only way to get into or out of Caesar's Palace was through the casino. It wasn't easy to safari through a crowd of gamblers, carrying dirty laundry stuffed in pillowcases.

Room service, three-meals-a-day for three weeks for so many people was impossible and expensive, so we brought electric fry pans and crockpots to cook dinner in our rooms. Dee Dee was such a master at this that she could prepare a seven-course gourmet sit-down dinner for twelve in one frying pan.

At around 6:30 p.m. or so, we would begin getting ready for the show, each of us doing our own hair and makeup. We would meet downstairs around 7:30, where Kathy would re-style Dee Dee's hair. (Dee Dee admits that she's rotten at fixing her own hair.)

Our Caesar's Palace dressing room is unbelievably luxurious, especially when compared to the men's locker rooms we had at every arena, or the horse stables under the grandstands at state fairs. We like sharing the same dressing room, because it's easier to help one another dress, and we enjoy just being together. Kathy takes care of the costumes herself, because it has to be done right, and truthfully she's the only one she can trust. Kathy nags us a lot, but perhaps we would never all get onstage if she didn't.

"Five minutes!" The call comes over the speaker in our dressing room. Hurriedly we make last-minute touch-ups. I'll admit my hardest job is to tear myself away from the mirror. At that moment, I want to change everything—my hair, my makeup, my weight.

Just before showtime, the four of us retire to a quiet corner of the backstage area and say the same prayer we have said before every engagement for thirty years. It happens to be the prayer we were taught by the nuns to say before volleyball games in grammar school. And it works just the same . . . win a few, lose a few.

Then we separate to our appropriate corners; Peggy and Dee Dee await the cue on one side of the stage, and Kathy and I take our places on the other side.

Kathy:

Sometimes!

One summer night at the Las Vegas Hilton, we received our five-minute call, and Janet wasn't even in her costume yet. So Dee Dee and I went upstairs to get ready, while Peg, being a nice guy, stayed downstairs to help Jan dress. In every show on The Strip, the sweep second-hand of the clock reaches 8:00, and the overture begins, ready or not! That night, I was certain that Dee Dee and I would end up performing as a duet. We were supposed to start our opening number out in the audience, and as the musical introduction began, we heaved a great sigh of relief as Jan and Peg rushed through the curtain and ran down the dark aisles to where we were standing. As the spotlight came up, I handed Jan her microphone, and we started singing, "What Are You Doing Tonight?"

Then I saw her. Jan had on only one shoe. There she was with her foot up on a table of a booth, trying to buckle her shoe strap with one hand and hold her microphone with the other, as she alternately sang and gasped, "What are you doing (excuse me, please) tonight (I'm so sorry)." The lady on whose lap she was practically standing was laughing, thank heavens. Then, as Jan walked ahead of me up the stairs and onto the stage, I noticed her zipper was down. Luckily I was close enough to pull it up before she brought down the house. Will we ever learn to live with Jan's narrow escapes as well as she does?

Peggy:

Dinner shows are always the most difficult. The patrons are busy sawing their steaks, and are still in a state of shock over the prices they are paying. Some are bragging loudly over their winnings, others are licking the wounds from losing at the gaming tables or the one-armed bandits. We have to work all the harder to win them over. A big challenge is convincing some of the men in the audience to relax and allow themselves to be entertained. Usually, the wives are the ones who have insisted on seeing The Lennon Sisters, and their husbands are there without a smile, thinking they would rather be watching Ann-Margret. It's gratifying to us to see the surprise on their faces when they realize that we've finally grown up and do more than just stand and sing.

During the song "Cabaret," dressed in our red satin corsets, we sit at the edge of the stage and sing to the men at the closer tables. We have to laugh at the diverse reactions initiated by our silly flirting. We've all become adept at quick character-study. We can immediately spot the "happily marrieds" and the "miserables." Either the husband laughs, while the wife nudges him teasingly, or the man stares over our heads, while the woman glares at him as if to say, "Don't you dare enjoy this." If we were marriage counselors, we could give instant advice—to some, "You've got it made," and to others, "It'll never last."

The experience we four enjoy onstage is filled with a mixture of highs and lows. Dee Dee, Janet, Kathy, and I have talked a great deal about those intimate moments together. I believe the lows come when we are standing backstage and the questions run through our heads, "What am I doing here?" "My legs are just going to refuse to step out on that stage one more time." "How can I possibly smile?" "I don't feel like singing tonight at all."

Whether we perform for twenty people or twenty-thousand, our stomachs quiver and our knees shake. Much of the enthusiasm and determination that compels us to perform at our highest level is due to fright. After more than thirty years of entertaining, the fear that we may not be accepted by the audience is still present. We work very hard, and we are proud of the variety of changes in our act, yet we still have that inner desire that everyone enjoy our performance as much as we enjoy performing for them.

Fortunately, at most clubs or arenas, we don't have time to dwell upon these anxieties. But, one year when we were with Andy Williams at Caesar's, we had too much time. For ten minutes, we were seated upon four swings suspended 25 feet above center stage, while Andy did his opening songs and monologue. It was dark up there. It was hot and smoky up there. It was HIGH up there. Through the scrim, the sheer black curtain hanging in front of us, we could see the flickering blue candles at each table that allowed us to discern only hints of faceless bodies. The only brightness was the beam of light enveloping Andy as he introduced us.

"I'd like you to meet four girls whom I love very much," he said. "You've seen them on television for many years. Some of you, I'm sure, have never seen them perform onstage before. They've grown up. They sing great; they dance great; and I'll tell you another thing—and this is the truth—it's a lot more fun sharing a dressing room with them than it was with The Osmond Brothers. Ladies and gentlemen, for your pleasure, my friends The Lennon Sisters!"

At that moment our thought processes switch from manual to automatic. Janet's husband John, our conductor, alerts the orchestra with the count-off for our song. In that instant, we complete a mental checklist: "Shoes, dress, makeup, earrings, hair, microphone. Now, smile!"

The curtain rises and the music swells, the first rush of adrenalin surges through our bodies, bringing with it an overwhelming feeling of self-confidence. At the same time, four bright spotlights cut through the smoke-filled showroom and slap us in the face. The startling brilliance of the lights causes a momentary distortion of our vision that makes our eyelashes glisten, and we feel as though we are peering through fine wet cobwebs. Our mirrored swings descend to the sound of whispered "oohs" and "aahs," and the reflections from our beaded gowns sprinkle the audience with a myriad of shimmering lights. Then, at that moment, we soar to the glamor and the excitement of being onstage. It's the only times we admit to ourselves that we feel like stars. And we are stars.

Seeing one another from across the stage, we communicate by our smiling eyes that this singing and dancing and working together is actually fun. It is a natural high, a singular fulfillment. We also acknowledge in these moments many of the feelings we have for one another. Although normally not flamboyant with our emotions, we let them fly onstage, and all the love and pride we feel as sisters surrounds us, and we share it with the audience. It is thrilling for us to hear our four voices meld into one in a blend that is ours and ours alone. At times, we become totally suspended in a union of spirit that experiences to the fullest the talent that God is sharing with, and through, us.

On opening nights we are anxious, awaiting the reactions of our mentors. Harold Cohen, our manager, is always gracious and complimentary, whether he believes it or not. Andre Tayir gives us hugs, criticisms, notes, and changes, served with a glass of white wine. But it is Phyllis Cohen, Harold's wife, who is our loudest critic. Phyllis flits about our dressing room in her basic black dress, her gorgeous strands of pearls bobbing up and down in rhythm to her clicking highly polished fingernails—the epitome of the society model, her hairstyle soft and casual. She is a sleek lady, in the best sense of that word, tall and truly classy. She checks out our hair: "Dee Dee, your new coiffure is deevine!" And our bodies: "Kathy, you look so skinny! I told you to fatten up for this engagement." "Peggy, I'm so proud of you. You did hold your tummy in better this time." And our voices: "Oh, my dear Janet, you didn't whisper your solo tonight. You were suuuuuper!"

Dianne:

When Peg's last two babies were born, our working schedules were naturally thrown off-kilter. At first we were panicked as to what to do. We had commitments with Andy Williams for Vegas and Lake Tahoe. Peg had managed, accidentally, to schedule her babies at the same time. So, from our large family, we came up with the perfect solution—another sister.

Mimi was wonderful. She worked hard and looked adorable. We were all terribly proud of her. It took a great deal of courage for her to accept the offer to perform with The Lennon Sisters. She began her career at the top, with Andy Williams at the Sahara Tahoe and Caesar's Palace.

Within three weeks, she had her costumes fitted, her choreography rehearsed, her hair cut and styled, and—spending every evening with Peg—learned her harmony part. She was eighteen years old, nervous, terrified, and a surprise to everyone, including herself.

Opening night at the Sahara, Mimi looked at me just before we went on and announced, "I think I'm going to throw up."

"Oh, no, you're not!" I exclaimed and shoved her out onto the stage.

After that case of opening night jitters, she loved it. "I loved the bright lights and seeing and hearing all the happy clapping (and sometimes drunk) people," Mimi said. "The costumes and makeup and all the glitter that many associate with the stage were exciting to me. But the greatest thrill of all was being on the stage with my big sisters, singing and dancing, smiling and laughing. It was an overwhelming feeling of love that will never leave me. What a thrill it was being a 'star,' even for that brief while."

Before our eyes, Mimi blossomed into a beautiful young woman (while Peg blossomed further into motherhood).

Our children also benefited greatly from our visits to Las Vegas.

They learned to be courteous and quiet in a restaurant; they know that, when they are waiting for an elevator, they must let people out before they can pile in; they are careful not to splash adults sitting around the pool, even if the adults *are* sitting by the only place shallow enough for little children. I think they have had experiences not many children will know.

For instance, the experience of my little Tommy Gass. The first time we appeared in Las Vegas, I made a special point of telling my three children how to keep from getting lost if we should become separated from one another. Particular attention was given to the elevator. "Now kids, if you get caught alone in the elevator, don't panic. Just push the Number 6 button, and that will take you up to our floor. Wait until the red Number 6 light goes out up above the door, and then step out and wait for Mommy. I will know to find you there."

One afternoon, returning from the pool, four-year-old Tommy ran on ahead and jumped into an empty elevator just as the door began to close. I caught a glimpse of his little blue L. A. Rams bathrobe and white styrofoam swim-ring disappear behind gold doors. Then five-year-old Dee Dee began screaming at the top of her voice. "My brother is in there! Oh, somebody, do something! Help, help! Oh Tommy! Help!"

Mary, being the oldest sister at age six, put her arm around little Dee Dee, trying to console her hysteria.

I attempted to calm her down by telling her that Tommy knew what to do. "Now, Dee Dee, you girls know you would do the proper thing, and Tom will, too." (Meanwhile, I was praying that Tom was tall enough to reach the 6 button of the elevator.)

We caught the next elevator, but when we reached the sixth floor Tom was not there. I dragged the two girls to our rooms.

Nana, who was babysitting, opened the door to the room, and I shouted out, "Is Tom here?"

"Oh, yes," Nana said. "He's in the other room, coloring."

In the other room coloring! While Marybo, Dee Dee, and I were at wits end with worry, Tom was in the other room coloring.

"Tommy, oh, Tommy." The girls surrounded him as if he had been lost from them for months.

"Hi, Mom," he said. "Well, I just came up ahead of you."

I was quite amazed he (and we) had weathered this first storm so well. Then about five minutes later, Tom came into my room. "Mom, you know, what I said wasn't really what happened," he confessed. "I got in the elevator, and when the doors closed I got scared, so I remembered what you said and pushed the number 6 button; then I stood back all alone, stuck my fingers in my ears, and screamed as loud as I could all the way up here."

Another crisis we won't forget was the time we were awakened about 5:30 a.m. by the sound of the hotel fire alarm. I jumped up and ran to the door—I was not as quick as Dick, who got there first. He looked up and down the hallway, but saw no one, no smoke and no flames. Then he heard some man yell, "Let's get the hell out of here!" Dick ran back into the room and tried to reach the hotel operator over the telephone. There was no answer, and the thought raced through his mind that they were the only ones left alive in the hotel. "Dee Dee, get the kids up," he said. "I'll run across the hall and get Janet."

Janet, always slow to come out of sleep, did not care about what was going on, because she was going nowhere without her false eyelashes on. To make matters worse, she could not find her sunglasses. For Janet, it was either lashes and glasses or burn. Dick Gass, a safety representative for the telephone company, knew that the first rule in escaping a fire is "don't use the elevators."

"Quick, guys, down the stairs," he commanded.

All this time, there was not another soul around. The alarm blasted away, and we started frantically down the twelve flights of stairs. Tommy, his pillow tucked under his arm and wearing his blue robe, led the way. We did not encounter anyone else, but as we reached each floor, the fire alarm seemed to blast louder, echoing off the cement walls of the stairwell.

At the bottom, we opened the door into the casino and were shocked to see people milling around, pulling slot machines, yelling at each other, and having a wonderful time, completely oblivious to the impending doom. Nobody cared. There we stood, barefooted evacuees, in the middle of Caesar's Palace, under the statue of Julius himself. I had managed to grab my purse and a jacket, but I will not account for the dress of the others, except to say that Janet had her coat on over her shortie pajamas and stood the whole time with her face against Caesar's tummy, her hands held over the sides of her face. And still people just rushed by. Nobody cared.

Dick sneaked through the casino in his bathrobe, very few people showing any surprise at his garb. At the front desk he asked if anything was wrong. To his embarrassment, he was told that it was a false alarm. He slinked back through the array of gamblers at their tables and slot machines and herded his weirdly attired family into the nearest elevator. People crushed in on us, glasses of booze in their hands, singing loudly and generally carousing. Nobody cared.

We were all at the pool the next morning, and Dick asked Peg what the Cathcarts were doing during all the mayhem the night before. "What are you talking about?" she asked.

"The fire alarm. Didn't you hear it? I know you were down at the other end of the floor, but that clanging could have been heard a mile away."

"You mean," she exclaimed, "the fire alarm went off last night? We surely didn't hear it." Then with tongue in cheek, Peg asked, "You bums, why didn't you come to our room to make sure we were up? Thanks a lot!"

Dick Gass replied, "Nobody cared."

Peggy used to give her kids instructions too, and she harped on manners constantly. "I don't want you kids to grow up as snobs, but I do want you to have manners and respect. You should never use vulgar words. That only shows your lack of knowledge of the English language. Vulgarity embarrasses other people and should embarrass you. It doesn't matter whether you are rich or poor, as long as you have respect for yourself and others and do the proper thing at the proper time. It's not being snobby—it's called having 'a little bit of class.' "

That bit of wisdom cropped up one night when Dick and Peg took their children to eat dinner at the Piazza Restaurant at Caesar's. They were seated at a round table with two high-chairs placed near Mom and Daddy for the baby girls. Peg admits that the children were on particularly good behavior, and she was basking in the glory of being the "perfect mother."

Midway through dinner, a large group of people came crashing through the normally sedate Italian restaurant, swearing, waving wine bottles, and yelling at the waiters. Joey, who was about eight years old, asked his daddy if he could leave his chair and walk around to where his mom was sitting. Permission granted, he quietly made his way to Peg and whispered in her ear. "Mommy, those people behind us don't have any class, do they?"

Triumph!

Jan recalls an incident in which it took all her power of concentration to keep from laughing. She was preparing to take her children to dinner and asked them to please go to the bathroom before they went downstairs. "You know the bathrooms are way across the casino, and I'm not going to get up during dinner for any of you, so you'd better go now." The children scurried off and returned in record time.

Downstairs, after they were seated at the table and had ordered their food, Goober said, "Mommy, I have to go to the bathroom."

"I'm sorry, Goober. I told you to go when we were upstairs, and if you didn't go to the bathroom then, you can just wait now."

When their dinner had arrived, Goober said once again, "Mommy, can I go now?"

"Goober, it's just impossible to get through that casino from here. Just finish your hamburger, and on the way out I'll take you."

He sat there for a few minutes, hands in his lap, eyes down. "What's the matter? Why aren't you eating your dinner? Come on, Goobs."

"Okay, Mom, but it sure is hard eating a hamburger with only one hand," he said in his slow drawl.

Peggy:

We can only scratch the surface of what it's like to try to keep a sense of humor for three weeks, cooped up in eight rooms with about 25 people, on a working vacation.

There is no place on earth like Las Vegas; and there is no other place like Lake Tahoe. It is a beautiful spot all year. We have seen many summers there while appearing with the Welk band and on our own. But we had never seen the white splendor of the Tahoe winter until our first introduction to it at Christmastime, 1971. We were scheduled to appear at the Sahara Tahoe Hotel for ten days with Andy Williams, and we were looking forward to that White

Christmas. It was not merely the snow that we anticipated, but also that Christmas was going to be our first Christmas away from home.

Home came with us, however. The contract for that engagement was unlike any we had ever signed. It contained unique requirements. To induce the four of us and our families to leave Venice, the hotel agreed to many provisions: (1) our usual four sets of double connecting rooms, with four refrigerators, (2) four decorated Christmas trees, (3) a home on the lake for our mother, grandmother, five brothers, two sisters (their girlfriends and/or boyfriends), and, naturally, the family dog Mutt, (4) a room for Kathy's mother-in-law, (5) a tall, decorated Christmas tree and extra cots sufficient to bed the entire family.

It was quite evident that somebody wanted The Lennon Sisters to work there, because the management went far beyond those requests, even to delivering food from the hotel kitchen every day— turkeys, roasts, fruits, vegetables, desserts. We were also provided with snow sleds and logs for the huge fireplaces. It was ideal! Christmas Eve found all of us together at Mom's home on the lake, with snow falling in great abundance. And for our children the miracle of Christmas was how Santa knew to come to that house instead of our own homes in southern California.

The snowfall became a snowstorm, blocking all the roads. We voiced our hope that we might be snowbound and therefore unable to work that night. We were snowbound, but the hotel (they had provided everything else) sent a snowplow to clear the roads.

Christmas morning we awoke to a white Christmas. Attending Mass at the new church in the pines was like pictures we had only seen on postcards or in movies; everyone bundled up, trudging through the snow toward the little church in the forest. The holiday dinner was, as it had always been for us, a big family affair. Seated around two large round tables, we enjoyed turkey and all the trimmings, with the snow-covered pine trees glistening right outside the windows. God was a great set decorator that year.

For the first few days, we could not get enough of the snow. We jumped into it, slid down it, made snowballs of it, and ate it. The newness did wear off in time, but still the snow fell upon us and Lake Tahoe. The little kids loved it though, running in and out of the house all day long. Every time a hand got cold or a bottom was wet, there was another trip to the fireplace hearth where warmth was found. There was a constant stream of wet, soggy mittens, hats, and socks shoved into the clothes dryer. I learned to appreciate what mothers back east must go through every winter.

That Christmas night, we bundled up warmly, and caroling, we plodded through the snow, over the hill to our neighbor's house. It belonged to a man who was also entertaining in Tahoe that season. It seemed fitting that we wish the neighbor and his wife and children and all his grandchildren a very Merry Christmas. For Perry Como is a dear friend. And Christmas is for friends.

Our traveling today, in the 1980s, has been yet another change for us. For so many years we limited our traveling to only those places close to home, where we could take our children with us. But in the last decade, emphasis in our field of entertainment has shifted from west to east, as Atlantic City became the new Las Vegas. Musical variety shows on television have become almost obsolete; situation comedies, soap operas, and rock videos have flooded the screen. Our opportunities for working in our own backyard were rapidly disappearing. We were getting calls from major clubs and theaters around the country, and it was only sensible that we consider their importance to The Lennon Sisters. We decided that the demands of our career and our finances necessitated that we do more long-distance traveling. (A simple case of mathematics: our salary is divided by four, our expenses are multiplied by four.)

When at all possible our husbands travel with us, but because each has his own profession, it's never often enough. We try not to book more than two weeks of work at any one time. When our children were babies, we thought that that was the most important time to be with them. Now, as mothers of teenagers, we *know* that these are the years when our children are most vulnerable. So, we limit our out-of-town appearances to around six or seven weeks throughout the year.

The style of traveling is certainly less complicated today than previously. We take with us our conductor, Jack Feierman, our drummer Evan Diner, and our choreographer/stage manager/producer, Andre Tayir. The many technical problems we had always had to face alone are skillfully handled by these professional men. Consequently, our job on the road has become less of a hassle and much more enjoyable.

The most frustrating part of going on the road for me is the attitudes of the others. They think of little else but food. I'm really not exaggerating when I say that three-quarters of their conversations center on the where, when, and what of mealtimes. Even before we get on the plane they wonder if breakfast *and* lunch will be served. Upon landing, before the seatbelt sign has been turned off, they are planning where to have a long, leisurely dinner. All of them know the greatest restaurants in each city, and they try to visit them all at least once. I've had salad in all of them.

Kathy is the funniest. She orders conservatively, and then, with an "I Love Lucy" stare, she listens with rapt attention as everyone else orders. When the food is brought to the table, she raises her fork in expectation. Then, her hand darts in and out, up and down the table, tasting and sampling. We've threatened to buy her a gold fork to hang around her neck! And she's always so skinny!!!

The only other one who can compete with Kathy's appreciation for food is Jack Feierman. Most of the time he eats sparingly, but when he decides to have a really big meal, he's a joy to watch. His problem is that, when he overeats, he sneezes. We all know when he's had too much, and he alternately sneezes and laughs through his dessert.

Andre is a finicky eater, unless everything is covered with garlic butter. Evan is a finicky eater, unless everything is covered with catsup—even his pineapple sherbet. Dee Dee will eat anything, as long as it's not fast food, and Janet and I just love food, fast or otherwise, but it is always covered with guilt. Our life on the road now really centers on cameraderie at mealtime. Good wine, good food, good friends.

Since we are traveling through the Midwest and East more often now, we've been able to renew old friendships with many people we met while traveling with the Lawrence Welk band. Wherever we travel, we have been able to meet with members of our fan club, most of whom we knew only by name. Thanks to Ruth Hirschoff, our fan club president, our fans receive periodic newsletters, pictures, and information on our next performances. Many of our fans travel hundreds of miles to be with us. The wonderful thing about them is that they respect our right to privacy, they don't try to monopolize our time or interfere with our routine. But they do offer support, and quite often they bring homemade gifts, cookies, *etc.* We always manage a breakfast or lunch together, and sometimes we'll all go to the closest shopping mall, spending the day browsing and visiting. Even though these friendships began as fan-and-performers, they have become much more than that, and will far outlast our singing career.

Through the years we have remained very close to Lawrence Welk, Jr. Growing up together through the rough teenage years on the road created a special bond between us. Larry is now president of Teleklew Productions, Lawrence Welk's organization. From time to time, we have worked with Larry on various projects, the most recent being an album of inspirational music for Ranwood Records, Teleklew's recording company. We also were featured on Lawrence Welk's 1984 Christmas Reunion Special, with all our families. Doing this TV show for Larry was a nostalgic experience, reminiscent of the first show we did for his dad.

In 1980, The Olympics were held in Moscow. Because Russia had recently invaded Afghanistan, President Jimmy Carter made the decision to boycott the competition. It was a very controversial decision and one that affected the whole world.

The President attempted to make up to our athletes for their frustration and disappointment by inviting each one of them to Washington, D. C., for a week of festivities. He presented specially designed medals to those men and women who were unable to represent the United States at the competition for which they had trained—some for most of their lives.

We were invited by the U. S. Olympic Committee, along with a small group of other artists, to entertain the athletes in a special night of tribute at the Eisenhower Theater of The Kennedy Center. It was an honor to meet and perform for those Olympians, the climax of which was dinner on the White House lawn with all of them, after a personal meeting with President and Mrs. Carter and Amy. The President and his family graciously posed for pictures with each and every athlete and performer.

All of that celebration could not fill the void for those Olympic competitors, but the four of us were left with mixed feelings of pride, sympathy, and elation.

In the last few years, we have been many places and performed for many people. But, an outstanding highlight took place right in Los Angeles. We were honored by Mayor Tom Bradley and the

City Council for our talent, community service, and our part in spreading the good will of the people of Los Angeles throughout the nation. It was a memorable and somewhat humbling experience. At the same time we were asked by the Mayor to be present at City Hall on Reagan Day, January 13, 1981. This was a salute and farewell to Ronald Reagan as he left California to take up residence in Washington, D. C. Eighty mayors of California cities were gathered in Council Chambers. The Reagans were behind schedule that day, and we were called upon to ad-lib a program to keep the mayors entertained. We got many of the mayors up to sing and had the news media reveling in the extra news footage of their mayors' performing.

When President-elect and Mrs. Reagan arrived, they were greeted by Mayor Bradley and presented with a large jar of jelly beans. At the close of the ceremonies, we sang "America The Beautiful," and as we left the platform the Reagans shook our hands. "Thank you, girls, beautifully done. I've watched you for so many years. That song always brings a tear to my eye," Mr. Reagan said warmly.

We have met and sung for six presidents during our career. And we know that, no matter what one's political affiliation, it is always a thrill and a privilege to meet the President of The United States.

16

Hail! Hail! The Gang's All Here (Relatively Speaking)

The Lennon Sisters:

Mom

Webster defines the word "mother" as "a female parent, to attribute to a particular person the maternity or origin of." Well, he may be able to explain or define a "mother" with words, but for us, it is nearly impossible. Yes, she was and is our "female parent" and gave us our "origin." From the moments of our births, she was our main source of life, love, and guidance, and she has been much more.

She was Dad's partner and helpmate, and we know she has earned a special place in heaven for her patience and understanding of him. While Dad was the more gregarious of our parents, Mom was the quiet, solid rock. She seemed always to be there when we needed her. Without forcing her views upon us, she was instrumental in helping us to form and express our own opinions.

Home was her dominion, maybe because she had had an unstable home life as a child. She seemed to relish all the chores of being a housewife, but most of all, she loved having us—and any of our friends we happened to bring home—all underfoot. It was just a matter of fact that, when we came home from school each day, we yelled "Mom!" And her voice always answered, "Here I am."

We don't think she ever had time to herself alone, but it never seemed to us that she wanted it. On television, we see mothers taking a leisurely bubble bath before dinner. Mom could hardly stay awake long enough to enjoy a quick dip in the tub after her long day. As children, we wondered why moms never took baths, and kids had to take them several times a week. As we grew older, we realized that Mom did slip into the tub, only after she had slipped all of us into bed.

Mom's cooking is the best. Though there were many children and few dollars, our meals were well-balanced and delicious. She could pull the leftovers out of the refrigerator and make some of our favorite dinners, which we called "Stuff." And making ten or eleven sandwiches from one small can of tuna was almost comparable to the Biblical parable of the loaves and fishes. The things our mom could do with a little of this and a little of that would make a great cookbook. If someone happened to drop by at mealtime, well, there was always enough for one more, or three, or five. It was quality, not quantity, that we came to appreciate and consume with great relish. None of us ever realized that people were allowed more than one piece of bacon or one pork chop at a meal, until after we had left home.

Mom's hands were exceptionally strong—especially when she braided our hair. She could pull our braids so taut (to keep them in place all day) that even with her blue eyes Dee Dee looked Oriental. But her hands were gentle when she washed our hair. When we were very young, she would lay us down on the kitchen sink counter to wash our hair while telling us a story. After rinsing our hair with cold vinegar, she sat out on the back steps with us and towel-dried our hair with her unique way of rubbing and touching. We had her all to ourselves for a few moments.

Although Mom didn't tell many jokes or try to upstage Dad, she had a great sense of humor and saw the funny side of things. As each of us reached school age and brought home the same old first-grade jokes, second-grade jokes, third-grade jokes, she managed to laugh as if it were the first time she had ever heard them. As opposed to Dad's reaction. He would wait until the punch-line and then blurt it out ahead of us. "Why pretend?" he'd say. "I already knew it."

Mom is a fine athlete. It was one of the qualities Dad admired most in her, and some of their best times were spent playing golf together and attending various sporting events. Dad loved to brag about her, "If your mom had not been so crazy about me, and begged me to have a million kids, she could have been the greatest woman athlete in the world."

If Mom has a fault, perhaps it is that she saves everything—not just useful, good things, but anything and everything. Her basement on Harding Avenue is cluttered with costumes, old vases, decorations for holidays, suitcases, used wrapping paper and ribbons, snow clothes, *etc*. But if any of us need anything unusual, we know where to go.

One word can describe our mother. She is a *Giver*. An unconditional giver. We can never remember any selfishness on her part.

In the years since Dad's death, we have watched our mom face the extraordinary challenges that the younger generation presented during the 1970s. As a single parent, she raised five sons and two daughters who were true products of that era.

She put no conditions on her love for her children. They sought her advice and counsel, and she was an active listener. She allowed them to make their own choices in life. And for that, she gained their greater respect.

She manages to accept whatever comes her way. Her strength is her faith in the Lord. She has always said, "God will provide. He will never send us more than we can bear."

She is young. She is pretty. She is an optimist and fun to be with. And she is ours.

Brothers And Sisters

With feelings of pride, happiness, respect, and concern, we have watched our younger brothers and sisters grow. When they were babies, they were the main reason we decided to accept the responsibility of working a weekly television show. Even when we were very young ourselves, we considered them our "little kids." In a fleeting moment called time, we were robbed of our "babies," and now our "kids" are our grownup brothers and sisters, and in a sense, we are all the same age. In some ways, their generation is quite removed from the one in which we grew up—we were "fifties-sixties," they were "sixties-seventies." They are much more open with their feelings, and to our way of thinking, sometimes too open. But because of their honest, outspoken ways, we have grown to respect and understand a little better the intricate and delicate feelings of today's young people. Their openness has helped us to relate and communicate more easily with our own children.

As big families often do, we have formed a special vocabulary with meanings that are ours alone. To other people, our "code" phrases, or verbal shorthand, is unintelligible. They may not understand how an old TV cartoon or the theme-song for "I Married Joan" could have such great meaning.

Once every few weeks, we all gather with our families at Mom's house, to celebrate the birthdays-of-the-month. Ironically, the eleven of us were born in eleven different months. These are times of great disorganization. In the midst of the madness, *we* know what is happening and savor even the smallest incidents.

Although each brother and sister has moved out, none have moved away. Everyone lives close enough to drop by Mom's with laundry; on their way to the Maytags, they can grab a cold piece of French toast off the stove and a quick glass of orange juice before saying, "Thanks, Mom. I'll pick up the clothes later."

For several years, four of our brothers ran their own furniture repair and restoration shop in Venice, specializing in antiques. Dan, the boss, Pat, the craftsman, Bill, the artist, and Joe, the apprentice, loved working together because it allowed them to mix business and pleasure. While refinishing furniture, the boys would sing four-part harmony by the hour, mostly for their own enjoyment, but also as rehearsal for their occasional local club appearances.

Little Kippy grew up one day and became Kipp Lennon, Entertainer. He makes his living singing for movies, television, and commercials. Unlike the four of us, he lives to be onstage, whether that be Mom's living room or in clubs with VENICE, the pop group in which he sings with our brother Pat and cousins Mike and Mark Lennon.

With all the varied musical styles and sounds, all eleven of us have performed in concert many times. Standing onstage together, we experience a oneness of voices and souls. As a family we are quick to laugh and quick to cry. We love to poke fun at each other, sometimes moving the victim of our jokes to tears. If one of us makes a foolish mistake of any kind and another happens to see or hear it, the mista*kee* had better be prepared for a brutal teasing from the rest of the family. At the risk of becoming Mistakees, we have assembled a thumbnail sketch of each brother and sister. As their personalities are different, so are their recollections.

*

[**Kipp**—*Low man on the totem pole, cartoonist, spoiled; artistic, self-confident, a performer, spoiled, trendy dresser, still plays with Captain Action dolls, comic book collector, spoiled, loving and lovable; great huge dimples, generous, spoiled, our baby, little Skipper.*]

Kipp Lennon:

The twenty years that separate Dee Dee from me make me a member of another generation, although I'm her youngest brother and the "baby" of the family. Needless to say, my musical influences have been different from my sisters', and the ideals and aspirations of a young singer now are different from those of four girls singing to America's living rooms in the fifties and sixties. But there is one beautiful thread that connects all the great singers and performers together as far as I'm concerned. Whether it's the fire in the eyes of Ol' Elvis, or the rich, happy sadness in the voice of Al Jolson, or the perfect timing of Jack Benny, or the sheer thrill of the Beatles, or the perfect grace of Dionne Warwick. I've never found a word for this thing—but as they say, "you either got it, or you ain't got it." And it transcends time or fads or fashion.

It's a gift, and when used to its utmost it can thrill you to your soul. When my sisters sing, there are moments like that when they shine above the din of everyday life with a sound that shouts "Life!" And when we are all singing together, the feeling of pride and beautiful sadness is just overwhelming . . . and so good.

As I get older I see the way they grew up in the public eye as "America's Sweethearts" and see the way some people have labeled them "dated" or "too wholesome." It makes me sad to think they

Christmas, 1978, with our children. *(The Lennon Family Collection)*

A Christmas Special, singing with Mom. *(The Lennon Sisters Collection)*

The Lennon family album: Top row, Dan and Ginny Lennon; Pat and Nancy Lennon; Bill Lennon and fiancee, Gail Lopata. Middle row, Mimi and Danny Macias, with children Mary and Elizabeth; Joe and Ellyn Lennon. Bottom row, Annie and Mike Suzuki; Mom, Kipp Lennon, and Nana. (*The Lennon Family Collection*)

sometimes aren't appreciated for the talent that they have by the kids of my generation. There are lots of people, from Dylan to Springsteen, who have spoken for the people of my generation, hitting the nail on the head and getting all the praise they deserve.

Now some people might say that Norman Rockwell misrepresented the war years by not showing the blood and pain and violence. But they miss the point. Some artists just want to paint the prettiest picture they can. To help people forget their problems and just laugh and love. Boy, can my sisters paint.

And I hope to use the same colors, because we're all just trying to make it a little sunnier around here.

*

[**Annie**—*Dream-teller, clown-lover, wife, babysitter, telephone talker, poet, considerate, artistic, self-conscious; long dark hair; huge round black eyes, baby sister.*]

Annie Lennon Suzuki:

I don't really know what memory of my sisters stands out the most. It seems there are so many. I know it was hard for me at such a young age to realize why my sisters came and went so often. I remember how hard I tried not to cry when Kathy would tell me they were leaving again. They said they would only be gone a short while, but to me it seemed like years. When they finally did come home, I don't know which I was happier to see—them or the presents they had brought me.

I also remember the excitement of getting to appear on the Lawrence Welk Show. The wardrobe department took us all to Western Costume Company, where we were outfitted in all kinds of costumes. From their clothes hangers hung my dreams, as well as my nightmares, and I still don't know whether I was excited to be there or just plain scared to death.

There have been advantages and disadvantages to having famous sisters, although the good ones have outweighed the bad. At school, for instance, if one of the kids was upset with me, instead of yelling about what I did, it was "Just because you are a Lennon." In the same way, if I won some kind of election or office at school, it was "Because you are a Lennon." There were the kids I hardly even knew who, after finding out my sisters were the Lennon Sisters, would immediately be my "best friends."

But, like I said, there are so many good things I've enjoyed because my sisters are who they are. I've loved the excitement of going down to the studio and watching all the tapings, and I know how lucky I am to have been able to meet so many of the TV stars I've looked up to.

As I've grown older, we all seem to have become the same age. They've been through so much with me. I feel lucky to have such a close relationship with *all* my sisters. So, above being great performers, my sisters are also four of my best friends.

*

[Joe—*A romantic, gentle, intelligent;stubborn, artist, adventurer, the bottomless pit for food; determined to find the Loch Ness Monster; still watches Saturday morning cartoons; has a St. Francis of Assisi face and sad, round, basset hound eyes, the "Doc."*]

Joe Lennon:

A few months after beginning my studies to become a Doctor of Chiropractic, the financial burden of staying in college started to take its toll on my bank account. It must have showed in my face, because a fellow student asked me why I looked so down. As I began my reply, my new friend interrupted with, "What do you mean, financial difficulty? Your sisters are The Lennon Sisters! You could probably buy this whole college!"

How many times had I heard something like that? My thoughts went back to grammar school and the taunts of the tough kids, "Hey, rich kid.... Hey, stuck-up.... Hey, sissy, you gonna sing on

TV again this week? . . . You're teacher's pet 'cuz your sisters are famous . . . ."

I never understood why I had to hear those remarks at least once or twice a year from children who were otherwise my friendly playmates. My sisters weren't really that famous, were they? The Lennon Sisters? No, they were "the girls," just like my brothers were "the guys." In fact, my sisters were "the guys," too. They weren't celebrities, they were Janet-who-listened-to-rock-n'-roll-up-in-her-room, Kathy-who-took-us-to-the-beach, Peggy-who-sewed-together-Christmas-ornaments, and Dee Dee-who-made-French-toast-like-Mom. The Lawrence Welk Show was just their job, like Jerry's dad was a gardener, or Kim's sister was a nurse.

Because I was not really conscious of their celebrity status, growing up with show business was just a normal part of my life. I remember I wouldn't wait until it was my turn to go to "the show" to see all the costumes and lights and cables and stage props and cameras. The electricians and sound men and members of "the crew" as I knew them would show me the magic they performed to produce a television program, and then would treat me to a cheeseburger and fries at the Commissary. (I still have nightmares in which I can't run fast enough past the stairs that lead to the sound booth, where—I was told—"the giants" lived. I wonder if the crew didn't want me up there?) Also, on my special day, I would get to sit in the empty seats where the audience would be later, and listen to my sisters pre-record. I could help in the dressing room during rehearsal, or run errands to the make-up room or sewing room. That night, I would fall asleep on one of my sisters' laps, listening to them practice their song one more time as we drove home.

Because of The Lennon Sisters, one of my biggest dreams came true when I was four years old. I got to meet and talk with my favorite hero, Zorro, and poke Sergeant Garcia's fat belly. And how many guys do you know that have slept with Debby Boone? (We were both six years old and had fallen asleep in front of Mom's television set watching Disneyland.)

A few more months after that first incident at college, another student approached me after class. "I just found out your sisters are The Lennon Sisters," she said, smiling. "You know, I grew up with them, too. Every Saturday night, I would just watch them and pretend I was their other sister. But you *really* grew up with them as your sisters. That must have been neat."

Yes, it was.

*

[**Mimi**—*One half of Campbell Soup Kids; tiniest girl in the family, good listener, concerned mom, picks at food, morning grouch, athletic, peaches-and-cream complexion, sweet, graceful, friend to everyone, a talented, funny lady.*]

Mimi Lennon Macias:

When I was little, I never knew my sisters to be any more than my four big sisters. In fact, when I was about three years old, Kathy asked me if I knew who The Lennon Sisters were, and I told her, "Yeah, I met them down at the studio once."

It was also at that time that the Welk Band nicknamed me "Screaming Mimi." It seems that anytime anyone who wasn't family came within ten feet of me, I would let out a tremendous yell that could be heard all around the studio. To this day the name still sticks!

I couldn't wait until it was my turn to go down to the studio. There are so many memories I retain of the Welk Show. I remember sitting in the make-up chair and having Rudy put rouge on my cheeks and thinking I looked like my sisters.

Although I loved being behind the scenes, I hated being in front of the camera. I was on the show numerous times, but you could always count on my performance being the same each time: dress rehearsal, I was all smiles and joking around, but when it came time to sing on live TV, panic set in—and I froze. No smiles, no nothing, just great big tears in my eyes and throat.

In my growing-up years, I began to see my sisters in a different light. Along with being my "second moms," I realized that they could be my friends, too.

And now that we're all the same age, I don't know what I would do without them. I feel fortunate to have been blessed with so many years of growing to know my sisters. I only hope that my two daughters will share in that same sisterly love.

*

[**Bill**—*Thinker, inventor, reader, dreamer, schemer, intellectual, vegetarian; moon-faced, slow but sure, artistic, teases Mom, never eats, great with our children, disappears a lot, has Dad's mannerisms, wears little round glasses, has baby skin with old-man eyes; the other half of The Campbell Soup Kids.*]

Bill Lennon:

I never thought of the girls as stars. I realized they were on TV once a week, and I had seen the crowds that greeted them on their tours, yet it all seemed normal. Maybe it was a lack of glitter that a young mind associates with stardom. My sisters weren't and aren't really that flashy. They just sing as well as any four people have a right to. I've always felt that. Growing up through the 1960s, there were times I felt my sisters were real corny and out-of-date, but that certainly didn't stop me, and still doesn't, from getting chills every time I listen to them. My sisters' blend is so sweet in their performances. I can't imagine a better blend.

But my sisters aren't stars. They just sing great. My Dad was no star, but he sang better than those who were and are. And the rest of my family is just as incredibly talented. Our sisters just weren't considered any more important (*i.e.*, stars) than the rest of us. I mean, they would be on TV one hour, and the next they would be home washing our dishes. Don't think they aren't very special people, though. They're as special as the rest of this weirded-out family, and they're the best singers I've ever heard.

*

[**Pat**—*Surfer, plant-lover, wine-lover, Cheerios-lover, free spirit; shy, happy with himself, sensitive to others; wilderness-lover, kind to everyone and everything; with his fine blond hair, he reminds us of a Hummel figurine.*]

Pat Lennon:

My wife Nancy and I have been avid campers for the past ten years. We enjoy camping along the California coast. That gives us the opportunity to meet a variety of people. When introducing ourselves, the question that invariably comes up is, "Where are you from?"

Our mutual answer is, "Venice," since we were both born and raised there.

More often than not, we get a reply something like, "Oh, Venice. I have a relative that used to live there . . . used to live right down the street from The Lennon Sisters." Or, "Oh, yeah. Venice. That's where The Lennon Sisters live."

Once I let them know that I am a Lennon brother, the conversation flows easily. A lot of people seem to mention the fact that they watched the girls grow up and felt them to be a part of their families.

We once befriended an older couple that loved to talk of Lawrence Welk and The Lennon Sisters. At the end of an enjoyable evening, they brought us fresh apple pie and vanilla ice cream. What a treat . . . especially when camping.

I am really impressed to come in contact with such a wide array of people who still care so much about my sisters. This makes me all the more proud for them.

*

[**Dan**—*Firstborn son, big brother, athlete, scholar, teacher, worrier, searcher, chain-smoker; passionate, sensitive, high-strung, aesthetic, and a sentimental slob.*]

Dan Lennon:

When my sisters were on the road, we would go weeks sometimes as a shell of a family. Everything would seem okay, but it was too quiet; and in bed at night, I would have difficulty remembering what Dad looked like. I missed Janet especially. She was like a big brother to me. And then Saturday morning would come, and we would sit, hearts pounding, staring into the street. A station wagon pulled into the harbor, docked, and we seagulls ran screaming and veering to greet the passengers. I grabbed Dad's knees and his huge, dark coat, burying my face in the cool smell of Father. He seemed to bring home with him snow from Cleveland, cold from Boston, darkness from the streets of New York City. It was like a child hugging a priest, something about feeling alone, but somehow comforted by a huge presence that would never go away. And the girls would be laughing and giving us surprises, and telling us stories about all the crowds and oddballs they met; yet, then, I never understood that part of their lives. They were just my pals.

In college, I began to realize they were almost an American institution, or failing that, at least a fairly well-acknowledged symbol of wholesome, middle-class American womanhood. At times I felt somewhat antagonistic toward their maintenance of this goody-goody image, when I knew them as people and found them more individualistic, interesting, and experienced than their press clippings would imply. But you must realize that at this time I was fairly cynical about everything—the world just didn't seem fair, and their "duplicity" was one of the reasons.

Yet, as I grew older (and now I am so wise and experienced), I began to see how their image was not a lie at all. Basically, they are all—to different degrees—wholesome American women. And in each one of my sisters is a private personality, a whole world of realities that does not belong in the public eye. They are different, yet I love each of them specially. Since they work in a world that will make a public image of anything they may say or do, they respond, as all of us do, by creating a working relationship with society, then living their personal lives as best they can. Beyond my unintended smoke screen of excess wordage lies a basic message—I am proud of my sisters for dealing with the world strongly, honestly, and successfully. They are still "regular guys," whom I respect. And though our tastes in music aren't identical, I believe they are among the most talented vocalists in show business. I sometimes forget how beautifully they sing, especially when I see them onstage, flopping around and flashing arms and legs and melding with the brassy orchestra. Yet at family reunions I hear that sweet, sad blend of humanity that makes music the key to my emotions, that perfect sound of people who love to sing and love each other; no band, no costumes, no makeup. Just that indescribable moment that they can create for me sometimes.

Most of the time, I don't think about "The Lennon Sisters" very much, though. They are Janet, Kathy, Peggy, and Dee Dee. My sisters, just like anybody's.

Mom:

When I sit out in the audience and see and listen to all eleven of my children singing on that stage together, it is almost too much for me to grasp. It's hard to believe they are all my babies and they are the same children whose bottoms and noses I wiped for so many years. If I couldn't detach myself in some way, I would be torn apart inside. It makes me feel so close to their dad. He's always right there. I am filled to overflowing.

Peggy Lennon Cathcart and Janet Lennon Bahler.

Dianne Lennon Gass and Kathy Lennon Daris.

17

Same Song—Separate Voices

Janet:

This memoir may be a rarity, because it is the life of four people. We are very attuned to one another, but we are very much individuals. We don't try to be different one from the other; we just are.

I sometimes feel that, if I didn't attempt to keep a lid on this huge can of worms I call me, I would explode into a thousand little pieces of contradiction. After years of both professional and self analysis, I am still basically the same shy/outgoing, loving/aloof, comical/ serious, woman/child I've always been. Only now I'm better able to accept myself. Whoever I am, I'm happy.

All of my life I have felt loved and appreciated by my family, friends, and even the public.

Growing up in the public eye didn't seem out of the ordinary to me. I felt secure and protected in our goldfish bowl existence. I never viewed our fans as faceless, cardboard characters, but as friends. I believe they viewed us in the same way.

After more than thirty years of performing, I still don't know how I really feel about being an entertainer. I have alternately loved it, despised it, and reveled in it. I know that I'm thankful for its education and opportunities. But I don't believe, if circumstances had allowed me a choice, that I would have ever chosen to be an entertainer. (I had fantasized about being a novelist or social worker.) As it turns out though, I have the best of two worlds. I'm the wife and mother I've always dreamed of being, and I have a career that only takes me away from home eight or ten weeks a year. My life is a healthy balance.

The one sustaining, positive force throughout all my personal losses and glories has been my deep faith in God. He has been my companion, counselor, and sounding board. My relationship with Him is personal and individual, and I'll leave any preaching to those better qualified.

One of the winning hands that God dealt me came to me in the person of John Bahler. I met John in the summer of 1971, when Andy Williams hired him to arrange and conduct our entire Vegas show. I remember being impressed by his kindness and patience with the orchestra, and by their respect for him. We developed a deep friendship even from the beginning. After a few working engagements, John moved on to other opportunities in the music business, and we didn't see each other for some time. In 1975, when John had heard through mutual friends that Lee and I had separated, he called me. We talked for what seems like forever, and he asked me out to dinner. At first I said "No." I was scared to go on a "date" again, after so many years. I pictured Rona Barrett lurking in every restaurant corner. Eventually though, we did get together, and our relationship fit us like an old pair of comfortable shoes. Eighteen months later, on September 25, 1976, we were married in a small chapel in San Diego, California.

Just 24 hours later, we faced our first big challenge together. We arrived home from our one day honeymoon to face our own instant "Brady Bunch!" (John's two, Greg and Michele, and my three, Billy, John, and Kristin.) All the chaos was nothing new to me, but it was hard for John to get used to waiting in line for my attention. Peace and quiet seemed only a figment of our imagination. I'm reminded of a wonderful quote: "It's too bad that all children have to be raised by inexperienced parents." My sentiments, exactly! What a job!

Combining our families was even harder for me than singing an eight-bar solo. Don't get me wrong. I love being a mom, and I think I'm a good one, but *WOW!* It's tough.

For years we had family meetings every Sunday, to air our grievances and learn to know each other better. In no time at all, we were one big confused, normal, mixed-up, happy family.

Our oldest son Greg probably taxed my maternal patience the most, throughout his teenage years. Our personalities are so completely different. But Greg and I developed a very deep Mother/Son bond of love. He is a handsome, loving person. In fact, as I was writing this, Greg surprised me with a visit and brought me a bouquet of flowers, "Just because . . ."

Michele is our trendy independent one. With her beautiful dark looks, she could be a model, but she has aspirations to be a surgeon. Michele and I have long conversations and love to share make-up tips and clothes.

Billy, with the laughing eyes, is my firstborn. He looks very much like his Grandpa Bill Lennon, and has inherited his quick wit. I've never been able to successfuly discipline Billy, because he always makes me laugh (and cry sometimes, too). He hopes to end up in the music business and is happy for now playing guitar in a band with his brother and cousins.

John (Goober) is our scholar, competitive wrestler, artist, and humorist. He plays bass in the band with Bill and his cousins. He is handsome like his father, and is deeply sensitive to others' feelings.

Kristin is our baby—outgoing, self-confident, and delightful. She looks very much like me, is a straight "A" student, sings on commercials, and is an incredible athlete.

All of our children have become sensitive, loving people. Responsible? Not always, but they're working on it!

John and I are among the millions of parents who have stated, "As our children grow, we hope they will be able to come to us with anything and everything and feel free to discuss it." Be careful what you wish . . . . Our wish has come true.

On the one hand, we feel great that they can come to us; on the other, we bite our lips a lot. There have been some real heavy-duty discussions with the children on subjects I didn't even know existed when I was their ages. I try to sit poised, like the rational, intelligent woman I am, and nod and comment and interact to agree or disagree. And then, after the discussion is over, I allow my "mom" feelings to come to the surface. I calmly walk to my room, shut my door, and proceed to bite through the back of my fist, while stifling a scream.

I do feel that, although our children may not always like us, they think us fair parents. That's most important to me.

Billy, John, and Kristin not only have one great dad, but two terrific dads. John and Lee, who call themselves "husbands-in-law," agree wholeheartedly on how to raise and discipline the children.

These paternal partners periodically get on my case about being too lenient with the kids and embarrass me into cracking the whip a little harder.

I have to change hats a lot. Sometimes it's hard to make a smooth transition from entertainer to mom to wife and back again. It's a humbling experience though, to go from standing ovations one day to standing in the kitchen doing dishes the next. Mostly, I love it. But sometimes, if my timing isn't just right, my brain heads south for the winter. Thank God, John is understanding. Some days he comes home after a long, hard day to find a mere semblance of a wife, a shell of the intelligent woman he married.

I probably haven't been the best troop leader, but I've certainly given it my all. I don't know what I'll do without all the commotion. I'm already suffering withdrawal pains at the thought of the children moving out. They're my friends. And we laugh a lot. I have a feeling they'll never be that far from home.

Sometimes I can even relax. One of my favorite ways to unwind is to cook. I love to cook. I love to eat. The only thing I love more than cooking is eating my cooking. I also love to play golf. Daddy taught us to play when we were still teenagers. John and I play whenever we get a free moment, oftentimes on the road.

We live in a ranch community in the San Fernando Valley and have Arabian horses in our backyard. John and the girls ride their horses in local gymkhanas (obstacle courses organized for horseback) and have rooms full of trophies and ribbons. The boys used to have their own horses too, but sold them when they realized horses didn't have carburetors or long blond hair and blue eyes.

We are all Trivial Pursuit nuts. Once in a while the kids let John and me win.

John runs his own business, John Bahler Associates, in Hollywood. He and his staff create, design, and produce music for radio and television commercials. They also compose musical scores for motion pictures and television. I have so much respect for

John's musical genius. Among his many talents, he's one of the rare breed called "the studio singer." These talented people can (and do) walk into as many as five recording sessions a day, pick up the sheet music, and sight read all the notes correctly first time.

Sometimes, when John wants a certain sound on one of his commercials, he has me sing on it. He's a sensitive producer, and the atmosphere is easy in his studio. We love working together onstage and in the studio. After we were married, John became The Lennon Sisters' musical conductor and arranger again for a few years. When he decided to devote himself full-time to his production company, he stopped going on the road to conduct for us, but he still writes our vocal arrangements. Occasionally, when our regular conductor, Jack Feierman, has a conflicting date, John agrees to fill in for him. I love these times together, but there's something that happens when we look at each other onstage that fills us with pride, admiration, and a wonderful spark of physical attraction for one another.

Although we have many common interests, I feel that it's our differences that keep John and me so stimulated by each other. You might say we're a modified "Odd Couple." I've helped John to take the edge off of his Felix Unger, and he's helped me to "neaten up" my Oscar Madison. He has taught me to recognize the serious side of life, and I've taught him to see more of the humorous. We're a nice complement.

I love to write poetry as a way of capturing my elusive feelings. It's hard for me to express my true emotions. I often hide behind my humor. But when I write, I am able to transfer my deeper feelings onto paper.

On my love for John (a portion of my first poem to him):

> And still, my friend,
> Each time we meet,
> Each time we touch,
> Each time we love,
> There is a precious new moment of discovery
> Of unmatched wealth,
> And because we are reflections
> Of each other's inner souls,
> I've discovered that in loving you with all my heart
> I also love myself.

On the reality of the peaks and valleys of our years as husband and wife:

> He came like a bolt of lightning
> On a pure white horse and in shining armor
> He swept me up with him,
> And together we traveled a long, fine road;
> Flower laden it was,
> And the sun shone bright and warmed our hearts.
>
> But as the road began to bend,
> Clouds began to form on the horizon,
> And they brought winter to the summer of our lives.
> And as the rain began to fall, it dampened our spirits
> But never our souls, for they are strangely intertwined.
>
> And now the horse is not as white
> Nor the armor so shiny,
> But we ride together still,
> For we know that when the sun shines again,
> It will be brighter and warmer than before,
> And we will see it through different eyes
> And wonder what it is like to feel the raindrops.
> And yet know that we will be better prepared
> To face again the clouds that may form
> over our horizons.

I would like to take this opportunity to publicly thank my three big sisters for their individual and collective influences on my life.

To Dee Dee—for braiding my hair all of those years and putting up with my fussiness at having to look perfect; for being my shining example of graciousness and composure. When I was little, I thought of her as a Sister Superior, and I would never disagree or contradict her, out of respect for her position. Somewhere along the way though, I grew up, and we became peers. Now I consider her one of my best friends and confidantes. I would very much love to have her face and hair, and her golf swing.

To Peggy—for coming to my rescue when I was pressed for time, and writing a poem for me that won me an "A" from my fourth-grade teacher. For being my example of holiness. I can remember looking at her when we were in church together and thinking she would ascend to heaven at any moment; and later, sharing motherhood hints, carpools, and life philosophies. I wish I had her big brown eyes and big smart brain (and her skill in making stuffed manicotti).

To Kathy—for being my best pal my whole life. For our childhood years of sharing every thought, experience, and cute outfit. (Although I do wish she hadn't shared with me her discovery that there was no Santa Claus. I was only five.) For double-dates, more support than I deserved and for being there during my most traumatic times. She still takes care of me, and I still let her. I would give anything to have her singing voice, her small waist, and her self-confidence. (And her mink jacket.)

To the singing Lennon Sisters with whom I've performed for over thirty years; thanks for the tremendous career highs, the belly laughs, and for a lifetime of incredible harmony, working with my best friends.

Kathy:

Me, in show business thirty years?

No. Impossible—you must be talking about Bob Hope!

Every year, I have been "going to quit." I just want to stay home and be normal—what is normal?

To be married and have a big family.

God had other plans for me. The physical pain I had experienced through my teenage years culminated in a cancerous tumor on my ovary. So a hysterectomy had to be performed in 1971.

I was 28 years old and childless, and the emptiness inside me has never been completely filled. I long for this fulfillment of my womanhood. My body aches for the feel of a moving child within me, for the loving pain of childbirth, and to hold my needy, nursing infant. I believe it is a blessing to be God's vessel in the perpetuation of life, which is His greatest miracle. When new souls are constantly being mistreated in today's society, it disturbs me in my aloneness. I wonder when I return to God if I will care to ask "Why?" All the singing or applause in the world will never replace the longing in my heart.

It took me many years of struggle and turmoil to accept the fact that I was not a failure in life because I failed in marriage. I believe desperately in the bond of marriage, and to come to terms with my inner being took some counseling and lots of time. I always felt I should be perfect. I wanted everyone to like me. I tried to be everything to everybody and make everyone happy. And my main objective was never to disappoint anyone.

I've changed a lot since my first marriage. I have learned through pain to be the best I can be and not try to be something I'm not. In my first marriage, I tried to recreate the relationship my parents had with each other, and found out every situation is totally different, and should be. I was trying to remold what was not mine to change, and I have now learned to accept without conditions.

I was 36 years old when I met Jim Daris. That devastating year of leaving one life and entering into another was a new beginning that changed my world.

Out of a very deep trusting friendship grew an undeniable love. I was vulnerable and scared at the time, and it took a while for me to accept that I was desperately in love. Soon my life before Jim seemed to be just a movie I once saw.

His enthusiasm for life was incredibly exciting and very contagious. He was totally giving, and right out of a romantic novel. He was six-foot, five-inches tall, with dark black eyes and salt-and-pepper hair. He brought me flowers, the wine, the candy, and special gifts. He also brought the comfort to help me take risks again. I began to relax, to stop to enjoy the sunsets. I had felt I was on a treadmill for so long, and slowly I began to feel the wind blow through my hair and to breathe the fresh air. I began to laugh again. He allowed me freedom to love without being smothered.

Soon we became committed to each other. We wanted to be together forever. And once again, the old ghosts of the past cropped up into my mind. Was I doing what was right? Is this what I'm supposed to do? To reach out for help, I turned to what I felt was necessary for me to drop the weight of the past.

We went to a minister and friend, and we bared our souls. I needed this draining, cleansing session. The minister said something to me that will be with me all of my days. As I tearfully poured out my feelings of failure and guilt over my divorce, and how I was anxiously grasping to enter my new marriage without fear of carrying over that guilt, he said, "Kathy, we are all sinners, and you tell me you believe in the Death and Resurrection of Jesus Christ. Now, you can stay in the pain of The Cross and Good Friday, or come on over to the Resurrection and New Life with the rest of us." All my life I believed Jesus died for my sins, but not until that very moment had I understood the full meaning of His Life and Death on Earth.

And on April 24, 1982, I became Mrs. James Daris.

Jim is a Chiropractor who specializes in Applied Kinesiology. After many years of dedicated practice, he has decided to take a sabbatical and apply his own philosophy. In his own words, "I want to see, feel, and hear life, while I'm still young enough, and not wait to retire when I'm too old to walk the steps of the Acropolis."

Our life is full. We love being together, and we laugh a lot. He helps me to open up when things bother me. That has been difficult, because I constantly try to avoid any kind of confrontation. He continually asks, "What about you—are you okay?" That is one of the kindest questions a husband and friend could ask. Jim is an only child. And by saying "I do," he instantly acquired ten brothers-in-law and ten sisters-in-law, and all the nephews, nieces, relatives he could ever hope for. Also, his Chiropractic hands are not laid to rest as long as my family is around. We both crave our mothers' cooking. His momma, Sophie, is constantly sending us home with her Greek goodies, and my mom continues to send home her chocolate Bundt cakes. Good thing we are both avid exercise nuts.

Because my touring was strictly limited to singing engagements, I had never traveled for pleasure. I really didn't know there was such a thing. Leaving home had been such a negative experience through the years that I was shocked to find it can be fun. In fact, it can be incredibly wonderful. My fear of flying is still present, but not as obvious. I can even let go of the arms of the seat in the plane so I can pretend to be eating the pretend-food. Jim and I take advantage of The Lennon Sisters' schedule, and before or after each engagement, we rent a car and travel through various towns, to soak in as much history and different lifestyles as possible. He took me for three months to Germany, Austria, Italy, France, Yugoslavia, and Greece, his parents' homeland. I then found out what is meant by the "old world." I am surprised to be able to say that every canal, cobblestone street, castle, church, and ruin begs me to "come back."

We are both real beach bums and draw a sense of peace from the tranquillity of the ocean. I never take for granted my view from our home of the ocean and its glorious sunsets. I never take for granted our time as partners in love.

I still don't know what I want to do in my future. I love to sing. The joy I experience when interpreting the lyrics and notes contained in a song is so fulfilling. My body becomes warm all over when I know what I am singing is real. I try to live each song with the vitality of its first conception. I love the emotion it stirs.

I love to organize. If everybody would just do it my way, everything would be under control. My secretarial skills are in full use coordinating The Lennon Sisters' schedules. Bookings and billings are my self-designated responsibility, and these pressures sometimes really get me down. Out of necessity, the phone has become an intricate part of my day, and I confess at times I let it become too important. Each time a professional decision has to be made, I have to call three other households, and the juggling begins. First I call Jan:

"We have been asked to sing the National Anthem at the Dodger game Friday or Saturday night. Which is better for you, if either?"

"Well, I think Friday, but I must drive Billy to work, and Kristin has a soccer game! But if we don't have to be there until six-thirty I can work it out."

Then I call Dee Dee: "Deed, we have been asked . . . ."

"I promised to watch Mimi's girls Friday night, and Tommy needs my car on Saturday! But if you can pick me up and bring me home, Saturday is best for me."

I dread calling Peggy: "Peg, we've been asked . . . ."

"*What?!* You're kidding. This weekend? You know I'm producing the school play. I have three sets to paint and two-hundred choir robes to staple together. I'll have to bring my little girls with me, so you have to get two extra tickets. Oh well, just tell me where and when, and I'll be there!"

By the time I get around to asking myself if *I* can make it, I'm exhausted.

Our singing career is not always our first priority. I not only act as business manager, but I also handle the caring and storing of the costumes and the music filing. Our publicity over the years has resulted in trunks of pictures, write-ups, and awards; along with these, I've saved paper dolls, coloring books, and all our recordings, as mementos for each family. Now a thirty-year collection for four people is condensed four trunks high into one 7-by-9 room, upstairs at Mom's house. Do children ever move out?

It is thrilling to realize how many options I still have to explore in my lifetime.

If I could give my sisters a gift, it would be the fulfillment of these wishes:

Dee Dee—May you always have your arms filled with a warm child.

Peggy—May you have an instant clean house every day so you can enjoy sharing your mind without guilt of neglecting your *duties* at home.

Jan—May you finally believe you are the best!

How do I feel about the Book? Every family of two or more should take up a decade and write out their history. It makes no difference what walk of life one comes from, the experiences of sharing memories—all of them—cleanses.

Peggy:

Dick and I live in the San Fernando Valley, in a four-bedroom, "no headroom" home. I say that because our six children, along with their various possessions that they can't live without, take up every inch of space. Dick and I will be married twenty years as I write this. Our relationship is all I could ever want, and yet it still seems to grow and become stronger as each day goes by. I have always felt that Dick and I possess a special love, perhaps because of the circumstances of our ages and the problems we have had to endure in order to be together, or it could be that I'm too romantic—but I don't think so. I shall always remember how Daddy, who had had misgivings about our marriage, admitted to us his changed feelings. Dick and I were seated at the dining table after our son Michael was born, and Daddy put his hand on the back of my neck and said, "Honey, I can see you are so happy. You and Dick have a relationship that took your mom and me many years to cultivate. You are so fortunate."

There are many times each day that I get bogged down or frustrated, and I take a minute to calm myself. My immediate thought is of Dick, because he is the calming center of my existence. His love is so steady and so strong that I derive strength from the mere thought of him. Then, all the other problems of the day are just outside annoyances that can be handled or ignored, because my center is there, still and warm and forever.

Dick is tolerant of my faults, and understanding when I need it most. I know there are times when he could throw up his hands at the incompetence surrounding him in our home. He is tidy and meticulous. I can't even imagine the patience he must have to muster to be able to live amicably with the rest of us slobs. He certainly was not prepared in his earlier life to cope with nine children.

As the much younger baby in a family of four sons, he led a quiet, almost "only child" type of existence in Michigan City, Indiana. His father was an accomplished musician and taught his sons at early ages to play various musical instruments. They have all had careers in the music field and are excellent performers. While Dick was growing up, his music came first. He enjoyed playing in many of the Big Bands, and led a rather solitary life on the road—not much preparation for the chaos that was to make up the rest of his life.

It's not that Dick doesn't enjoy his family. It's just that there's so *much* to enjoy. When the kids were little, he couldn't understand broken toys. He would hit his toe against a cracked Spiderman Web Shooter and yell, "How can you let this happen? I remember when I was in the Army. My mom wrote me a letter asking if she could give my electric train, tin soldiers, and games to the little boy across the street. They were kept in perfect condition in a box in the attic. I kept those things for years. They were perfect. You kids just don't appreciate anything."

His statements were absolutely true, and the kids knew it. But they liked to make their daddy laugh, and they would continue his lament. "Yeah, Daddy, we know, and I'll bet you walked to school five miles in a blizzard with no shoes, carrying a branch to erase your tracks so that wolves couldn't follow you."

Most of our children have grown out of toys, and all that Dick has to trip over now are records, guitars, headphones, and tapes. I tell him how lucky he is that they are on the floor and not on the machines blasting through the speakers! He doesn't laugh.

When I think of our older children—Carrie, John, and George—I feel a wide range of emotions. For one thing, I've always

had a difficult time putting a name to Dick's children. I hate the word "stepchildren," it sounds so witchy. And if I say "Dick's children," I sound as if I want nothing to do with them. There should be a much more loving word invented for such wonderful children as I've had the fortune to mother.

Carrie now lives in Breckenridge, Colorado, with her husband Toby Sadaski and her two daughters. Heather and Heidi, our granddaughters, are the same ages as our daughters Jennie and Betsy. Carrie and I have had a great time raising our girls together and sharing the joys and frustrations of four babies all at once.

Georgie (when will I ever learn to call him George?) is a design draftsman for an electronics company and lives close by. Close enough to drop in for a home-cooked meal and some guitar sessions with his brothers. Like most young people today, he spends most of his time trying to pay bills on time and trying to save enough for a date or two. Come to think of it, most of us old people are doing the same thing.

In May of 1983, our Johnnie was killed in an automobile accident. I think the shock I felt at his death was stronger even than that I had felt at the deaths of my sister Mary and Dad: Mary was a baby going home to her Father; Daddy had had a full and rich life. But John was so young and vital and eager for life. His wife of three years, Missy, was expecting their first child in July, and I can remember how proud he was at her baby shower.

For the first time, I questioned the validity of my concept of God. He was not the God I had formed in my heart and mind throughout my life. He had permitted death to have power over John. It was a struggle that I had to fight for a long time, and in some ways I still feel confused and afraid. But the faith that God in His goodness has given me, and the love of His Son, sees me through each day. Death is not a product of God, but an absence of Him. Yet the Lord has the last laugh. He draws all souls to Himself.

The last time I was with John, he took me out to see the new golf club he had refinished, and as I was turning away from his truck, I happened to notice a bumper-sticker on the fender. John was always vocal about his dislike of bumper-stickers. This one read "Mine eyes have seen the Glory of the Coming of the Lord."

John and Missy's daughter, Sarah Elizabeth Cathcart, was born on July 11, 1983.

Of our six younger children, I have millions of memories and

The Gass family: Diane, Dick, Dee Dee, Tom, and Mary. *(The Lennon Family Collection)*

The Cathcart family: surrounding Peggy and Dick, clockwise from bottom left, Jennie, Chris, Mike, Juli, Joe, and Betsy. *(The Lennon Family Collection)*

Kathy and Jim Daris. *(Photo by Charis/The Lennon Family Collection)*

The Bahler family: seated are Kristin, Janet, John, Michele. Upper row: Bill, John, and Greg, *(The Lennon Family Collection)*

impressions, some vivid, some just out of reach.

Julianne Mary was born on St. Patrick's Day, March 17, 1965, and I think that must have been the reason for her Irish red hair. From the first, she was an intelligent child, and her big black eyes always looked as though they were recording events for later appraisal. My brothers thought she was a witch and took care not to make her angry for fear of being zapped into a frog. My sisters said she was a Communist spy, sitting there, silent, observing, remembering. And I just thought she was perfection. I could take her anywhere, confident that she would behave with excellent manners and decorum. She's still that way, always the lady.

Blond, blue-eyed Christopher Richard was born February 27, 1966. (He loves to tease Juli that for three weks every year he's the same age as she.) I remember the night he was born. I sat on the window sill of my darkened hospital room, staring at the street lights. How does one overcome the feelings of total elation enough to sleep? I couldn't.

God gave Chris to me twice. When he was ten months old, Christmas week, he came down with a chest cold. I had taken him to the doctor for shots twice that week and so was not prepared for the extent to which his illness had progressed by New Year's Day. He had double pneumonia and a massive larynx infection that totally closed his trachea, and an emergency tracheotomy was performed, and then the long, interminable convalescence. I would go to see him almost every day in the intensive care unit. Big tears rolled down his cheeks, but no sound. The trachea tube bypassed his vocal cords, and I remember how this affected Dick—to see his baby cry or talk or laugh without success was almost more than he could bear. This time was extremely difficult for Dick. We had been in an automobile accident the week before, and my left hand was broken and in a cast. I was also in my fourth month of pregnancy, and my concern over Chris was affecting my health. When I couldn't be at the hospital, the nurses became Chris's mommy, and he loved them. They knitted him sweaters and made him clothes, and I shall always be grateful for their kindness to me. They showed me how to suction his tube, which is a scary operation at best, and they let me bring Juli to see him.

For six weeks, Dick and I prayed and waited for the doctor's reports. Finally, they were able to remove the tube, which meant Chris could live a normal, active life once again. He came home on his first birthday, a day I had thought we would never see. That night, he took his first steps alone. What a perfect day! And the joy of hearing him laugh and talk again can't be described. Even today I never look at him but that I don't marvel at the presence of him there near to me, whole and perfect. And when I think of his voice, my mind wanders back to the words he always used at the age of two when he felt especially close to me: "You is mine boy, huh, Momma?"

"Mine boy" is now nineteen.

On June 29, 1967, Joseph William was born. Dick was working at Lake Tahoe with the Lawrence Welk band, so my brother Danny had to take me to the hospital. It was midnight. Danny was seventeen, and I could hear whispers as we went down the hospital corridors, Danny carrying my suitcases: "My, what a young father!"

Joey has curly red hair, big dimples, and blue eyes. He was my most sensitive child, in a state of perpetual motion, either falling on the ground crying or leaping into the air screaming with happiness. That has stood him in good stead. He's a senior yell-leader at school. (Mostly on the ground crying; we have a terrible team!)

Michael Matthew was born July 7, 1968, another redhead with black eyes like Juli's. Mikey's first great ambition was to be a trash can at MacDonald's. But I think he will be an artist. He's never without a pencil or piece of charcoal in his hand. That may sound like an exaggeration, but I have taken pencils out of his fingers when he is sound asleep. I have seen him in the bathroom with his sketchpad on his lap, and even at the dinner table I've caught him eating left-handed so he could draw with his right.

Mike's artistic ability is not limited to drawing. One birthday, I asked Mike what he wanted as a gift. "Oh, ten feet of chicken wire and some fur." So that's what he got. And he created a spectacular, four-foot-in-diameter black widow spider.

On another occasion, I went into his room to change the linens on his bed, but I couldn't find his pillow. "Mike," I yelled, "where is your pillow?"

"Oh, yeah," he mumbled, "I remember now—there it is."

He pointed to the window sill, and there sat four brand new puppets all with long white beards he had gleaned from his pillow stuffing.

For four years after Michael was born, our household was

peaceful, and we settled into a pattern that became easier as the boys outgrew their diapers and bottles. But God had other plans for us. Much to the children's delight, I became pregnant again. This was the first baby any of them would remember. Juli was just three years old when baby Mike was born, and all four of the children just grew up together. But now they had a baby sister, Jennifer Lora, born January 22, 1973. Juli felt I had done her a personal favor by having a girl. After three brothers, she was ready to play house with a real live doll. Jennie is a dishwater blonde with blue eyes. She is delicate, feminine, and her aunts think she looks like a kitten. She is extra sensitive, extra bright, and loves gymnastics.

Close on the heels of Jennie—and surprise of all surprises to Dick and me—Elizabeth Anne was born June 21, 1974. She is the complete opposite of Jennie in looks. Betsy has black eyes, dark brown hair, and a deep olive complexion. Finally, after five children, the sixth resembled me. When I brought her home from the hospital, the older kids immediately nicknamed her. For several months they had been watching the Vietnamese refugee children coming into this country, and Betsy, with her dark hair, almond-shaped eyes and Cathcart "no nose," was dubbed "Soo Ling." She and Jen are real buddies, and where one goes, the other follows. It is such fun to have two girls together for a change.

All six children, and not one is like the other. It fascinates me how I can make a simple statement and get six altogether different reactions, from tears to whoopees.

What do I want for my children? What most parents want. Success. By that I mean that I hope they can attain a degree of contentment in their lives, an ease in being able to handle daily problems, a belief in and love for themselves and others, and a fulfilling relationship with their God. Their choices in life will be their own. I don't think many will coincide with what my choices would be for them. But I won't discourage them, though in one area I haven't been exactly pushy—I've never encouraged them to work in entertainment. Having experienced the problems and having seen the industry falling further away from my own values and standards, I made sure my kids were aware of the pitfalls. Unfortunately, I overlooked one thing. They are extremely talented, and they love to perform. Juli spent most of her high-school days as assistant director on all the drama productions. She is a marvelous actress and singer, and would love to be a director in films.

Chris and Joe, along with Bill and Goober Bernhardi and Tom Gass, and their childhood buddy Mike Mazza, have a pop rock band that plays local clubs and high-school and college dances. Their musicality and sense of harmony makes a refreshing addition to the raucous rock beat.

Mike has a band with three of his friends, and they are busy many weekends at high-school parties and dances. Mike plays beautiful jazz guitar and has his Dad's heart and soul for music.

Jennie and Betsy are busy quite often recording jingles for television commercials. Their uncle John got them started in his studio when he needed some kiddie voices owned by sharp minds and quick thinkers. Jen and Bets jumped right in. I don't mind this type of work for them, because they have learned a sense of professionalism without the pressures and egos of "on camera" performances, and they're saving their money for school.

It is not easy for Dick and me to raise our children in today's world, and frankly, it worries us. It seems that so much of what we try to show them by example or teach them through our talks is constantly being threatened by television, records, books, and movies. And we cannot speak from personal experience about the problems unique to their generation, namely, drugs and socially acceptable immorality. But these frightening elements do post a threat to their lives, and we and our children will have to face it the only way we can—with God's help, one day at a time.

My life now is filled with complex and compound days of myriad things to do. Some of them, I love. Some, I detest.

I don't like housekeeping. It doesn't like me. So we rarely see each other. Not that I'm not a good cleaner. When I clean something, it's perfect. But I find so little time to do all there is to do that the monster that takes over my house grows bigger and bigger. Right now my laundry room is my biggest problem. I wash clothes every day, sometimes four or five times a day. Then there are the days that the kids clean their rooms, and bring in every lost sock and towel in the house, and the washer goes on 24-hour duty.

Sometimes I get the clothes folded, ofttimes not. So I will empty the dryer into large laundry bags and put them in the corner to be folded later, like two or three months later. The only part of this that is in any way redeeming is the fact that the laundry room has become the "sulking room." Whenever one of the kids has a problem or a grouch, in he goes to the laundry room, plops down on the soft warm bags of laundry, puts his feet up on the washer, and pouts. Sometimes I hear a "Mom, can I talk to you in private?" Then I retire to the confines of that little room, and dispense love and psychology to the plunkety-plunk of the dryer and the smell of soap.

I'm constantly on a diet. Deed and Kathy are skinny, and Jan and I hate them. They drink banana milkshakes before bedtime and eat chocolate cake for breakfast, just to keep their weight up. Jan and I can look at a glass of water across the room and both gain five pounds. It's unfair, and it's not fun. And I lack the same qualities of determination in my dieting that I do in my housekeeping. Therefore, I am a yo-yo: weight up, weight down, *etc* . . . , but I'm working on it.

Aside from my work with my sisters and the running of my household, I am a director of our two-hundred-member grammar school drama club. And I teach five days a week at the local Catholic High School. Crazy? You bet! But an important part of my life right now. Because my sisters and I choose to work only eight to ten weeks a year, and by its very nature a musician's work is sporadic, it was very difficult for Dick and me to be able to afford to send our children to Catholic High School. And so, when I was asked if I would be interested in teaching a religion class at the school my boys attend, I jumped at the chance. I could help pay tuition costs, and I could *teach*, something I had always wanted to do.

So, for the last four years, I have taught ninety-five students per semester, three fifty-minute classes a day. They have been wonderful, because I love teaching seventeen-year-old boys who know it all and know nothing, and terrible because I have come to realize that I'm not a very good juggler. It's rough on my children when I not only have to struggle with their homework, but mine as well. Rough on Dick because, for the first time, we don't have our daytimes together.

But we have survived, are surviving—barely. (If we just didn't have to work on the Book.)

And after the last child is out of high school, I'll only have about three more years of teaching until tuition is paid off.

I guess what I wish most these days is more time to spend with Dick. This last summer I had an opportunity to be with him while he was performing at various jazz festivals throughout the country. What a joy to be able to hear him play. There's not a sweeter player in the world. How proud I am to be his wife!

Peg on Peg

I'm writing my autobiography. I don't know how.
Who am I?
How do I feel about my brothers and sisters?
Why was I given the winning ticket in
Families? Why me? Such joy!
They don't judge me—well, sometimes they find
"Guilty, Temporary Insanity!"
So individual; so together. THEY MAKE ME LAUGH!
How do I feel about Mom?
How does she do it?
What does she have and give that I don't?
She's love.
I don't talk to her enough.
I wish my hugs said aloud all the words.
Does she know the depth of my admiration?
How do I feel about my Sisters?
They love me; they know me and they still love me.
I'd love to be skinny for Kathy. I'd love to be more
Quiet, like Deed. I'd love to be able to handle my
Home like Janet. They are my best friends. They are
Me.
How do I feel about my career?
It's something to do until I grow up and can choose
What it is I want to do. I don't feel highly
Emotional about my work—yet many emotional
Things happen at work.
Would I choose entertainment as a career?
No!—Yes!—No!—I love to talk, tell a
Good story: I love to make people laugh or smile
Or be deeply concerned.

Center of attention? Entertainer? NO! YES! NO!
I don't know.
Am I a good wife?
I bring him tea each morning, and rub his back.
I love him completely. I can't find enough time to
Spend with him. The time we do have is wholly
Fulfilling. He's so understanding, so supportive in
Every way. He knows I love him.
Am I a good mother?
Yes, and No. Yes, I give a lot. No, I yell a lot.
Yes, I listen. No, I preach. They know I love them
Unconditionally. I spank, I hug. I try.
What are my faults?
I'm lazy. Is it because I'm too
Tired? Why don't I take better care of
Myself? Then I wouldn't be too tired. I'm
Too tired! I'm too emotional, too quick to open my
Big mouth. I can hurt someone before I
Know it.—Oh! How much that hurts me! Why do
I continually open my mouth? I think I'm so
Smart, that's why!
I'm so dumb.
Am I a good person?
Yes, a lot of room for improvement. Am I surface
Good? Sometimes.
Am I deeply good? Sometimes.
Being good makes me feel Good. Am I looking for that
Feeling as a reward? I don't think so. It makes me feel
Close to the Lord. Is that my reward?
I'll take it!

Dianne:

As I begin to put down on paper all my thoughts and memories, I suddenly realize that my life seems almost like a fairy tale—oldest daughter in a large family where the mother and father really cared; oldest sister to eleven brothers and sisters, all of whom like each other and never fought; mother of three children, all healthy and reasonably happy; and wife to a man with whom I share my innermost feelings and from whom I receive the respect and love every woman needs.

But there have been many trials and sorrows that, at times, seemed unbearable. Somehow there is a balance, and life continues.

I have savored and still savor my different roles—in fact, I am almost selfish with them. It is difficult for me to open up my personal life to others; with my family and friends, I am completely honest and sharing, sometimes to a fault. I am extremely sensitive, especially when children are involved—an unexpected smile or hug will bring instant tears. And my life has been filled with children.

Our three children have been the center of our lives; each bringing us pleasure. We feel we have been doubly blessed because we know the joy of both "selecting" and "expecting" a child. Our first-born, Mary, was an unexpected bonus in our lives. These words tell the story:

> Not flesh of my flesh
> Nor bone of my bone
> But still miraculously my own.
> Never forget for one single minute
> You weren't carried *under* my heart,
> But *in* it.

Shortly after Dick and I were married, we were told that I would probably never be able to conceive or bear a child. It was very hard to accept, because we had planned a large family. But God had other plans. After undergoing major surgery and countless fertility tests, I still was not pregnant. It was then we decided to adopt. Blond-haired, blue-eyed Mary Estelle entered our lives when she was a day-and-a-half old. We finally had our own baby! Three weeks after her birth, I thought I had stomach flu. But after two weeks of extreme nausea, the doctor confirmed what we suspected. I was pregnant! But I had to stay in bed for three months. So Dick, Mary, and I moved in with Dad and Mom, until I could be up and around again. When the three months were over, I had no more problems. And in October of 1964, Diane Isabelle joined our family—nine months and three days after Mary's birth. She was a miracle.

When Diane (Little Dee Dee) was six months old, I went to the doctor for a check up. I showed him a mole on my leg that seemed to have grown very quickly since she was born. He did not seem too concerned, but decided to remove it in his office right then, just as a precaution. Later that day, he telephoned me and said that the lab report showed that the tissue he had removed was a malignant melanoma—black mole cancer. The next day I went to see a specialist, and within two days I was in the hospital to have further surgery. I had to sign a release stating that the surgeon had permission to remove my leg if he deemed it necessary. My world had suddenly turned upside down, and I was scared.

The surgeon removed a large portion of the muscle tissue in my leg, hoping that he had excised all of the diseased area. I returned home from the hospital, not knowing whether I would eventually have to return for more surgery—still, there was the possibility of losing my leg. The next year was a nightmare. I returned for checkups every few weeks and dreaded every one. There I was with two little babies, not knowing if I had a chance to live to raise them. Through it all, my family rallied around me and gave me mental and spiritual support. And I leaned on them. Dick was constantly reassuring me that God had finally given us the children we wanted, and that he was sure He wanted us to raise our daughters together. It was a big turning point in my life, and I decided to leave it all in God's hands. And once again, He let me know that He had plans for me contrary to what the doctors believed. Though the odds were not in my favor, no re-occurence ever appeared. (A year later, I learned that my sister Kathy had told Mom that, if I should be unable to care for my family or should die from the cancer, she would spend her life helping Dick to raise our girls—even at the price of not having her own children. I had no words to express my feelings to her.)

Nine months later, I was again surprised by morning sickness. After the rabbit died, which erased all doubts, I was once again ordered to bed. But how does one go to bed for ninety days with two small children, one not even walking and both still in diapers? We couldn't move in with Dad and Mom again. They still had seven children at home, and four more people would be too hard on Mom.

For me the answer was Betty Sanford. The lady, upon whom the Lennon family had already relied so many times before, was now nursemaid, housekeeper, and babysitter at the Gass home. She drove me to the doctor's office every other day for shots and intravenous injections. She washed and combed my hair, cooked and fed me what little food I could keep in my stomach (mainly lima bean and ham soup and avocado sandwiches), and she cuddled and spoiled our little girls. She was as determined as Dick and I that I was going to carry this baby. Her loving determination paid off. In March of 1966, Thomas Richard was born. Three children in 27 months! And we couldn't have been happier.

We have had more than a few anxious moments concerning our brood, as most parents have. The ones that stand out in my mind are these:

The time two-year-old Tom bit through an electrical extension cord and burned away half of his bottom lip; the night I sat rocking three-year-old Mary in the steam-filled bathroom until the sun came up, never having seen asthma before; making a tent over six-week-old Dee Dee's playpen and filling it with steam so as to remove the congestion in her chest, and sleeping on the floor next to her all night with my hand on her little, heaving breast; three different hurried trips to the emergency hospital for stitches in Tom's head, once during his "pirate" birthday party when he was taken to the emergency room still dressed as Long John Silver; and the time Mary climbed out of her bed and then helped Dee Dee out of her crib to indulge in a "tea party"—of baby aspirins.

Many times Mom has said that parents worry about their children forever—and I can see now that it is true. We have raised our children all in the same way, and yet, they are different from one another. Somehow I believed that they would be exactly as I planned them to be. And as children, they were. I relived much of my childhood happiness through them, spending every moment I could with them. They were everything I could ever hope for.

But they are not copies of us. They have their own likes and dislikes, and they developed their own personalities, while Dick and I watched with pride and awe.

Mary is working as a medical assistant for three pediatricians and attending night school to become a Registered Nurse. She wants to marry and have five or six children. Knowing Mary, she will.

Diane, little Dee Dee, is currently caring for toddlers at a day care center every day. She also is attending college and singing in a jazz group. She hopes to eventually become a commercial singer. That type of work will enable her to fulfill her childhood desire—to be a mom and raise her children at home. She will be a good one!

Tom is working for his uncle, John Bahler, learning the recording business from the bottom of the ladder. He has played guitar since he was six and plays many nights well after everyone else has gone to bed.

Though they are still living at home, I miss them. They are very busy with their own lives, and I have to admit that I have a hard time accepting the fact that they are no longer my little children—for I have had children around me all my life. I enjoy the close moments I now share with each one. Mary will often sneak up behind me while I'm cooking and give me a bear hug or ask me to tuck her in at night; Dee Dee surprises me occasionally with a single red rose and an accompanying card, "Just because you're Mom!"; and Tom will jump in the car with me while I go on an errand, just to talk for awhile. I love who they are, and I'm proud of them, but it's hard to let them go. I know I'll always want to take care of them—and I think they'll do the same for me.

For the first time in my life, I find I now have time for myself—and at first, I didn't know what to do with it. Each day I would get everyone off to work after a good breakfast, do my housework, and then face the task of deciding what to do for the next five or six hours, before I would start cooking dinner. I took up reading books—lots of books—and for awhile it sufficed. I did some sewing and even had time to polish my toenails. My girlfriend Jane and I spent a lot of time together wallpapering, shopping, laughing, playing tennis, and talking over coffee, as only best friends can do. But I still felt as though I wanted to be around children. And so, in 1979, I volunteered to help teach reading at St. Mark Grammar School, which my family had all attended. Now I'm teaching kindergarten, and have found it rewarding. The innocence and inquisitiveness of those five-year-olds brings tears of laughter and joy to my eyes; and their constant hugs given so unashamedly are returned just the same way.

And for almost 25 years, I have had the companionship of a man who makes me feel all the things a wife and lover wants to feel. We grew up together as husband and wife, sharing for the first time all the events that enrich a marriage. He understands me, and I understand him. Dick was the oldest of eight children, and out of necessity took on some of the duties of a parent to his younger brothers and sisters. When we married, he had already spent many years as a "father" and brought to our life a maturity that few men of 23 possess. Though he has a very serious side, it is his wonderful way of being a child at times that has kept me infatuated with him. He still surprises me with little gifts that mean "I understand," or "You're the best." We laugh a lot, which helped us get through our three teenagers' years. (I have to admit that I was able to laugh a little more than he was.)

If he has a fault, it is that he spends too little time for himself. He is in public relations for General Telephone Company, and as such, he sees first-hand the need for community involvement by each and every citizen. There are certain organizations with which he is involved that take up much of his time even after hours—especially charities concerning children. I share in some of his commitments—and wholeheartedly.

But I'm sure that there are times when I bug him when I declare, "Life's too short. Don't get so involved." (Look who's talking!)

I love to hold his hand. I'm proud of him. I love him. And I am sure of his love for me.

When our kids were little, we spent most of our weekends at the beach—sand castles, volleyball, hamburgers, picnics—always together. Now that our children are young adults, our time as a family is infrequent. And I know it bothers each of us in a different way—but life changes . . . .

So now Dick and I are back to our relationship before we had children, but with wonderful memories. We are not travelers, nor are we real socializers. We spend most of our evenings at home, possibly because we both spend our days with large groups of people. (Although kindergarteners are not exactly people!) We play golf together every Sunday. I gladly gave up my golf clubs for fifteen years while I raised my children; now golf is my therapy at the beginning of each week.

Dick spends his Saturdays at Venice Beach playing paddle tennis. If anything could ever come between us, I guess it would be "the beach." I love the beach—he is *in* love with the beach. But he needs the exercise, and he still looks like that guy I married in October of 1960.

We have a varied array of friends that keeps us dabbling in football, basketball, paddle tennis, Trivial Pursuit, and many other assorted activities.

If the next forty years of my life are as full as the last forty years, I will savor them with the same selfishness. For I am happy.

I have been married to Dick for 25 years now, and have been "married" to Peggy, Kathy, and Janet for thirty—and, living with them for almost forty!

We have supported each other through good times and bad, for richer or poorer, in sickness and in health. Yet we have all gone our separate ways, each standing on her own two feet and living her personal life according to her singular beliefs. I admire all three of them for the good women they are—both in mind and spirit. They each have characteristics that I would like to take from. Peg has an ability to put to memory every bit of knowledge she acquires, and yet she is not pompous. Kath has a very simple way of expressing her feelings and is not afraid to do it. And Jan is a person who is very willing to make an effort to change with the times.

They are good wives, and I would "marry" them all over again. I thank God for selecting three very special people to be with me . . . "till death us do part."

The Last Word

James Davis:

I married Kathleen Mary Lennon on April 24, 1982, and that day I acquired enough relatives to influence the outcome of a presidential election. Do *you* know any family that sings "Happy Birthday" every two weeks?

I had been the chiropractor to Kathy's mom, to three of her brothers and a sister (Dan, Bill, Kipp, Annie), and to assorted aunts, uncles, and cousins. I *still* have to remind Kathy of my loss of the thousands in income when I became "family."

Unless you lived in a cave all your life, you know who The Lennon Sisters are. You watched them grow up on television like I did. Now you're going to get the real truth about the Lennons.

You think Dee Dee is sweet, pretty, and all-American? Bah! Humbug! Not true! She's perfect. The perfect mom, the perfect homemaker, the best legs; but worst of all, she beats me at golf.

Peggy—I *hate* her! She always wins at Trivial Pursuit. She wins all games, in fact. You can discuss anything with her, and she's well-versed on the subject. She paints, she sews, and if you discuss theology it sounds as though she had lunch with God.

Janet—you're going to say I can't pick on Janet because she's the baby. She's so sweet, her little bangs, her shy way, never says much. HA! Vicious, that's what Janet is! She makes Joan Rivers look like Mother Theresa. Why one day I heard her say "Shucks!" Another day, when one of her boys did something wrong, I overheard her whisper, "Darn you." How can anyone live under that kind of pressure?

Kathy—worst of all of them. She only taught me what real, unselfish, unconditional love is all about. It means giving with the total heart. She is Pied Piper of children. The Woman, who is beauty, brains, the perfect figure, and still possesses the genuine humility of Joan of Arc. Is it easy living with a woman like that? Especially for a man who thought it was permissable to hate at least three people in a lifetime. Not only is it easy, it's magical.

To give an overview of the Lennon family we have to discuss first the real villain of the tribe. In reality, a She-devil. I'm talking about Mom. That's what they call her—Mom!

This planet is worried about world hunger? Forget it! Send them all to Mom's house. This woman is intent to see that Fat is Fun! (Not for her; she's svelte.) It's for anyone who passes through the portals of her pantry. She is the fastest cake in the West. She knows that no one has eaten for four days, and when you leave her house you don't get a doggie bag, you're handed an elephant trunk! She's brought twelve children into this world, and in all the years I've known her I've never seen or heard her raise her voice, complain, or be negative about anything. Nothing! Zilch!

She is The Mom every man, woman, boy, girl, puppy, kitten, or tarantula ever wanted, and I guarantee her chocolate bundt cake will destroy the world. That recipe is what the Russians are really after.

I'm the husband with the least amount of seniority, but I still say I've never known a family like this one. There are seven more children I haven't discussed, all suffering from their own individual, distinct, wacky personalities. The whole gang, including Nana, have a relationship that's very special, a sense of humor that stretches from a belly laugh to the bizarre. They have a world of togetherness that no one can enter, and all can enter. No matter if it's a baseball game in the backyard at Mom's after a barbecue or all the holidays, their house glows with love. If you choose to sit on the sidelines they will coax you in, but if you don't join them you'll miss the fun.

I can sit on Christmas Eve and watch the eleven Lennons sing together (which they do every Christmas, Thanksgiving, July Fourth, Labor Day, Birthdays, Anniversaries, Halloween, Valentine's Day, St. Patrick's Day, and Ground Hog Day, you get the idea?) and watch their faces, and I, being an only child, envy the love they share together. It's real, it's deep. it's mesmerizing.

Kathy and I have a special relationship, but when she is with her family they have something no one can participate in completely. I'm just happy to be able to be there for the fallout.

Kathy and her sisters worry about their goodie-goodie image. No one has to worry that The Lennon Sisters are *too* nice. I put all fears to rest. They *are* too nice. I see the spell they cast everywhere they perform. I look at the eyes of their fans; *they* know the Lennons have what the whole world needs—LOVE.

And I can say anything I want to about the Lennon kids. You know why? Because Nana *likes* me . . . . and their mom is crazy about me . . . .

John Bahler:

My grandmother really did make me watch The Lennon Sisters every Saturday night. Nanny thought "little Janet was sooo cute," and so did I, as soon as I was old enough to fully understand that girls were not just soft boys!

I met the Lennons in 1971, while conducting for Andy Williams. I remember walking into the first rehearsal and seeing four of the most beautiful women I had seen in my life; they were working in their dance routine. I turned to Andy and asked, "Who's the blonde?" Andy looked me in the eye and said, "Her name is Janet, and they're all married, and they're all Catholic!"

Well, that didn't matter. I was in love. Then and there. Although Janet didn't know I existed at that time, the good news is that she does now!

Knowing the "girls" and being a part of their family has been the highlight of my life thus far. You have to spend some time around them to get the real picture. What you see is what you get. The girls are real!

I may have a different perspective from the other husbands, because I worked with the girls and we were friends first. It was hard for me to believe how anyone with their kind of popularity and success could be so normal. Well, I finally figured it out. They are more concerned with how people feel than they are about their careers. The most important things in their lives are their husbands and their children.

Being accepted into the family is important to an outsider. They seem to feel and act in unison. Their family strength lies within the love and respect they have for each other. The odd thing is that, if you get any one of them alone, he or she is totally different. Their strength is in numbers.

I never knew Bill Lennon, their father. But every year at the Lennon family Christmas gathering I feel his presence. I even hear him talk to me. Now, I'm not a great believer in the "spirit world," but in this case I'm a believer. The man lives on through his family. By knowing the family, you know Bill. His loving, caring attitude toward mankind displays itself in every one of his children. They're so close that an outsider has to deal with all of them acting as one. I don't mean to imply that the family makes an outsider feel like an outsider. Quite the contrary. In my case I was welcomed; but one has to learn how to deal with the family.

The girls' sense of humor is their saving grace. Many of us would collapse under the pressures of having a career, being a marriage partner, and being a parent. But they are able to find the funny side of life and make it bearable, not only for themselves but for their loved ones.

I must say that the girls are the biggest blessing God has bestowed on me as a vocal arranger. It's one thing to write notes, chords, and phrasing that you hear in your head. That's exciting. However, no matter how good I think something I've written is, the girls take it and turn it into a pure soulful communication. They breathe life into an arrangement. They make it come alive, because they feel each note, each harmony, each phrase. That is what makes the girls so special to me.

I thought it would be tough to be married to a celebrity. With Janet, nothing is tough except maybe cleaning the kitchen after she's cooked one of her wonderful specialities.

Janet taught me how to love. I had never really committed myself to another person before I met her. I couldn't, because I was not able to trust anyone. Janet proved not only can people be trusted, but you can also be in love with your best friend in the whole world! We share secrets like best friends, we support each other in times of emotional need like best friends, we disagree just the way best friends do. What we have together is as close to perfection as anything I've ever known. We really complement each other. Janet's messy, I'm neat; Janet's funny, I'm serious; Janet's gorgeous, and I'm . . . .

Janet spoils me rotten. The women's movement will probably choke on that, but you know, I'm not going anywhere. She gives me total freedom. Freedom that I could never even give myself! And along with that freedom comes devotion and faithfulness from me the likes of which I have never, ever in my life, given anyone. Janet is "special." Everyone says it! *She* can't see it. But then, if she could, she might not be so special.

Janet wants to be many things that she's not. She finds fault with almost everything about herself. And the reason? She can't find anyone to compare herself with! Now, if that isn't "special," what is?

Dick Cathcart:

When I first met Peg some 22 years ago, I was absolutely amazed. Now, after twenty years of marriage and six children, I'm still amazed—only more so. Her loving exuberance has never diminished. Through thick and thin, feast or famine, she has always kept the boat floating.

In the days before we married (and didn't know then if we ever could be), we used to have a lot of long-winded conversations about almost anything, just to be together. Sometimes her seemingly dream-world naivete worried me. After all, I had been in the music business for over twenty years then, and I had a few bruises to show for it. That's when I tried to educate Peg with a few hard facts of life. I still try now and then, but it never has really worked. I realized a long time ago that Peg isn't wearing rose-colored glasses. She enjoys a basic security, a product of her faith in a Higher Power, her ties to her family, and her faith in the inherent goodness of people.

Meeting a large family like the Lennon family can be pretty overwhelming. I found that out the first time I was invited to dinner. Eleven brothers and sisters, all different and clamoring for recognition, a father who stepped right out of a Joe Miller joke book, and a mother who patiently put up with it all. And then, there was Nana, resident humorist. Quite an experience the first time around.

I was not prepared for this sort of mayhem, but I think over the years we've all reached an understanding or, at least, a reasonable level of compatibility. When things get a little hectic for me at one of those family gatherings, I'm the one who retires to the library and sticks his nose in a good book. Sis does have a marvelous library.

I suppose I could have had some trepidation about being accepted into such a close-knit family, but I didn't really think about it. As much as I loved them all, I never planned on becoming a Lennon, any more than I expected Peg to become a Cathcart—God forbid! We were marrying each other, not families, because we loved each other and we wanted to spend the rest of our lives together.

I didn't plan on having all those kids either. But God has been good, I think. Our children are all healthy, and they're all nuts too, lovably so, like their grandfather Bill. A good combination for domestic chaos.

The often disorganized state of our household can be distracting and even downright infuriating, until I remember I'm no Felix Unger myself. And with our brood, housekeeping is no picnic. The last full-time housekeeper we had actually fled the country.

However, I must say Peg is an excellent cook and likes to create culinary delights when she has the time. (She also likes to use every pot and pan and dish available. She feels that if you have a clean utensil left over, you just haven't tried.)

Peg is not fond of printed instructions, even the simple ones like "Open on dotted line." The cereal boxes in our house look like they were opened by a starving raccoon.

On the other hand, I tend to place too much emphasis on routine and organization. My hobbies are woodworking, model railroading, and golf, and I'm a professional musician. All of these activities require attention to detail, so I guess I'm overboard in that direction.

In any case, it all evens out, and the only thing that really matters is this—there's an awful lot of love in our house, and if anyone wants a Peggy in their house, they will have to find their own, 'cause I plan to hang on to mine.

Dick Gass:

Can't tell you how many people have asked me, "How the hell did *you* luck out and get Dee Dee for a wife?" I always look them right in the eye with a straight face, and answer: "I had her convinced I had a lot of money."

Far from the truth—being the oldest of eight children and living in a two-bedroom house in Venice doesn't exactly mean you're financially set. However, growing up in a large Catholic family had its advantages—love and happiness. Dee Dee also grew up in the same environment; and being the oldest of large families, we have much in common.

I knew immediately when Dee Dee and I started dating that she was the girl I wanted to marry. Besides being beautiful, she loved sports, living in Venice, and going to the beach. What more could I ask for?

I spent two years as a paratrooper in the 82nd Airborne Division, and when I returned to Venice, once again I convinced Dee Dee that I had a ton of money. Somehow, she still believed me, and we married. We've lived in Venice ever since, and have raised three great children—Mary, Diane, and Tom. Each of them love Venice and love going to the beach.

I will be ever grateful to one person for raising Dee Dee to love sports and the beach. Dee Dee's dad, Bill, was a special kind of guy, and I loved him very much, from the time I was a young kid growing up on the streets of Venice. I could write a book on the crazy things we used to do together. Bill was a true friend to kids. We miss him very much—it's difficult to believe he was taken from us so soon.

Now Dee Dee and I are beginning to kick back and watch our three children grow into adults. Dee Dee still tucks them in, and I wonder when they will be moving out on their own. Whenever the kids and I discuss their eventual move into that big world outside, Dee Dee sneaks into the kitchen, heats up three bottles, and promptly tucks each of them into bed with their favorite blanky and teddy bear. Oh, the joys of parenthood!

I know it's corny, but I admit I'm the luckiest guy to have Dee Dee as my wife. The real secret though has been the ability to hold on to her all of the years. At least once every six months, when we're at a public function or with large groups of friends, I announce to Dee Dee, loudly: "Dee Dee, I don't really care if you leave me. But I'm going with you."

Don't laugh—it works!

Kathy, Dianne, Janet, Peggy—The Lennon Sisters. *(Courtesy of Harry Langdon)*

Index

Cedar Rapids (IA), 127, 174
"Champagne Lady," *See* Lon,
   Alice
Channing, Carol, 119
Chaplin, Charlie, 229
Chaplin, Emily, *See* Denning,
   Emily C.
Charlie McCarthy, 40
Chestnut's Drug Store, 255
"Chestnuts Roasting on an Open
   Fire," 67
Chicago (IL), 20, 127
Christmas, 44, 62, 66, 67, 78, 96
   119, 127, 260, 284, 285, 334
Chrysler Corporation, 31, 103,
   131 167
Cilurzo, Vince, 86
Cisco Kid, The, 40
Clark, Dick, 102, 120
Cleveland (OH), 150, 302
"Climb Upon my Knee, Sonny
   Boy," 235
Cobb, Peggy, 130
Cocoanut Grove, 264
Cohen, Harold, 237, 269, 278
Cohen, Phyllis, 278-279
Colorado, 317
Como, Perry, 119, 120, 173, 175
   228, 285
Confessions of St. Augustine,
   The, 4
Confidential magazine, 118
Coogan, Jackie, 234
Cook Brothers, 50
Corn Palace (SD), 170, 171
Correspondents Association
   Press Club, 163
Crawford, Johnny, 118, 175
"Crescent City," 202
Crosby, Norm, 228
"Cruising Down the River," 49
Culver City (CA), 15, 21, 189
Culver, Harry, 21

Dagwood, 65
Dahl, Bill, 84

Dale, Dick, 126
Dallas (TX), 128
Damone, Vic, 229
Darin, Bobby, 116
Daris, James (Jim), 11, 312, 313
   333-335
Daughters of Mary and Joseph,
   78
Davidson, John, 120
Davies, Marion, 63
Davis, Mac, 120
Davis, Sammy, Jr., 120, 228,
   264
Deaf, School of the, 130
Dee, Sandra, 116, 148
Del Conte, Ken, 205, 206
Demoff, Lolly, 50
Denning, Danforth (Grandpa),
   29-31, 45-49, 72, 83
Denning, Danforth Jr. (Dan),
   30, 31
Denning, Emily Chaplin, 29
Denning, Frank, 29
Denning, Isabelle Emily, *See* Len-
   non, Isabelle
Denning, Reina Ysabel Alvarez
   (Nana), 3, 15, 29-34, 37, 40-42,
   45, 46, 49, 50, 52, 53, 63, 64, 70,
   188, 240, 260, 280, 334, 335,
   338
Denver (CO), 127
Des Moines (IA), 133
Detroit (MI), 169
De Young, Peggy, 50
Diner, Evan, 285
Disneyland, 153, 298
Disney Show, 182
Disney, Walt, *See* "Mickey
   Mouse Club"
Dodge, *See* Chrysler Corp.
Donaroma, Pat, 91
Don Ho, 228
Dorothy (of Oz), 40
Douglas Aircraft, 34, 41, 249
Douglas, Mike, 120, 228
"Dry Bones," 16